Italian Grammar for Beginners
Textbook & Workbook Included

Supercharge Your Italian With
Essential Lessons and Exercises

TalkinItalian.com

Also available:

Italian Short Stories for Beginners (https://geni.us/italianshorts)

TABLE OF CONTENTS

INTRODUCTION

Grammar is one of the most challenging - not to mention, boring - parts of learning a language. Unfortunately, it's something that can't just be learned as an afterthought.

If you truly want to know how to express yourself in Italian - and not just barely get by - and you want to speak Italian using clear and precise language, you need to build a strong and solid foundation in Italian grammar.

Here in this book, we strive to help you do that. We lay down all that you need to learn about Italian grammar for beginners, and we help you build an effective learning habit in the process.

This book is divided into 25 lessons and one lesson is meant to be tackled each day. After 30 days of consistently studying every day, you will be able to build a learning habit that will be useful in helping you reach your learning goals in Italian.

But why the need to build a learning habit?

At our website talkinitalian.com, one of our learning philosophies is centered around building a daily habit. Let's face it, language learning is difficult, tedious, and requires long hours of intense study. That's precisely the reason why a lot of learners stop halfway or lose interest without achieving their learning goals.

The key to successful Italian language learning? Build a habit. Instead of sporadically studying "whenever the mood strikes" or "off and on for several years", do it consistently each day. A learning habit will help you get past the most boring and challenging parts of learning Italian even when your motivation is at its lowest.

Italian grammar, simplified

This book also strives to discuss grammar using the simplest yet most thorough explanations. Italian grammar rules can be quite complicated, so instead of burdening you with wordy explanations and unnecessary jargon, this book simplifies Italian grammar in a way that makes it easily digestible and easy to grasp.

We hope that with this book, you'll be able to build the strong grammar foundation that you need to eventually reach fluency in Italian.

Grazie, thank you,

Talk in Italian team

Important! The link to download the Audio Files is available at the end of this book. (Page 288)

LESSON 1: SALUTARE IN ITALIANO – ITALIAN GREETINGS

Greetings are the very first words we utter when we meet someone. And when you're meeting someone for the very first time, knowing how to greet properly helps you make a great first impression! In this lesson, we'll be talking about basic Italian greetings. Learn how to say "hello" as well as other greetings in Italian, both for formal and informal situations.

Let's begin!

How to say "Hello" in Italian

You're probably already familiar with "ciao", but it's not the only way to say hello in Italian. In fact, some situations call for other more appropriate ways of saying hello. Let's take a look at the different ways of saying hello!

Listen to track 1 (Don't forget. You can find the link to download the audio at Page 288)

Ciao!

Ciao means both 'hi' and 'goodbye'. Cool, right? Fewer words to memorize. But wait! Contrary to what some people think, you can't really use *ciao* with everyone and at all times.

Think of it as like saying 'hi' in English - it's not very appropriate to say it in highly formal situations. But when you're with friends or family or in a casual setting, feel free to say 'ciao'!

In some cases, Italians can even say it over and over at the end of conversations, like *"ciao ciao ciao ciao ciao!"*

You can also say *"Ciao a tutti!"* (hi to all!) and *"Ciao ragazzi!"* (hi guys!) when addressing a group of people. It means "hi everyone!" or "bye everyone", depending on the context.

Listen to track 2

Salve!

This might sound a little odd to non-Italians, but if you find yourself in a situation where you are among people you are not really familiar with, *"salve"* is the proper way to say hello.

If *ciao* is more like "hi" in English, *salve* is somewhere near the more formal "hello". It can also be used to say goodbye, just like *ciao*. Now say it with me, "sahl veh". There you go.

Italian greetings for different times of the day

While *ciao* and *salve* can be used any time of the day, you also need to learn how to greet people during specific times of the day. Time-specific greetings are considered even more formal than *salve* but you can still use it in casual situations among your friends.

How to say "Good morning" or "Good day" in Italian

Listen to track 3

Buongiorno!

In the morning until early afternoon, you say *buongiorno* as a greeting. Take note that, though the word is made up of two words, *buon* (good) and *giorno* (day), it's written as a single word.

Quick tip: *Buongiorno* is used as a greeting, but if you want to wish someone 'a nice day', you say "**buona giornata!**"

How to say "Good afternoon" in Italian

Listen to track 4

Buon pomeriggio

When it's past noon, you do still hear Italians say *buongiorno*, but the more accurate greeting would be *buon pomeriggio*, which you're likely to encounter in places like Bologna.

However, this is used less often as most would either just say *buongiorno* until early afternoon and *buonasera* after siesta time.

How to say "Good evening" in Italian

Listen to track 5

Buonasera

It might seem a bit early to wish someone a good evening when work resumes in the afternoon - or even at four in the afternoon - but that is the case in Italy.

You could also say *buonasera* to say goodbye, but "*buona serata!*" (have a good evening!) works just as well.

How to say "Good night" in Italian

Listen to track 6

Buonanotte!

When it's late in the evening and you're turning in for the night, you say *buonanotte* to wish someone good night and sweet dreams.

How to say "How are you?" in Italian

Of course, greetings don't end the moment you say hello or good day. You always have to follow it up with some form of "How are you?" Let's take a look at the formal and informal ways of say this in Italian.

Listen to track 7

Come sta? - How are you? (formal)

The polite way to ask someone how they're doing is "*come sta*".

Come stai? - How are you? (informal)

When you're among friends or family, you can say "*come stai?*" instead of "*come sta?*". *Sta* and *stai* come from the Italian verb *stare* which means "to stay" and *stai* is the informal *tu* form.

Come va? - How's it going? (informal)

Another informal way to ask how someone is doing, when you're with people close to you, is to say "*come va?*".

Ways to respond to "How are you?" in Italian

Now let's talk about how to respond when someone asks how you're doing.

Listen to track 8

Bene, grazie!	Fine, thanks!
Molto bene, grazie!	Very well, thanks!
Bene, grazie, e lei?	Good, thanks, and you?
Non c'è male.	Not bad.
Così così.	So-so
Va benissimo, grazie.	It's going very well, thanks.
Tutto a posto!	Everything's going well!

To sum up...

- A very informal greeting, *ciao* is the equivalent of 'hi' in English and can also be used to mean 'bye'. Use it with friends and family or in a casual setting.
- A relic from Latin, *salve* is a neutral way to say 'hello'. Use it with people you are not really familiar with.
- Time-specific greetings change depending on the time of the day. *Buongiorno* (good morning) is generally used in the morning until early afternoon.
- *Buon pomeriggio* (good afternoon) should be used in the afternoon, but most Italians skip it and just use *buongiorno*.
- *Buonasera* (good evening) is to be used after siesta time.
- Say *buonanotte* (goodnight) to wish someone good night.
- The polite way to ask someone how they're doing is "*come sta?*".
- When you are among friends or family, you can say "*come stai?*".
- "*Bene, grazie*" (fine, thanks) is the most common way to respond when someone asks how you're doing.

Workbook Lesson 1. Italian Greetings

Exercise 1.1: Tick the right answer:

1. Roberta is a friend of Laura's. She would ask her:
   1) Come stai?   2) Come sta?

2. It's morning. Marco wants to say 'good morning' to Francesco. He would say:
   1) Buon pomeriggio   2) Buongiorno   3) Buonasera

3. To wish someone a good night, you would say:
   1) Buongiorno   2) Buon pomeriggio   3) Buonanotte

4. You want to ask your boss how he is, so you say:
   1) Come stai?   2) Come sta?

5. To say «everything's going well», you should say:
   1) Non c'è male   2) Così così   3) Tutto a posto

Exercise 1.2: Translate from Italian to English and vice versa:

Italian	English
1- Buongiorno	.....
2-	How are you (informal)?
3-	Well, thank you.

4- E tu?	.....
5-	Good night

Exercise 1.3: Translate this conversation from English to Italian:

English	Italian
You: Good morning. How's it going?	You: _____?
Your friend: Not bad. And you?	Your friend: _____?
You: Everything is going well. Bye!	You: _____!
Your friend: Bye!	Your friend: _____!

Exercise 1.4: Tick the right answer:

1. You are talking to your boss. You would say:
   a. Io sto bene, grazie. E tu?   b. Io sto bene, grazie. E lei?

2. If somebody asked you « come stai? », you would answer:
   a. Bene, grazie.   b. Ciao!   c. Come va?

3. To say 'good night', you say:
   a. Buongiorno   b. Buonasera   c. Buonanotte

4. Your friend asks you « come stai? ». You're not feeling great, so you would say:
   a. Così così   b. Bene, grazie   c. Tutto a posto

5. To ask someone « how's it going », you say:
   a. Come sta?   b. Come stai?   c. Come va?

Exercise 1.5: Translate this conversation from Italian into English:

Italian	English
Tu: Buongiorno. Come sta?	Tu: _____?
Il tuo capo: Bene, grazie. E lei?	Il tuo capo: _____?
Tu: Tutto a posto, grazie. Arrivederci.	Tu: _____.
Il tuo capo: Buona giornata.	Il tuo capo: _____.

Answers:

Exercise 1.1:

1) Come stai? / 2) Buongiorno / 3) Buonanotte / 4) Come sta? / 5) Tutto a posto

Exercise 1.2:

1. Good morning / 2. Come stai? / 3. Bene, grazie. / 4. And you? / 5. Buonanotte

Exercise 1.3:

You/Tu: Buongiorno. Come va?

Your friend/Il tuo amico: Non c'è male. E tu?

You/Tu: Tutto a posto. Ciao!

Your friend/Il tuo amico: Ciao!

Exercise 1.4:

1) Io sto bene, grazie. E lei? / 2) Bene, grazie. / 3) Buonanotte / 4) Così così / 5) Come va?

Exercise 1.5:

You: Good morning. How are you?

Your boss: Well, thank you. And you?

You: Everything is going well, thanks. Goodbye!

Your boss: Have a nice day.

LESSON 2. PRONUNCIA ITALIANA – ITALIAN PRONUNCIATION

Before we proceed, let me start with some good and bad news.

The good news!

- **Italian is a phonetic language.** That means, words are often pronounced the way they are spelled!
- **Italian pronunciation rules are constant.** They won't trick you into thinking you got the rules down pat only to stab you in the back with exceptions to the rules.
- **There are no silent letters in Italian (except H, that is)!** But in general, each letter is always spoken with the same corresponding sound.

The bad news

There's no bad news actually. The Italian sounds you hear might be intimidating at first, but with constant listening and speaking practice, you can easily (*okay, not that easily but you can learn them quickly enough*) learn to speak Italian words the way native Italians do.

Some tips before we proceed

- When speaking Italian, **feel free to exaggerate the sounds!** Never mind if you feel silly. That's simply the Italian way to do it, and practice is key.
- **The Italian intonation patterns follow simple rules**:
  - The stress is usually in the second to last syllable. For example: bub-BON-e, bam-BI-ni.
  - The exception is with words that have accent marks on the last letter. This puts the stress on the last syllable.
- **Always find time to listen!** As with any other language, always practice listening. This will give you the correct tools to navigate any pronunciation issues. It will also make producing the sounds so much easier!

Now let's begin the lesson! Ready?

The Italian Alphabet

Let's start by getting familiar with the Italian alphabet. As you'll notice, it's exactly the same as the English alphabet, but with fewer letters. So - YAY!

In the table below, you can see in the first line the name of the letter as you know it, followed by what the letter is called in Italian. Then on the third line, you can check out some Italian example words that make use of these letters/sounds prominently.

Listen to track 9

Letter in English	Letter in Italian	Example Wors in Italian
Aa	A	*Abbazia, ala*
Bb	Bi	*Bambini, bubbone*
Cc	Ci	*Ciuffo, cecio*
Dd	Di	*Dado, addio*
Ee	E	*Aereo, bere*
Ff	Effe	*Zuffa, Fifa*
Gg	Gi	*Bigio, gengiva*
Hh	Acca	*Hotel, Herpes*
Ii	I	*Idillio, igienico*
Ll	Elle	*Livello, cellula*
Mm	Emme	*Mamma, melodramma*
Nn	Enne	*Nonna, insonnia*
Oo	O	*Comodo, goloso*
Pp	Pi	*Pappa, appropriato*
Qq	Cu	*Qualunque, quadro*
Rr	Erre	*Orrore, ramarro*
Ss	Esse	*Sasso, gassoso*
Tt	Ti	*Intatto, trattenuta*
Uu	U	*Usufruire, multiculturale*
Vv	Vu	*Ravvivare, evviva*
Zz	Zeta	*Zozzo, zizzania*

Take note that the letters j, k, w, x, and y rarely appear in Italian words. When they do, it's mostly with words that are borrowed from other languages.

2. Italian Vowel Sounds

Now that we have gone through the different letters in the Italian alphabet and some corresponding example words, we'll take a look at the different vowel sounds you'll encounter in Italian.

Listen to track 10

A sound in Italian

In Italian, the 'a' sound is always the same. You say it like 'ah' as in car in English but with a slightly exaggerated open sound.

/a/ - *cane* (dog), *mare* (sea)

Listen to track 11

E sounds in Italian

There are two 'e' sounds in Italian: the closed one [e] which is nearer in sound to 'hey', 'say', or 'day' in English. Then there's the open 'e' [ɛ] like met or bet.

Some examples:

/e/ - *chiesa* (church), *vedere* (to see)
/ɛ/ - *ieri* (yesterday), *stélla* (star)

Listen to track 12

I sound in Italian

There's only one way to pronounce the 'I' sound in Italian - like how you would say the 'ee' sound in 'knee' or 'see'. But keep the 'ee' sound shorter than you would in English!

/i/ - *vino* (wine), *vivo* (alive)

Listen to track 13

O sounds in Italian

O in Italian makes one of two sounds: an open O sound like 'doe' or 'store' and a second one like 'hog' or 'bot'. Just remember that in Italian, unlike in English, the 'o' sound is made without rounding your lips too much towards the end of the 'o'.

/o/ - *amore* (love), *croce* (cross)
/ɔ/ - *oro* (gold), *porta* (door)

U sound in Italian

Listen to track 14

The 'u' sound in Italian, like the other vowels we've discussed so far, is quite simple. You form it with the same sound as 'oo' in 'hoot' or 'shoe', but make it shorter and without rounding your lips too much. Try to remember that there's no rounded sound in Italian, then you're good!

/u/ - *tutto* (all), *muro* (wall)

So, still doing great so far?

Awesome.

Let's move on to the rest of the letters in the alphabet. Next up, consonants!

3. Italian Consonant Sounds

In this section, we'll go through each of the consonants and all of the sounds they're used for in Italian. It should be a breeze for you actually, as most of the sounds are essentially the same as in English, with just a few tricks here and there.

Ready? Let's go!

B sound in Italian

Listen to track 15

The 'b' in Italian is exactly the same in English. No surprises here!

/b/ - bolla, burro, bosco

C sound in Italian

Listen to track 16

There are two 'c' sounds in Italian: the 'ch' sound like chocolate and the 'k' sound like cola. The major rules you have to remember here are:

/tʃ/ - when the 'c' is before i and e, the 'c' sounds like ch.

Examples: *cipolla, ciliegia, Cina*

/k/ - when the 'c' is before any consonant or the vowels 'a', 'o', and 'u', the 'c' sounds like 'k'. Examples: *casa, cambio, costo*

Listen to track 17

D sound in Italian

D in Italian sounds very much like it does in English. The only difference, however, is that in Italian, the 'd' sound is harder and more pronounced than its English equivalent.

/d/ - *dedica, dire, dado*

F sound in Italian

Listen to track 18

Another one that sounds the same as in English! Easy-peasy.

/f/ - *ferro, fango, furia*

G sound in Italian

Listen to track 19

Just like the Italian 'c' sound, 'g' in Italian has two different sounds and two rules to follow. The first 'g' sound is a hard sound similar to good, great. The other 'g' sound is the softer one like gem.

Here are the key things to remember:

/g/ - when 'g' is before the vowels 'a', 'o', and 'u'.

Examples: *gara, ruga, godo*

/ʤ/ - when the 'g' is before 'e' or 'i'.

Examples: *gioia, gelo, gioco*

H sound in Italian

Listen to track 20

This one is super easy to remember because 'h' is silent in Italian!

/h/ - *hanno, hotel, herpes*

L sound in Italian

Listen to track 21

Think of the Italian 'l' sound as a more serious 'l' version of its English counterpart. To produce the sound like a native does, you have to dwell longer on the 'l' sound and exaggerate it a bit.

/l/ - *palo, luce, perla*

There's also another 'l' sound in Italian - a more difficult one - that can be formed when you have the letters 'gl' together. There's no similar sound in English so you need to practice this one: say 'lyi'!

/ʎ/ - *sbadiglio, coniglio, consiglio*

M sound in Italian

Listen to track 22

The 'm' is pronounced the same way in English and Italian, so no worries here!

/m/ - *mare, mosca, ramo*

N sound in Italian

Listen to track 23

In Italian, you have three sounds that can be produced by the letter 'n'. The first one is the regular 'n' sound, as in noon or never.

/n/ - *nero, nuvola, renna*

The second sounds like the 'ng' in swing or singing. But in Italian, it is formed by the letters 'n' and 'c' together.

/ŋ/ - *banca, anche*

Take note that *banca* would therefore sound like [bang-ka] while *anche* sounds like [ang-ke].

The third 'n' sound is a lot harder to process by the non-native tongue. It is formed when you have the two letters 'g' and 'n' side by side and is pronounced as 'nya'. But you do know how to say lasagna, right? So, you're good to go!

/ɲ/ - *gnocchi, cognome, legna, pigna*

P sound in Italian

Listen to track 24

The 'p' sound is basically the same in English and Italian, except for one tiny thing. Try saying the word 'speak'. Then say the word 'put'. Do you notice a difference with how you pronounce the p sound?

When you said 'speak', you didn't put a puff of air into the 'p' sound. But when a word starts with 'p', such as 'put' or 'ponder', there is that puff of air. For your reference, the 'p' sound in Italian is the same as the 'p' in 'speak'. You don't aspirate the 'p' in Italian.

/p/ - *pepe, pane, crepa*

Qu sound in Italian

Listen to track 25

The letter 'q' in Italian cannot stand on its own and is always accompanied by the letter 'u'. When joined together, 'q' and 'u' together make the same sound as in the English words question or quick.

/kw/ - *quando, quarta, quarantina*

R sound in Italian

Listen to track 26

The English 'r' sound is different from the Italian 'r' and this often stumps non-native speakers. How is it different, you ask? For starters, the Italian 'r' is called the 'trilled r' or a 'slightly rolled r'. You pronounce it by tapping your tongue against your gums at the back of your upper teeth.

/r/ - *raro, ruba, caro*

But pronunciation of the 'r' doesn't end there. In Italian, you will notice that some words have double consonants. When you see this, it means you have to prolong the consonant sound and exaggerate it further. Try these examples of words with double 'r':

/rr/ - *carro, ramarro, porro*

S sound in Italian

Listen to track 27

With the letter 's', it's not as straightforward in Italian as it is in English. You basically have two types of 's' sound in Italian: the regular 's' sound like sweet, and the 'z' sound like zebra.

Here are the rules to know which 's' sound to use:

/z/ - use the 'z' sound when the 's' is sandwiched between two vowels or when it comes before the letters b, d, g, l, m, n, r, and v.

Examples: *raso, posa, sgabello, svelto.*

/s/ - use the regular 's' sound in all cases apart from the ones mentioned above.

Examples: *sei, sito, siepe.*

The 's' also figures in one more difficult Italian sound: the 'sc' sound. When 's' and 'c' go hand in hand, it produces a sound similar to 'sh' in English.

/ʃ/ - *sciarpa, riuscire, scena*

T sound in Italian

Listen to track 28

You'll be happy to know that 't' in Italian is pronounced the same way as in English!

/t/ - *tuono, tiro, prato*

V sound in Italian

Listen to track 29

The 'v' in Italian sounds exactly the as in English, too!

/v/ - *volo, vista, vaso*

Z sound in Italian

Listen to track 30

There are two sounds you can make in Italian when it comes to the letter 'z'. It could be either 'ts' as in 'bats' or 'ds' as in 'heads'.

/tz/ - *pizza*

/dz/ - *pranzo, zona, zio, zolla*

Other consonant sounds not covered above

We may not see the letters 'w' and 'y' in the Italian alphabet, but there are sounds for them produced by different letters. Here they are:

Listen to track 31

/w/ produced by the letters 'uo'- *cuoco, cuoio, vacuo*
/j/ produced by the letter 'I'- *piatto, siepe, pioggia*

Now let's do a recap of the different Italian consonant sounds and their examples:

Listen to track 32

Italian Consonant Sound	Examples
/b/	bolla, burro, bosco
/d/	dedica, dire, dado
/f/	ferro, fango, furia
/g/	gara, ruga, godo
/h/	hanno, hotel, herpes
/k/	casa, cambio, costo
/l/	palo, luce, perla
/ʎ/	sbadiglio, coniglio, consiglio
/m/	mare, mosca, ramo
/n/	nero, nuvola, renna
/ŋ/	anfora, angolo
/ɲ/	cognome, legna, pigna
/p/	pepe, pane, crepa

/ɾ/	raro, ruba, caro
/ɾɾ/	carro, ramarro, porro
/s/	sei, sito, siepe
/ʃ/	sciarpa, riuscire, scena
/tʃ/	cipolla, ciliegia, Cina
/ts/	marzo, ospizio, zappa
/d͡ʒ/	gioia, gelo, gioco
/t/	tuono, tiro, prato
/v/	volo, vista, vaso
/w/	cuoco, cuoio, vacuo
/j/	piatto, siepe, pioggia
/dz/	zona, zio, zolla
/z/	raso, posa, sgabello

Difficult Italian Sounds

Listen to track 33

Of course, we won't end this guide without dwelling further on the sounds most non-native speakers find difficult to pull off. These are 'gn', 'gli', and 'sci/sce'.

/gn/ - this one sounds like 'ny' + vowel (nya, nye, or nyo). Try to practice it with these Italian words: *gnomo* (gnome), *pegno* (pledge), *guadagno* (gain)

/gli/ - think of the words million and billion in English. That's how you pronounce this sound. Say 'lyi' as in *moglie* (wife), *scegliere* (to choose), and *figlio* (son).

/sci/ or /sce/ - though this sound isn't hard to produce for non-natives, the problem lies with habit. It takes time for most non-native speakers to immediately pronounce 'sc' as 'sh'. Try to practice this sound with the following words: *pesce* (fish), *scivolare* (to slide), *sciare* (to ski).

To sum up...

Italian is a phonetic language, which means that words are pronounced the way they are spelled.

- There are no silent letters, except 'h'.
- The 'a' sound is always pronounced like the 'a' in the word 'car'.
- 'E' can be closed (like the 'a' in 'day') or open (like the 'e' in 'bet').
- 'I' is always pronounced like the 'ee' in 'knee'.
- 'O' is pronounced like the 'o' in 'hog'.
- The 'u' sound in Italian is pronounced like the 'oo' in 'hoot'.

As for consonants, most of the sounds are the same as in English. Note that there are two 'c' sounds in Italian: the 'ch' sound like 'chocolate' and the 'k' sound like 'cola'.

- 'G' has two different sounds too: a hard sound similar to 'good' and a softer one like 'gem'.
- There are two types of 's' sound in Italian: the regular 's' sound like 'sweet', and the 'z' sound like 'zebra'.
- The Italian 'r' is called the 'trilled r'.
- 'Gn' sounds like 'ny' + vowel, 'sc' sounds like 'sh' and 'gl' is pronounced like 'lyi' in million.

Workbook Lesson 2. Italian Pronunciation

Exercise 2.1: Decipher the following words from the sounds of each letter. You should write down what the words are:

1. Esse, ti, i, vu, a, elle, e _____
2. Effe, i, o, ci, ci, o _____
3. Ti, a, vu, o, elle, a _____
4. Gi, i, o, ci, o _____
5. Emme, o, zeta, zeta, a, erre, e, elle, elle, a _____

Exercise 2.2: Decipher the following words from the sounds of each letter. You should write down what the words are:

1. O, ci, ci, acca, i, a, elle, i _____
2. Emme, a, enne, gi, i, a, erre, e _____
3. Erre, i, ci, e, ti, ti, a _____
4. Ti, a, pi, pi, e, ti, o _____
5. O, erre, o, elle, o, gi, i, o _____

Exercise 2.3: Spell the following Italian surnames:

1. Come si chiama? - Rossella Mancini. (What is her name? - Rossella Mancini)
   - Può farmi lo spelling? (Can you spell her surname?)

   - _____

2. Come si chiama? - Luciana. (What is her name? - Luciana)
   - E di cognome? Donati (And her surname?)
   - Come si scrive? (How do you write that?)

   - _____

3. Come si chiama? (What is his name?) - Michele.

- Come si scrive? (How do you write that?)

- _____

Exercise 2.4: Decipher the following words from the sounds of each letter. You should write down what the words are:

1. Pi, erre, o, vu, o, ci, a, erre, e _____

2. Ci, u, ci, i, erre, e _____

3. Zeta, o, pi, pi, i, ci, a, erre, e _____

4. E, elle, e, gi, a enne, ti, e _____

5. Erre, i, gi, acca, e, elle, elle, o _____

Exercise 2.5: Write some words beginning with the following letters:

1. GN: _____

2. CH: _____

3. ST: _____

4. CU: _____

5. GH: _____

Answers:

Exercise 2.1:

1. Stivale / 2. Fiocco / 3. Tavola / 4. Gioco / 5. Mozzarella

Exercise 2.2:

1. Occhiali / 2. Mangiare / 3. Ricetta / 4. Tappeto / 5. Orologio

Exercise 2.3:

1. Emme, a, enne, ci, i, enne, I / 2. Di, o, enne, a, ti, i / 3. Emme, i, ci, acca, e, elle, e

Exercise 2.4:

1. Provocare / 2. Cucire / 3. Zoppicare / 4. Elegante / 5. Righello

Exercise 2.5:

1. Gnomo / 2. Chiesa, chiave / 3. Stivale, stoffa / 4. Cucchiaio, curare / 5. Ghianda, ghetto

LESSON 3. ARTICOLI DETERMINATIVI E INDETERMINATIVI – DEFINITE AND INDEFINITE ARTICLES

The foundation stone of Italian grammar, **definite and indefinite articles** (*articoli determinativi* and *indeterminativi*) play a crucial role in Italian phrases, and it's essential for you to master them all in order to speak correctly.

In this lesson, we will show you how to use these small but important words. Let's get started!

Definite articles in Italian

Italian sentences rarely start with a noun that has no article. **Definite articles** (*articoli determinativi*) are used to introduce nouns which refer to a specific item.

As you know, in English there is only one definite article, "**the**". In Italian there are eight ways to say "the", and the **definite article** you use depends on the answer to three crucial questions.

1. Is the noun feminine or masculine?

Italian grammar has gendered nouns, which means that every noun can either be feminine or masculine. We use different *articoli determinativi* based on the noun's gender. When learning vocabulary, memorize if a noun is feminine or masculine.

2. Is the noun singular or plural?

The definite article you use must match in number with the noun it goes with.

3. What letter does the following noun start with?

The first letter of a word affects the **definite article** you pair it with. Italian nouns that begin with consonants use one article, while nouns that begin with vowels use another. Nouns that start with "z", "ps", "pn", "gn", "x", "y" and "s" followed by a consonant follow a different rule again.

This may sound complicated, but it is not too difficult. Here is your guide.

Masculine definite articles

Most Italian nouns end with vowels. Words that end in -o and -ore are almost always masculine. The definite articles to use with masculine nouns are *il, lo, l', i* and *gli*.

Listen to track 34

Il

You use *il* for masculine singular nouns starting with a consonant.

Here are some examples:

Il mare – the sea   **Il c**olore – the color
Il viaggio – the trip   **Il g**iornale – the newspaper

Listen to track 35

Lo

You use *lo* for masculine singular nouns that start with:

- **S + consonant**
  Lo studente – the student
  Lo scontrino – the receipt
  Lo spumante – the sparkling wine

- **Z**
  Lo zenzero – the ginger
  Lo zucchero – the sugar
  Lo zio – the uncle

- **Ps**
  Lo psicologo – the psychologist
  Lo pseudonimo – the pseudonym
  Lo psichiatra – the psychiatrist

- **Pn**
  Lo pneumatico – the tire
  Lo pneumologo – the pulmonologist
  Lo pneumografo – the pneumograph

- **Gn**
  Lo gnomo – the gnome
  Lo gnocco fritto – the fried dough
  Lo gnatologo – the gnathologist

- **Y**
  Lo yogurt – the yogurt
  Lo yacht – the yacht
  Lo yeti – the yeti

- **X**

    Lo xilofono – the xylophone

    Lo xenofobo – the xenophobe

    Lo xilitolo – the xylitol

Listen to track 36

L'

When a masculine singular noun begins with a vowel, *lo* contracts into *l'*.

L'aereoplano – the airplane

L'orologio – the watch

L'esempio – the example

L'uragano – the hurricane

L'intervento – the intervention

Listen to track 37

I

You use *i* for masculine plural nouns starting with a consonant.

I negozi – the shops

I medici – the doctors

I gatti – the cats

I trattori – the tractors

Listen to track 38

Gli

You use *gli* for masculine plural nouns that start with a vowel and with "z", "ps", "gn", "pn", "x", "y" or "s" followed by a consonant.

Gli aereoplani – the airplanes

Gli esempi – the examples

Gli interventi – the interventions

Gli orologi – the watches

Gli uragani – the hurricanes

Gli studenti – the students

Gli zii – the uncles

Gli psicologi – the psychologists

Gli pneumatici – the tires

Gli gnomi – the gnomes

Gli yogurt – the yogurts

Gli xilofoni – the xylophones

Feminine definite articles

Italian words that end in -a and -zione are almost always feminine. The definite articles to use with feminine nouns are *la, l'* and *le*.

Listen to track 39

La

You use *la* for all feminine singular nouns starting with a consonant.

La polvere – the dust

La sabbia – the sand

La domanda – the question

La pioggia – the rain

La relazione – the relationship

Listen to track 40

L'

When a feminine singular noun begins with a vowel, *la* contracts into *l'*.

L'anima – the soul

L'edicola – the news-stand

L'ironia – the irony

L'onda – the wave

L'udienza – the consultation

Listen to track 41

Le

Le is used for all feminine plural nouns.

Le camere – the rooms

Le infermiere – the nurses

Le scatole – *the boxes*

Le automobili – *the cars*

Listen to track 42

Note: the *articolo determinativo* you choose depends on the first letters of the word immediately following it, which may be a **noun** or an **adjective**. Compare the following:

Il giorno (the day) – *l'altro giorno* (the other day)

I bambini (the kids) – *gli stessi bambini* (the same kids)

Using Italian definite articles

The *articoli determinativi* indicate:

- abstract concepts
- something you have already mentioned
- a category of things
- a unique entity.

Sometimes the definite article is used rather differently from in English. In Italian, use it when:

Listen to track 43

- telling the time:

Sono le sette – It's seven o'clock

- referring to dates and years:

Alessandro è nato il 18 febbraio 2004 – Alessandro was born on February 18th 2004

Franco è andato in pensione nel 1998 – Franco retired in 1998

- using possessive pronouns:

Le mie sorelle – my sisters

La tua personalità – your personality

Le sue foto – her photos

I nostri ricordi – our memories

Le vostre biciclette – your bikes

I loro furgoni – their vans

- talking about geographical destinations, such as:

Listen to track 44

Continents: *l'Asia* – Asia

Countries: *la Grecia* – Greece

Regions: *la Lombardia* – Lombardy

Oceans: *l'Atlantico* – the Atlantic Ocean

Rivers: *il Tevere* – the Tiber

Lakes: *il Garda* – Lake Garda

Mountains: *il Kilimangiaro* – Mount Kilimanjaro

- mentioning days of the week to indicate a repeated activity:

Cosa fai di solito il sabato? – What do you usually do on Saturdays?

- talking about parts of the body:

Listen to track 45

Mi fa male la schiena – My back hurts so badly

Dammi la mano – Give me your hand

- talking about how much something costs per kilogram, square meter and so on:

Listen to track 46

2,95 euro al chilo – 2,95 euro per kilo

1000 euro al metro quadro – 1000 euro per square meter

- talking about rates, percentages and speed:

150 km all'ora – 150 km an hour

Il 45% della popolazione – 45% of the population

- referring to pseudonyms and nicknames:

Listen to track 47

Il Perugino (Italian Renaissance painter Pietro di Cristoforo Vannucci)

Il Canaletto (Italian painter Giovanni Antonio Canal)

In Italian, the definite article is used before the name of a language, except when the verb *parlare* (to speak) comes before it.

L'italiano è una bella lingua – Italian is a beautiful language

*Carlo sta imparando **il** giapponese* – Carlo is learning Japanese

Stephanie non parla una parola di Italiano – Stephanie doesn't speak a word of Italian

Using Italian definite articles with prepositions

When you use a definite article after a preposition, you make something similar to a contraction in English and the **preposition combines with the definite article**. Check out the most common combinations.

Listen to track 48

A (to)

- a + il = **al**
- a + l' = **all'**
- a + lo = **allo**
- a + la = **alla**
- a + i = **ai**
- a + gli = **agli**
- a + le = **alle**

Da (from)

- da + il = **dal**
- da + l' = **dall'**
- da + lo = **dallo**
- da + la = **dalla**
- da + i = **dai**
- da + gli = **dagli**
- da + le = **dalle**

Di (of)

- di + il = **del**
- di + l' = **dell'**
- di + lo = **dello**
- di + la = **della**
- di + i = **dei**
- di + gli = **degli**
- di + le = **delle**

In (in)

- in + il = **nel**
- in + l' = **nell'**
- in + lo = **nello**
- in + la = **nella**
- in + i = **nei**
- in + gli = **negli**
- in + le = **nelle**

Su (on)

- su + il = **sul**
- su + l' = **sull'**
- su + lo = **sullo**
- su + la = **sulla**
- su + i = **sui**
- su + gli = **sugli**
- su + le = **sulle**

In English, you can use *some* (un po') with singular and plural nouns. One way of expressing the idea of *some* in Italian is to use *de* (of) together with the definite article.

Listen to track 49

Dello zucchero – some sugar

Della farina – some flour

Degli studenti – some students

Indefinite articles in Italian

Indefinite articles (*articoli indeterminativi*) denote a non-specific noun. They have no plural and are equivalent to "a" and "an" in English.

Italian has four *articoli indeterminativi*. Which one you need to use depends on the gender of the noun it refers to and the initial letter of the word it precedes.

Masculine indefinite articles

The **indefinite articles** to use with masculine nouns are *un* and *uno*.

Listen to track 50

Un

Use *un* for masculine singular nouns starting with a vowel and most consonants.

Un programma – a program

Un diamante – a diamond

Un elicottero – a helicopter

Un regalo – a gift

Listen to track 51

Uno

Use *uno* for masculine singular nouns starting with "z", "ps", "pn", "gn", "x", "y" and "s" followed by a consonant.

Uno zaino – a back-pack

Uno psicologo – a psychologist

Uno pneumatico – a tire

Uno gnomo – a gnome

Uno yogurt – a yogurt

Uno xilofono – a xylophone

Feminine indefinite articles

The indefinite articles to use with feminine nouns are *una* and *un'*.

Listen to track 52

Una

Use *una* for feminine singular nouns starting with a consonant.

Una sorpresa – a surprise

Una sedia – a chair

Una libreria – a bookcase

Listen to track 53

Un'

When a feminine singular noun begins with a vowel, *una* contracts to *un'*.

Un'analisi – an analysis

Un'etichetta – a label

Listen to track 54

Un'istituzione – an organization

Un'ombra – a shadow

Un'uscita – an exit

Note: the *articolo indeterminativo* you choose depends on the first letters of the word immediately following it, which can be a noun or an adjective. Compare the following:

Listen to track 55

Una signora (a woman) – **un'**affascinante signora (a charming woman)

Un regalo (a present) – **uno** splendido regalo (a wonderful present)

Using Italian indefinite articles

Listen to track 56

Italian indefinite articles are used to indicate something mentioned for the first time or as part of a group. You generally use the *articolo indeterminativo* in Italian when "a" or "an" are used in English. There are some cases where it is used in English, but not in Italian. You don't use the *articolo indeterminativo*:

- in exclamations with *che* (what):

Che bella sorpresa! – What a nice surprise!

Che vergogna! – What a shame!

Che peccato! – What a pity!

- with the words *cento* (hundred) and *mille* (thousand):

Te l'ho detto cento volte, non attraversare con il semaforo rosso – I told you a hundred times, don't cross on the red light

Uno su mille ce la fa – Once in a thousand times

- when you translate a few (*qualche*) or a lot (*molto*):

Qualche giorno fa ho visto Simona in palestra – A few days ago I saw Simona at the gym

Prima di partire, Francesca prelevò molti soldi da un bancomat – Before leaving, Francesca withdrew a lot of money from an ATM.

Note: unlike in English, in general the *articolo indeterminativo* is not used when saying what someone's job is. You either leave out the article or use the verb *fare* (to make, to do) with the definite article. Look at the two examples below:

Mio zio è medico / *Mio zio fa il medico* – My uncle is a doctor

Paolo è avvocato / *Paolo fa l'avvocato* – Paolo is a lawyer

To sum up...

In Italian there are two types of articles:

- Definite articles (*articoli determinativi*) denote a specific noun, just like "the" in English.

Listen to track 57

Il labirinto – the maze (masculine singular nouns beginning with a consonant)

Lo stato – the state (masculine singular nouns that start with "z", "ps", "pn", "gn", "x", "y" and "s" + consonant)

L'idraulico – the plumber (masculine singular nouns beginning with a vowel)

La scrittrice – the writer (feminine singular nouns beginning with a consonant)

L'altalena – the swing (feminine singular nouns beginning with a vowel)

I fenicotteri – the flamingos (masculine plural nouns beginning with a consonant)

Gli attrezzi – the tools (masculine plural nouns beginning with a vowel and "z", "ps", "gn", "pn", "x", "y" or "s" + consonant)

Le bambole – the dolls (all feminine plural nouns)

- Indefinite articles (*articoli indeterminativi*) refer to a non-specific noun, just like "a" or "an" in English.

Un amico – a friend (masculine singular nouns beginning with vowels and most consonants)

Uno stagno – a pond (masculine singular nouns beginning with "z", "ps", "pn", "gn", "x", "y" and "s" + consonant)

Una volpe – a fox (feminine singular nouns beginning with a consonant)

Un'operazione – an operation (feminine singular nouns beginning with a vowel)

- In Italian, both definite and indefinite articles change depending on the gender and number of the noun that follows them.

Workbook Lesson 3. Definite and Indefinite Articles

Exercise 3.1: Choose the correct article:

1. ____ gatto dorme sul davanzale.
   1) Lo   2) Il   3) Le

2. ____ minestra è troppo calda.
   1) Le   2) Lo   3) La

3. ____ operai sono al lavoro.
   1) I   2) Gli   3) Le

4. ____ maestre sono giovani.
   1) Le   2) La   3) I

5. ____ palazzi sono nuovi.
   1) Le   2) Gli   3) I

Exercise 3.2: Complete these sentences with the right indefinite article:

1. Cerco ____ regalo per mia mamma. (I'm looking for a present for my mum.)
2. Lei è ____ bella ragazza. (She is a beautiful girl.)
3. Dammi ____ indizio! (Give me a hint!)
4. Questa è ____ eccezione. (This is an exception.)
5. ____ giorno andrò in Australia. (One day I will go to Australia.)

Exercise 3.3: Complete the following sentences:

1. ____ bambini giocano ____ spiaggia. (Kids are playing on the beach.)
2. ____ treno ____ 8 è in ritardo. (The 8 O'clock train is late.)
3. ____ zaini ____ studenti sono pesanti. (Students' backpacks are heavy.)
4. ____ telefono è ____ mia borsa. (The phone is in my bag.)
5. ____ suoi genitori non andarono ____ suo matrimonio. (His parents didn't go to his wedding.)

Exercise 3.4: Tick the right answer:

1. ____ stazione ____ treno è in ristrutturazione. (The train station is under renovation.)
   1) La, del   2) La, dello   3) Il, del

2. Se non ti piace ____ vino, prendi ____altra cosa. (If you don't like wine, have something else.)
   1) lo, un'   2) il, un'   3) il, un

3. ____ orso è ____ mammifero. (The bear is a mammal.)

    1) Il, un   2) L', il   3) L', un

4. ____ cane è ____ mia amica. (The dog belongs to my friend.)

    1) Il, della   2) Il, allá   3) Lo, della

5. ____ acqua ____ rubinetto non è potabile. (Tap water is not drinkable.)

    1) La, del   2) L', del   3) L', dello

Exercise 3.5: Translate the sentences from English into Italian:

English	Italian
1. The neighbor's bicycle is blue.	
2. The apartment costs one million euros.	
3. Twentieth-century paintings are exhibited in the museum.	
4. Curry is a mixture of spices.	
5. The boat is near the port.	

Answers:

Exercise 3.1:

1) Il / 2) La / 3) Gli / 4) Le / 5) I

Exercise 3.2:

1. un / 2. Una / 3. Un / 4. un' / 5. un

Exercise 3.3:

1. I bambini giocano sulla spiaggia.

2. Il treno delle 8 è in ritardo.

3. Gli zaini degli studenti sono pesanti.

4. Il telefono è nella mia borsa.

5. I suoi genitori non andarono al suo matrimonio.

Exercise 3.4:

1) La, del / 2) il, un' / 3) L', un / 4) Il, della / 5) L', del

Exercise 3.5:

1. La bicicletta del vicino è blu.
2. L'appartamento costa un milione di euro.
3. Nel museo sono esposti i quadri del Novecento.
4. Il curry è un misto di spezie.
5. La barca è vicina al porto.

LESSON 4: SOSTANTIVI – NOUNS

Nouns are the cornerstone of the Italian language and one of the most basic parts of speech. If you want to build a solid Italian grammar foundation, **gender** and **number** are two fundamental concepts to learn.

The gender of Italian nouns tends to be a sticky grammar point for native English speakers. In this lesson, we will give you a quick and easy introduction to these two important concepts. Ready? Let's start!

Gender of Italian nouns

Italian grammar has gendered nouns, which means that every noun can be either masculine or feminine. There is no neuter gender. All Italian nouns have a gender, even those referring to inanimate objects, places, qualities and ideas. This can be a strange concept to native English speakers.

Most of the Italian nouns agree with the following rules:

- masculine nouns end with **-o** for singular;
- feminine nouns end with **-a** for singular.

Here are some examples of masculine and feminine nouns.

Masculine nouns ending in -o
Listen to track 58

Tavolo (m.) – table
Vetro (m.) – glass
Mondo (m.) – world
Libro (m.) – book
Scoiattolo (m.) – squirrel
Corallo (m.) – coral

Feminine nouns ending in -a
Listen to track 59

Casa (f.) – house
Stanza (f.) – room
Lettera (f.) – letter

Nuvola (f.) – cloud

Cittadinanza (f.) – citizenship

Uscita (f.) – exit

Strada (f.) – street

There are a number of exceptions, though, like, for example, *problema* (problem) being masculine, and *mano* (hand) being feminine.

Some Italian words would seem to be feminine, since they end in **-a**, but are actually masculine. Here is a list:

Listen to track 60

Problema (m.) – problem

Sistema (m.) – system

Programma (m.) – program

Tema (m.) – theme

Clima (m.) – climate

Poeta (m.) – poet

Pianeta (m.) – planet

Profeta (m.) – prophet

Poema (m.) – poem

Some words would seem to be masculine, since they end in -o, but are actually feminine. Here are some of the most common ones:

Mano (f.) – hand

Eco (f.) – echo

Libido (f.) – libido

Pallacanestro (f.) – basketball

Pallavolo (f.) – volleyball

Pallanuoto (f.) – water polo

Pallamano (f.) – handball

(Sedia a) **sdraio** (f.) – deck chair

(Cerniera) **lampo** (f.) – zipper

Listen to track 61

Note: abbreviated nouns retain the gender of the words from which they are derived. For example:

- foto (f.) comes from *fotografia* (photograph), making it a feminine noun;
- cinema (m.) comes from *cinematografo* (cinematography), making it a masculine noun;
- moto (f.) comes from *motocicletta* (motorcycle), making it a feminine noun;
- auto (f.) comes from *automobile* (car), making it a feminine noun;
- radio (f.) comes from *radiotelefonia* (radiotelephony), making it a feminine noun;
- bici (f.) comes from *bicicletta* (bicycle), making it a feminine noun;
- metro (f.) comes from *metropolitana* (subway), making it a feminine noun.

Singular nouns ending in **-i** are usually feminine:

Listen to track 62

Crisi (f.) – crisis

Analisi (f.) – analysis

Tesi (f.) – thesis

Ipotesi (f.) – hypothesis

Paralisi (f.) – palsy

Diagnosi (f.) – diagnosis

Metastasi (f.) – metastasis

Psoriasi (f.) – psoriasis

Anamnesi (f.) – anamnesis

Nouns ending in **-à** are almost always feminine:

Listen to track 63

Città (f.) – city

Umanità (f.) – human race

Abilità (f.) – ability

Università (f.) – university

Qualità (f.) – quality

Unità (f.) – unity

Realtà (f.) – reality

Sanità (f.) – healthcare

Novità (f.) – novelty

Comunità (f.) – community

Note: **papà** (dad) is masculine.

Italian nouns ending in -e

Nouns ending in **-e** may be masculine or feminine, and the gender of these nouns must be memorized.

Listen to track 64

Masculine nouns ending in -e

Ambiente (m.) – environment

Animale (m.) – animal

Bicchiere (m.) – glass

Cameriere (m.) – waiter

Cane (m.) – dog

Carabiniere (m.) – carbineer, bully

Carattere (m.) – character

Cognome (m.) – surname

Cotone (m.) – cotton

Fiume (m.) – river

Giornale (m.) – newspaper

Latte (m.) – milk

Mare (m.) – sea

Mese (m.) – month

Nome (m.) – name

Ospedale (m.) – hospital

Padre (m.) – father

Paese (m.) – country

Pallone (m.) – ball

Pane (m.) – bread

Pepe (m.) – pepper

Pesce (m.) – fish

Piede (m.) – feet

Ponte (m.) – bridge

Presidente (m.) – president

Re (m.) – king

Ristorante (m.) – restaurant

Sale (m.) – salt

Sangue (m.) – blood

Sole (m.) – sun

Studente (m.) – student

Feminine nouns ending in -e

Listen to track 65

Arte (f.) – art

Capitale (f.) – capital city

Carne (f.) – meat

Chiave (f.) – key

Estate (f.) – summer

Fame (f.) – hunger

Gente (f.) – people

Luce (f.) – light

Madre (f.) – mother

Moglie (f.) – wife

Nave (f.) – ship

Neve (f.) – snow

Notte (f.) – night

Pelle (f.) – skin

Polvere (f.) – dust

Salute (f.) – health

Sete (f.) – thirst

Nouns ending in **-ore** are usually masculine:

Listen to track 66

Dottore (m.) – doctor

Signore (m.) – gentleman

Valore (m.) – value

Genitore (m.) – parent

Cuore (m.) – heart

Pastore (m.) – shepherd

Fiore (m.) – flower

Attore (m.) – actor

Rumore (m.) – noise

Promotore (m.) – promoter

Mentore (m.) – mentor

Gestore (m.) – manager

Pallore (m.) – paleness

Nouns ending in **-ione** are generally feminine:

Listen to track 67:

Ragione (f.) – reason

Iscrizione (f.) – enrolment

Stazione (f.) – station

Televisione (f.) – television

Alluvione (f.) – flood

Religione (f.) – religion

Nazione (f.) – nation

Visione (f.) – vision

Opinione (f.) – opinion

Rimozione (f.) – removal

Ustione (f.) – burn

Acquisizione (f.) – acquisition

The following words have a single form that refers to a man or a woman depending on which article is used:

Listen to track 68

Abitante (inhabitant): un/l'abitante, un'/l'abitante

Cantante (singer): un/il cantante, una/la cantante

Insegnante (teacher): un/l'insegnante, un'/la insegnante

Docente (lecturer): un/il docente, una/la docente

Supplente (substitute teacher): un/il supplente, una/la supplente

Parente (relative): un/il parente, una/la parente

Artista (artist): un/l'artista, un'/l'artista

Barista (bartender): un/il barista, una/la barista

Dentista (dentist): un/il dentista, una/la dentista

Giornalista (journalist): un/il giornalista, una/la giornalista

Farmacista (pharmacist): un/il farmacista, una/la farmacista

Turista (tourist): un/il turista, una/la turista

Nipote is the Italian word for grandson, granddaughter, nephew and niece, so regardless of gender.

Irregular feminine form

Some Italian nouns have an irregular feminine form. Here is a list of the most common ones:

Listen to track 69

Direttore (director) – direttrice (director)

Professore (teacher) – professoressa (teacher)

Scrittore (writer) – scrittrice (writer)

Imperatore (emperor) – imperatrice (empress)

Dottore (doctor) – dottoressa (doctor)

Presidente (president) – presidentessa (president)

Attore (actor) – attrice (actress)

Poeta (poet) – poetessa (poetess)

Pittore (painter) – pittrice (female painter)

Foreign nouns

Listen to track 70

As you might have noticed, most Italian nouns end in a vowel. Usually of foreign origin, nouns that end in a consonant are almost always masculine. Here are some examples:

Internet (m.)

Computer (m.)

Bar (m.)

Film (m.)

Sport (m.)

Business (m.)

Autobus (m.)

Parquet (m.)

Hotel (m.)

Yogurt (m.)

Dribbling (m.)

Scoop (m.)

Aerosol (m.)

Spoiler (m.)

Outsourcing (m.)

Foreign nouns ending with a vowel are generally feminine in Italian. Take a look at the following examples:

Pochette (f.) – purse

Boiserie (f.) – wainscoting

Paillette (f.) – sequin

Consolle (f.) – console

Couperose (f.) – blotches

Names of cars, like, for example, station wagon, city car and *Cinquecento*, are feminine in Italian.

Forming plural nouns in Italian

Listen to track 71

Pluralizing singular nouns in Italian is more difficult than in English. To turn a singular word into a plural one, you need to change the final vowel or the last couple of letters of the word.

Masculine nouns ending in -o take an -i ending in the plural:

Il libro (m.) → i libri – book/books

Il tavolo (m.) → i tavoli – table/tables

Lo scoiattolo (m.) → gli scoiattoli – squirrel/squirrels

Feminine nouns ending in -a take an -e ending in the plural:

La lettera (f.) → le lettere – letter/letters

La domanda (f.) → le domande – question/questions

La camera (f.) → le camere – room/rooms

Masculine nouns ending in -a take an -i ending in the plural:

Il problema (m.) → i problemi – problem/problems

Il sistema (m.) → i sistemi – system/systems

Il poeta (m.) → i poeti – poet/poets

Il pianeta (m.) → i pianeti – planet/planets

Il poema (m.) → i poemi – poem/poems

Il tema (m.) → i temi – theme/themes

Feminine nouns ending in -o do not change in the plural, except for mano (hand):

La mano (f.) → le mani – hand/hands

Turning Italian nouns ending in –e into plurals

Listen to track 72

Nouns ending in **-e** generally end in **-i** in the plural form. Remember to add the appropriate article.

L'abitante (m./f.) → gli abitanti (m.) / le abitanti (f.)

Il / la cantante (m./f.) → i cantanti (m.) / le cantanti (f.)

L'insegnante (m./f.) → gli insegnanti (m.) / le insegnanti (f.)

Il / la docente (m./f.) → i docenti (m.) / le docenti (f.)

Il / la parente (m./f.) → i parenti (m.) / le parenti (f.)

BEWARE: the plural form of nouns ending in **-ista** can be either -i if masculine or -e if feminine.

Il / la giornalista (m./f.) → i giornalisti (m.) / le giornaliste (f.)

Il / la turista (m./f.) → i turisti (m.) / le turiste (f.)

Il / la barista (m./f.) → i baristi (m.) / le bariste (f.)

L'artista (m./f.) → gli artisti (m.) / le artiste (f.)

Il / la dentista (m./f.) → i dentisti (m.) / le dentiste (f.)

Exceptions and irregular nouns

There are plenty of exceptions. It is crucial to know them when forming plural nouns:

- feminine nouns ending in **-cia** and **-gia** form their plural with **-ce** and **-ge** when a consonant comes before the suffix **-cia/-gia**:

Listen to track 73

La pelli**cia** (f.) → le pelli**ce** – fur coat/fur coats

La spiag**gia** (f.) → le spiag**ge** – beach/beaches

La fac**cia** (f.) → le fac**ce** – face/faces

L'aran**cia** (f.) → le aran**ce**– orange/oranges

- feminine nouns ending in **-cia** and **-gia** form their plural with **-cie** and **-gie** when a vowel comes before the suffix **-cia/-gia**:

La cami**cia** (f.) → le cami**cie** – shirt/shirts

La farma**cia** (f.) → le farma**cie** – drugstore/drugstores

La cilie**gia** (f.) → le cilie**gie** – cherry/cherries

- masculine nouns ending in **-co** and **-go** take **-chi** and **-ghi** in the plural, if the accent is on the second last syllable:

Il bu**co** (m.) → i bu**chi** – hole/holes

Il tron**co** (m.) → i tron**chi** – trunk/trunks

Il la**go** (m.) → i la**ghi** – lake/lakes

Il fun**go** (m.) → i fun**ghi** – mushroom/mushrooms

- masculine nouns ending in **-co** and **-go** take **-ci** and **-gi** in the plural when the accent is on the third last syllable:

Il medi**co** (m.) → i medi**ci** – doctor/doctors

Lo psicolo**go** (m.) → gli psicolo**gi** – psychologist/psychologists

Some words, like *amico/amici* (friend/friends) and *dialogo/dialoghi* (dialogue/dialogues) are exceptions.

- feminine nouns ending in **-ca** take a **-che** ending in the plural:

L'ami**ca** (f.) → le ami**che** – friend/friends

La tuni**ca** (f.) → le tuni**che** – tunic/tunics

La cioc**ca** (f.) → le cioc**che** – lock/locks

L'orti**ca** (f.) → le orti**che** – nettle/nettles

La luma**ca** (f.) → le luma**che** – snail/snails

- feminine nouns ending in **-ga** take a **-ghe** ending in the plural:

La ri**ga** (f.) → le ri**ghe** – line/lines

La tar**ga** (f.) → le tar**ghe** – plaque/plaques

La pie**ga** (f.) → le pie**ghe** – fold/folds

- feminine nouns ending in **-ea** change to **-ee** in the plural:

La d**ea** (f.) → le d**ee** – goddess/goddesses

La ninf**ea** (f.) → le ninf**ee** – water lily/water lilies

L'orchid**ea** (f.) → le orchid**ee** – orchid/orchids

- words ending with a grave accent do not change in the plural:

La citt**à** (f.) → le città – city/cities

La qualit**à** (f.) → le qualità – quality/qualities

La novit**à** (f.) → le novità – novelty/novelties

La virt**ù** (f.) → le virtù – virtue/virtues

- truncated words do not change in the plural:

La foto (f.) → le foto – photo/photos

La moto (f.) → le moto – motorcycle/ motorcycles

Il cinema (m.) → i cinema – cinema/cinemas

- foreign words do not change in the plural:

Il computer (m.) → i computer

Il bar (m.) → i bar

Il film (m.) → i film

Nouns with irregular plurals

Some Italian nouns are masculine in the singular form, and become feminine in the plural, ending with **-a**. Here is a list:

Listen to track 74

Il braccio (m.) → le braccia – arm/arms

Il dito (m.) → le dita – finger/fingers

L'osso (m.) → le ossa – bone/bones

Il ciglio (m.) → le ciglia – eyelash/eyelashes

Il sopracciglio (m.) → le sopracciglia – eyebrow/eyebrows

Il labbro (m.) → le labbra – lip/lips

Il ginocchio (m.) → le ginocchia – knee/knees

Il lenzuolo (m.) → le lenzuola – sheet/sheets

Il paio (m.) → le paia – pair/pairs

L'uovo (m.) → le uova – egg/eggs

The feminine noun **ala** (wing) ends in -a but changes to -i in the plural.

L'ala (f.) → le ali – wing/wings

Plural or singular?

Some words are plural in Italian and singular in English. Have a look at the following examples:

Listen to track 75

I miei **capelli** *sono lunghi e lisci* –My hair is long and straight

Fatti gli **affari** *tuoi!* – Mind your own business!

Le **notizie** *del giorno* – Today's news

Come dare buoni **consigli** – How to give great advice

Tutti i **mobili** *della camera da letto devono essere spostati* – All the furniture in the bedroom needs to be moved out

Non dire **sciocchezze!** – Don't talk nonsense!

In Italian, you use the singular form to refer to a piece of something:

un consiglio – a piece of advice

un mobile – a piece of furniture

una notizia – a piece of news

BEWARE: **gente** (people) is singular in Italian but plural in English, and requires a singular verb.

La **gente** *ama vivere qui* – People love living here

Feeling overwhelmed by all these rules and exceptions? Study and practice as much as you can, until you feel more comfortable. Practice makes perfect!

To sum up...

Italian grammar has gendered nouns, which means that every noun can be either feminine or masculine. There's no neuter gender.

As a general rule, feminine nouns end with -a and masculine nouns end with -o for singular, but there are plenty of exceptions. Some Italian nouns have an irregular feminine form.

As for pluralizing, most masculine nouns take an -i ending in the plural, and feminine nouns ending in -a take an -e ending in the plural, but there are a number of exceptions that need to be memorized.

Some Italian nouns are masculine in the singular form and become feminine in the plural.

Workbook Lesson 4. Nouns

Exercise 4.1: Tick the right answer:

1. _____ tavolo è di legno. (The table is made of wood.)
   1) La   2) Il   3) Lo

2. _____ minestra è bollente. (The soup is hot.)
   1) La   2) Le   3) Lo

3. _____ animale è socievole. (The animal is sociable.)
   1) Lo   2) Il   3) L'

4. _____ città sono affollate. (The cities are crowded.)
   1) La   2) Le   3) I

5. _____ gente lavora. (People work.)
   1) La   2) Le   3) I

Exercise 4.2: Classify the following nouns in the table:

Città, Cinema, Radio, Crisi, Bici, Papà, Cameriere, Capitale, Valore, Fiore

Il	La

Exercise 4.3: Translate the following sentences from English into Italian:

English	Italian
1. The problem	
2. The snow	
3. The health	
4. The blood	
5. The dust	

Exercise 4.4: Change the following nouns from singular to plural:

Singular	Plural
1. L'analisi (The analysis)	
2. L'ambiente (The environment)	
3. L'arte (The art)	
4. Il cognome (The surname)	
5. Lo studente (The student)	

Exercise 4.5: Change the masculine nouns to their feminine equivalent:

Masculine	Feminine
1. Il padre (The father)	
2. Il poeta (The poet)	
3. Il signore (The gentleman)	
4. L'attore (The actor)	
5. Lo studente (The student)	

Answers:

Exercise 4.1:

1) Il / 2) La / 3) L' / 4) Le / 5) La

Exercise 4.2:

Il: il cinema, il papà, il cameriere, il valore, il fiore

La: la città, la radio, la crisi, la bici, la capitale

Exercise 4.3:

1. Il problema / 2. La neve / 3. La salute / 4. Il sangue / 5. La polvere

Exercise 4.4:

1. Le analisi / 2. Gli ambienti / 3. Le arti / 4. I cognomi / 5. Gli studenti

Exercise 4.5:

1. La madre / 2. La poetessa / 3. La signora / 4. L'attrice / 5. La studentessa

LESSON 5: VERBI REGOLARI E IRREGOLARI – REGULAR AND IRREGULAR VERBS IN THE PRESENT TENSE

Italian verbs can be either regular or irregular. **Regular verbs** follow a set pattern in their conjugation, whereas **irregular verbs** don't follow the regular conjugation rules and you have to learn them individually.

In this lesson, we will show you how to form the **present tense** (*presente*) of regular verbs and you will get to practice some of the most common irregular verbs in Italian. Sound good? Ok, let's get started!

Constructing the present tense of regular verbs

To conjugate Italian verbs in the present indicative tense, you first need to take off the infinitive endings and add the appropriate endings to the remaining stem.

Let's have a look at **present tense verb conjugations** for each of the three types of regular Italian verbs.

First-conjugation verbs

To make the *presente* of **Italian regular verbs ending in -are**, take off the infinitive ending to find the root of the verb and add the following endings:

-o for "io"

-i for "tu"

-a for "lui/lei"

-iamo for "noi"

-ate for "voi"

-ano for "loro"

Listen to track 76

Parlare (to speak)

(Io) parl**o** – I speak

(Tu) parl**i** – You speak

(Lui/lei) parl**a** – He/she/it speaks

(Noi) parl**iamo** – We speak

(Voi) parl**ate** – Y'all speak

(Loro) parl**ano** – They speak

As you can see, the verb has different conjugations depending on who is doing the action. In Italian, verbs agree with subjects and subject pronouns. Here are some examples:

Parli italiano? – Do you speak Italian?

Chi parla? – Who's speaking?

Let's conjugate another **-are** verb just to reinforce what we just did:

Listen to track 77

Cantare (to sing)

(Io) cant**o** – I sing

(Tu) cant**i** – You sing

(Lui/lei) cant**a** – He/she/it sings

(Noi) cant**iamo** – We sing

(Voi) cant**ate** – Y'all sing

(Loro) cant**ano** – They sing

Second-conjugation verbs

To make the *presente* of **Italian regular verbs ending in -ere**, drop the infinitive ending to find the root of the verb and add the correct ending for the person you are talking about:

-o for "io"

-i for "tu"

-e for "lui/lei"

-iamo for "noi"

-ete for "voi"

-ono for "loro"

Listen to track 78

Vendere (to sell)

(Io) vend**o** – I sell

(Tu) vend**i** – You sell

(Lui/lei) vend**e** – He/she/it sells

(Noi) vend**iamo** – We sell

(Voi) vend**ete** – Y'all sell

(Loro) vend**ono** – They sell

As you can see, the 'io' (I), 'tu' (you) and 'noi' (we) endings are the same as **-are** verb endings. Let's conjugate another **-ere** verb:

Listen to track 79

Leggere (to read)

(Io) legg**o** – I read

(Tu) legg**i** – You read

(Lui/lei) legg**e** – He/she/it reads

(Noi) legg**iamo** – We read

(Voi) legg**ete** – Y'all read

(Loro) legg**ono** – They read

Easy, right? Regular **-ere** verbs follow this cookie-cutter way of conjugating. Memorize the present tense endings and you're good to go!

Third-conjugation verbs

There are two ways to conjugate verbs ending in **-ire** in the present tense, so every time you learn a new **-ire** verb, memorize which set of conjugations is appropriate for it.

To make the *presente* of most **regular -ire verbs**, take off the infinitive ending to find the root of the verb and add the following endings:

- **-isco** for "io"
- **-isci** for "tu"
- **-isce** for "lui/lei"
- **-iamo** for "noi"
- **-ite** for "voi"
- **-iscono** for "loro"

Note: the Italian letters "sc" have a /*sh*/ sound when followed by "e" and "i", and a /*sk*/ sound when followed by "o".

Listen to track 80

Pulire (to clean)

(Io) pul**isco** – I clean

(Tu) pul**isci** – You clean

(Lui/lei) pul**isce** – He/she/it cleans

(Noi) pul**iamo** – We clean

(Voi) pul**ite** – Y'all clean

(Loro) pul**iscono** – They clean

Some common **-ire** verbs, like *dormire* (to sleep), *aprire* (to open), *coprire* (to cover), *servire* (to serve), *soffrire* (to suffer), *sentire* (to feel, to hear), *offrire* (to offer), *seguire* (to follow), *scoprire* (to discover) and *partire* (to leave), do **not** add **-isc** to the root of the verb. The present tense endings of these verbs are as follows:

- **-o** for "io"
- **-i** for "tu"
- **-e** for "lui/lei"
- **-iamo** for "noi"
- **-ite** for "voi"
- **-ono** for "loro"

Listen to track 81

Dormire (to sleep)

(Io) dorm**o** – I sleep

(Tu) dorm**i** – You sleep

(Lui/lei) dorm**e** – He/she/it sleeps

(Noi) dorm**iamo** – We sleep

(Voi) dorm**ite** – Y'all sleep

(Loro) dorm**ono** – They sleep

Note: the subject pronouns are almost always omitted because the verb ending by itself makes it clear who is performing the action.

Listen to track 82

Dipende – It depends

*Mi **senti**?* – Can you hear me?

Nevica – It's snowing

How to make the present simple tense of irregular verbs

As mentioned previously, there are many Italian verbs that don't follow the same predictable rules for creating verb forms that regular verbs do. These include some very common verbs, such as **essere** (to be) and **avere** (to have). Their conjugations are as follows:

Listen to track 83

Essere (to be)

(Io) sono – I am

(Tu) sei – You are

(Lui/lei) è – He/she/it is

(Noi) siamo – We are

(Voi) siete – Y'all are

(Loro) sono – They are

Listen to track 84

Avere (to have)

(Io) ho – I have

(Tu) hai – You have

(Lui/lei) ha – He/she/it has

(Noi) abbiamo – We have

(Voi) avete – Y'all have

(Loro) hanno – They have

These are some more common irregular verbs:

Listen to track 85

Andare (to go)

(Io) vado – I go

(Tu) vai – You go

(Lui/lei) va – He/she/it goes

(Noi) andiamo – We go

(Voi) andate – Y'all go

(Loro) vanno – They go

Listen to track 86

Dare (to give)

(Io) do – I give

(Tu) dai – You give

(Lui/lei) dà – He/she/it gives

(Noi) diamo – We give

(Voi) date – Y'all give

(Loro) danno – They give

Listen to track 87

Venire (to come)

(Io) vengo – I come

(Tu) vieni – You come

(Lui/lei) viene – He/she/it comes

(Noi) veniamo – We come

(Voi) venite – Y'all come

(Loro) vengono – They come

Listen to track 88

Stare (to stay)

(Io) sto – I stay

(Tu) stai – You stay

(Lui/lei) sta – He/she/it stays

(Noi) stiamo – We stay

(Voi) state – Y'all stay

(Loro) stanno – They stay

Listen to track 89

Uscire (to go out)

(Io) esco – I go out

(Tu) esci – You go out

(Lui/lei) esce – He/she/it goes out

(Noi) usciamo – We go out

(Voi) uscite – Y'all go out

(Loro) escono – They go out

Listen to track 90

Vedere (to see)

(Io) vedo – I see

(Tu) vedi – You see

(Lui/lei) vede – He/she/it sees

(Noi) vediamo – We see

(Voi) vedete – Y'all see

(Loro) vedono – They see

Here are some additional groups of **irregular verbs** in the present tense.

1. Spelling changes

Piacere (to like, to be pleasing), *compiacere* (to appease), *spiacere* (to mind), *dispiacere* (to be sorry) and *giacere* (to lay) take a double "cc" in the **io** (I), **noi** (we) and **loro** (they) conjugations.

Listen to track 91

Giacere (to lay)

(Io) gia**ccio** – I lay

(Tu) giaci – You lay

(Lui/lei) giace – He/she/it lays

(Noi) gia**cciamo** – We lay

(Voi) giacete – Y'all lay

(Loro) gia**cciono** – They lay

Rimanere (to remain), *tenere* (to hold, to keep), *intervenire* (to intervene), *contenere* (to contain) add a "g" into their **io** (I) and **loro** (they) conjugations.

Listen to track 92

Rimanere (to remain)

(Io) riman**go** – I remain

(Tu) rimani – You remain

(Lui/lei) rimane – He/she/it remains

(Noi) rimaniamo – We remain

(Voi) rimanete – Y'all remain

(Loro) riman**gono** – They remain

Verbs ending in **-ciare** and **-giare**, like *cominciare* (to begin), *mangiare* (to eat), *rinunciare* (to renounce), *parcheggiare* (to park), *cacciare* (to hunt), *danneggiare* (to damage, to ruin), *intralciare* (to hinder) and *baciare* (to kiss), have a change in spelling when conjugated so that they maintain the expected pronunciation. An "i" is dropped from the end of the stem before the **tu** (you) and **noi** (we) endings, otherwise you would get a double "ii".

Listen to track 93

Mangiare (to eat)

(Io) mangi**o** – I eat

(Tu) mang**i** – You eat

(Lui/lei) mangi**a** – He/she/it eats

(Noi) mang**iamo** – We eat

(Voi) mangi**ate** – Y'all eat,

(Loro) mangi**ano** – They eat

Verbs ending in **-care**, like *applicare* (to apply), *praticare* (to practice), *codificare* (to codify), *bloccare* (to block), *dedicare* (to dedicate) and *cercare* (to look for, to search), add an extra "h" after the "c" in the **tu** (you) and **noi** (we) endings to preserve the /k/ sound of the infinitive.

Listen to track 94

Praticare (to practice)

(Io) pratic**o** – I practice

(Tu) prati**chi** – You practice

(Lui/lei) pratic**a** – He/she/it practices

(Noi) prati**chiamo** – We practice

(Voi) pratic**ate** – Y'all practice

(Loro) pratic**ano** – They practice

Verbs ending in **-gare**, like *piegare* (to bend), *collegare* (to connect), *allungare* (to extend), *negare* (to deny) and *dialogare* (to converse), add an extra "h" after the "g" in the **tu** (you) and **noi** (we) endings in order to preserve the hard sound of the infinitive.

Listen to track 95

Collegare (to connect)

(Io) colleg**o** – I connect

(Tu) colleg**hi** – You connect

(Lui/lei) colleg**a** – He/she/it connects

(Noi) colleg**hiamo** – We connect

(Voi) colleg**ate** – Y'all connect

(Loro) colleg**ano** – They connect

2. Stem changes

Apparire (to appear), *morire* (to die) and *sedere* (to sit, to be seated) have stem changes in the present tense.

Listen to track 96

Apparire (to appear)

(Io) appaio – I appear

(Tu) appari – You appear

(Lui/lei) appare – He/she/it appears

(Noi) appariamo – We appear

(Voi) apparite – Y'all appear

(Loro) appaiono – They appear

Listen to track 97

Morire (to die)

(Io) muoio – I die

(Tu) muori – You die

(Lui/lei) muore – He/she/it dies

(Noi) moriamo – We die

(Voi) morite – Y'all die

(Loro) muoiono – They die

Listen to track 98

Sedere (to sit, to be seated)

(Io) siedo – I sit

(Tu) siedi – You sit

(Lui/lei) siede – He/she/it sits

(Noi) sediamo – We sit

(Voi) sedete – Y'all sit

(Loro) siedono – They sit

3. Contracted infinitive verbs

Dire (to say) comes from the Latin *'dīcere'*, *fare* (to do, to make) comes from *'facere'* and *bere* (to drink) comes from *'bibere'*, and use their uncontracted stem in most conjugations.

Listen to track 99

Fare (to do, to make)

(Io) faccio – I do

(Tu) fai – You do

(Lui/lei) fa – He/she/it does

(Noi) facciamo – We do

(Voi) fate – Y'all do

(Loro) fanno – They do

Listen to track 100

Bere (to drink)

(Io) bevo – I drink

(Tu) bevi – You drink

(Lui/lei) beve – He/she/it drinks

(Noi) beviamo – We drink

(Voi) bevete – Y'all drink

(Loro) bevono – They drink

Listen to track 101

Dire (to say)

(Io) dico – I say

(Tu) dici – You say

(Lui/lei) dice – He/she/it says

(Noi) diciamo – We say

(Voi) dite – Y'all say

(Loro) dicono – They say

Note: the letter "c" followed by "e" and "i" has a /*ch*/ sound.

4. Modal verbs

Italian modal verbs are irregular in the present tense.

Listen to track 102

Volere (to want)

(Io) voglio – I want

(Tu) vuoi – You want

(Lui/lei) vuole – He/she/it wants

(Noi) vogliamo – We want

(Voi) volete – Y'all want

(Loro) vogliono – They want

Listen to track 103

Potere (can, be able)

(Io) posso – I can

(Tu) puoi – You can

(Lui/lei) può – He/she/it can

(Noi) possiamo – We can

(Voi) potete – Y'all can

(Loro) possono – They can

Listen to track 104

Sapere (to know)

(Io) so – I know

(Tu) sai – You know

(Lui/lei) sa – He/she/it knows

(Noi) sappiamo – We know

(Voi) sapete – Y'all know

(Loro) sanno – They know

Listen to track 105

Dovere (to must, to have to)

(Io) devo – I must

(Tu) devi – You must

(Lui/lei) deve – He/she/it must

(Noi) dobbiamo – We must

(Voi) dovete – Y'all must

(Loro) devono – They must

A few common irregular verbs have infinitives ending in **-rre**.

Listen to track 106

Comporre (to compose)

(Io) compongo – I compose

(Tu) componi – You compose

(Lui/lei) compone – He/she/it composes

(Noi) componiamo – We compose

(Voi) componete – Y'all compose

(Loro) compongono – They compose

Listen to track 107

Porre (to put)

(Io) pongo – I put

(Tu) poni – You put

(Lui/lei) pone – He/she/it puts

(Noi) poniamo – We put

(Voi) ponete – Y'all put

(Loro) pongono – They put

Listen to track 108

Proporre (to propose)

(Io) propongo – I propose

(Tu) proponi – You propose

(Lui/lei) propone – He/she/it proposes

(Noi) proponiamo – We propose

(Voi) proponete – Y'all propose

(Loro) propongono – They propose

Listen to track 109

Supporre (to suppose)

(Io) suppongo – I suppose

(Tu) supponi – You suppose

(Lui/lei) suppone – He/she/it supposes

(Noi) supponiamo – We suppose

(Voi) supponete – Y'all suppose

(Loro) suppongono – They suppose

Listen to track 110

Condurre (to lead)

(Io) conduco – I lead

(Tu) conduci – You lead

(Lui/lei) conduce – He/she/it leads

(Noi) conduciamo – We lead

(Voi) conducete – Y'all lead

(Loro) conducono – They lead

Listen to track 111

Produrre (to produce)

(Io) produco – I produce

(Tu) produci – You produce

(Lui/lei) produce – He/she/it produces

(Noi) produciamo – We produce

(Voi) producete – Y'all produce

(Loro) producono – They produce

Listen to track 112

Ridurre (to reduce)

(Io) riduco – I reduce

(Tu) riduci – You reduce

(Lui/lei) riduce – He/she/it reduces

(Noi) riduciamo – We reduce

(Voi) riducete – Y'all reduce

(Loro) riducono – They reduce

Listen to track 113

Tradurre (to translate)

(Io) traduco – I translate

(Tu) traduci – You translate

(Lui/lei) traduce – He/she/it translates

(Noi) traduciamo – We translate

(Voi) traducete – Y'all translate

(Loro) traducono – They translate

Listen to track 114

Indurre (to induce)

(Io) induco – I induce

(Tu) induci – You induce

(Lui/lei) induce – He/she/it induces

(Noi) induciamo – We induce

(Voi) inducete – Y'all induce

(Loro) inducono – They induce

To sum up...

In Italian, verbs agree with subjects and have different conjugations depending on who is doing the action.

Italian verbs can be either regular or irregular. Regular verbs follow a set pattern in their conjugation. To conjugate them in the present indicative tense, you need to take off the infinitive endings and add the appropriate endings for the person you are talking about.

To make the present simple tense:

- Regular -are verbs add **-o, -i, -a, -iamo, -ate, -ano**.
- Regular -ere verbs add **-o, -i, -e, -iamo, -ete**, -ono.
- Regular -ire verbs add **-isco, -isci, -isce, -iamo, -ite, -iscono**.

Note that a few -ire verbs add these endings: **-o, -i, -e, -iamo, -ite, -ono**.

Irregular verbs don't follow the regular, predictable conjugation rules and need to be memorized. These include some very common verbs, such as *essere* (to be), *avere* (to have), *andare* (to go) and *dare* (to give).

Workbook Lesson 5. Regular and Irregular Verbs in the Present Tense

Exercise 5.1: Conjugate the verbs between brackets in the simple present tense:

1. Io (andare) _____ in palestra 3 volte alla settimana. (I go to the gym 3 times a week.)
2. Noi non (bere) _____ alcolici prima dei pasti. (We do not drink alcohol before meals.)
3. (Potere) _____ aiutarci ad apparecchiare la tavola? (Can you help us set the table?)
4. I nuovi film (uscire) _____ al cinema il mercoledì. (New films come out at the cinema on a Wednesday.)
5. Il mio gatto (mangiare) _____ troppo. (My cat eats too much.)

Exercise 5.2: Change the following sentences into the plural:

Singular	Plural
1. Io ballo la salsa. (I dance salsa)	
2. Vuoi venire a casa mia? (Do you want to come to my house?)	
3. Lei non può uscire. (She can't go out.)	
4. Senza acqua la pianta muore. (Without water the plant dies.)	
5. Faccio sempre la doccia prima di dormire. (I always take a shower before sleeping.)	

Exercise 5.3: Change the following sentences into the singular:

Plural	Singular
1. Noi sappiamo tutto. (We know everything.)	
2. Loro giocano a scacchi. (They play chess.)	
3. Voi cucinate tutti i giorni. (You cook every day.)	
4. Noi andiamo al ristorante. (We go to the restaurant.)	
5. Voi scherzate sempre. (You always joke.)	

Exercise 5.4: Translate the following sentences from English into Italian:

English	Italian
1. He says we don't have to worry.	
2. I can only concentrate when it's silent.	
3. They study for the exam.	
4. We are looking for a solution to the problem.	
5. If you turn off the light I can't read.	

Exercise 5.5: Tick the right answer:

1. Io ____ ogni mese. (I travel every month.)
   1) viaggiare   2) viaggio   3) viaggiamo

2. Loro ____ sushi. (They eat sushi.)
   1) mangia   2) mangiamo   3) mangiano

3. Noi ____ il tango. (We dance the tango.)
   1) balliamo   2) ballano   3) ballare

4. Lei ____ una cartolina. (She writes a postcard.)
   1) scrivi   2) scriviamo   3) scrive

5. Loro ____ la verità. (They tell the truth.)
   1) dicano   2) dicono   3) diciamo

Answers:

Exercise 5.1:

1. Io vado in palestra 3 volte alla settimana.
2. Noi non beviamo alcolici prima dei pasti.
3. Potete/puoi aiutarci ad apparecchiare la tavola?
4. I nuovi film escono al cinema il mercoledì.
5. Il mio gatto mangia troppo.

Exercise 5.2:

1. Noi balliamo la salsa.
2. Volete venire a casa mia?
3. Loro non possono uscire.
4. Senza acqua le piante muoiono.
5. Facciamo sempre la doccia prima di dormire.

Exercise 5.3:

1. Io so tutto.
2. Lui/Lei gioca a scacchi.
3. Tu cucini tutti i giorni.
4. Io vado al ristorante.
5. Tu scherzi sempre.

Exercise 5.4:

1. Lui dice che non dobbiamo preoccuparci.

2. Riesco a concentrarmi solo con il silenzio.

3. Loro studiano per l'esame.

4. Cerchiamo una soluzione al problema.

5. Se spegni la luce non posso leggere.

Exercise 5.5:

1) viaggio / 2) mangiano / 3) balliamo / 4) scrive / 5) dicono

LESSON 6: NUMERI - NUMBERS

Today we're looking at something that seems so simple, but is actually one of the most important aspects of learning any foreign language: nailing your numbers. Whether you're counting to ten, asking for the time or writing the date, we've got you covered.

Learning your numbers in Italian really *is* as easy as 1, 2, 3. Luckily, the system is simple, regular and easy to follow. Don't worry: after you've read our top tips, you'll be counting in your sleep.

Simple numbers: 1 – 100

It may seem simple, but memorizing these numbers will give you a perfect starting point to help with all your number-related problems. Something as easy as paying in a shop or booking a table at a restaurant will require knowledge of these numbers – and that's where we come in.

We're going to break it down into chunks for you, AND give you the correct pronunciation.

You're welcome.

Let's start at the beginning. As Julie Andrews tells us, it's a very good place to start.

Numbers 1 – 10
Listen to track 115

1	Uno	oo-noh
2	Due	doo-eh
3	Tre	Treh
4	Quattro	kwat-roh
5	Cinque	cheen-kweh
6	Sei	seh-ee
7	Sette	set-the
8	Otto	oht-to
9	Nove	noh-veh
10	Dieci	dee-eh-chee

That's all there is to it! Practice counting to ten over and over again and before long, you'll start to get the hang of it.

Unfortunately, once we hit ten, the regular pattern starts to go a little out the window. The good news, though, is that after 20, we're all regular again. Phew! Read on to find out how to structure the 'teens'.

Numbers 11 – 20

Listen to track 116

11	Undici	oon-dee-chee
12	Dodici	doh-dee-chee
13	Tredici	treh-dee-chee
14	Quattordici	kwaht-tor-dee-chee
15	Quindici	kween-dee-chee
16	Sedici	seh-dee-chee
17	Diciassette	dee-chahs-set-eh
18	Diciotto	dee-choht-toh
19	Diciannove	dee-chahn-noh-veh
20	Venti	ven-tee

An easy(ish) way to remember this is that: after 16, the **'dici'** part flips over to the front of the word. The spelling, unfortunately, you have to remember for yourself.

Numbers from 20 – 99

Listen to track 117

We're now going to take a look at the way to structure numbers from 20 – 99. Thankfully, this follows a pretty clear pattern, which means that you won't have to memorize nearly 100 numbers. Woo-hoo!

Let's take the twenties as an example (because everyone knows that your twenties are the best years of your life).

21	Ventuno	ven-too-noh
22	Ventidue	ven-tee-doo-eh
23	Ventitré	ven-tee-treh
24	Ventiquattro	ven-tee-kwaht-troh
25	Venticinque	ven-tee-cheehn-kweh
26	Ventisei	ven-tee-seh-ee
27	Ventisette	ven-tee-set-the
28	Ventotto	ven-toht-toh
29	Ventinove	ven-tee-noh-veh

As you can see, the structure is really simple:

Venti + Number from 1-9		

Or, if there's a vowel at the beginning of the number (i.e. with 1 or 8):		

Vent' + Number		

And this pattern is followed all the way up to 100.

Let's take a look now at the multiples of 10, from 30 – 90 (all of which are super easy to remember).

30	Trenta	tren-tah
40	Quaranta	kwah-rahn-tah
50	Cinquanta	cheen-kwahn-tah
60	Sessanta	ses-sahn-tah
70	Settanta	set-tahn-tah
80	Ottanta	oht-tahn-ta
90	Novanta	noh-vahn-tah

So, using the same formula as above, you can work out any number that you could ever need between 20 and 99! For example:

*43 = Quaranta + Tre → **Quarantatre***

*67 = Sessanta + Sette → **Sessantasette***

*81 = Ottant' + Uno → **Ottantuno***

Larger Numbers: 100/1000 etc...

Now that you've mastered the simple numbers that lead up to 100, it's time to come to terms with those pesky big numbers. Even in your own language, these can seem overwhelming, but we're here to help you get fully equipped with anything larger than 100.

The Hundreds

Listen to track 118

These are super simple. Once you know the word for 100, this is your golden ticket to all the 'hundreds'. This magical word is:

Cento

To put it bluntly, just shove a number between 2 and 9 in front of this and *hey presto*! That's your number. Here's a table to help you remember (and show you the pronunciation):

200	Duecento	doo-eh-chen-toh
300	Trecento	treh-chen-toh
400	Quattrocento	kwaht-troh-chen-toh
500	Cinquecento	cheen-kweh-chen-toh
600	Seicento	seh-ee-chen-toh
700	Settecento	set-teh-chen-toh
800	Ottocento	oht-toh-chen-toh
900	Novecento	noh-veh-chen-toh

When you're looking for a specific number between 100 and 1000, it works pretty much in the same way as in English. HOWEVER, while we would say, for example,

Three hundred <u>and</u> fifty-two

The Italian construction is even simpler, as they drop the 'and'. So, this would literally be translated as

Trecento cinquantadue

(Three hundred fifty-two)

And it works this way for any of these numbers.

The Thousands

Before moving onto describing the thousands (which work in a similar way to the hundreds), I want to tell you about *DECIMAL PLACES*.

This probably sounds like something that wouldn't make a big difference. HOWEVER, the use of commas and decimal points (full stops) is totally different in English from Italian, and can sometimes cause a lot of confusion. A good example can be found in *CURRENCY*.

Let's take the figure:

£1,274.50

To anyone in the English-speaking world, this looks normal (albeit expensive). BUT, what you have to remember is that in Italian (and in many other European countries), the **commas** and the **full stops** are **SWAPPED**. So, the above figure, if written in Euros, is:

€1.274,50

And this is identical also for normal numbers (i.e. not currency-related). The decimal point is actually a decimal **comma**. Confusing, we know.

All that aside, let's talk about the *THOUSANDS*.

Listen to track 119

The structure of the thousands is actually pretty similar to the hundreds, but this time our key word is:

Mille

Which obviously means 'thousand/one thousand'. BUT as soon as we move to more than 'one thousand', **mille** becomes **mila**. Don't ask us why.

Let's look at the pattern in one of our trusty tables:

2000	Duemila	doo-eh-mee-lah
3000	Tremila	treh-mee-lah
4000	Quattromila	kwaht-troh-mee-lah
5000	Cinquemila	cheen-kweh-mee-lah
6000	Seimila	seh-ee-mee-lah
7000	Settemila	seht-teh-mee-lah
8000	Ottomila	oht-toh-mee-lah
9000	Novemila	noh-veh-mee-lah

So, how do we construct a number between 1,000 and 10,000? By using the same method as we've already seen with the hundreds, of course. Have a look at this example:

One thousand, seven hundred <u>and</u> twenty-six

In Italian, by dropping the 'and' again, we can easily construct any number within this bracket.

Mille settecento ventisei
(One thousand seven hundred twenty-six)

And it really is that simple! Once you get the hang of the patterns, you'll find that Italian numbers are a piece of cake.

Ordinal Numbers

'What on earth are those?' we hear you ask. **Ordinal Numbers** is just a fancy name for saying 1st, 2nd, 3rd, 4th and so on. Luckily, Italian ordinal numbers are actually much more regular than their English counterparts, and after '10th' all use the same ending. Yay!

Let's take a look at the first 10 numbers.

Listen to track 120

1st	primo
2nd	secondo
3rd	terzo
4th	quarto
5th	quinto
6th	sesto
7th	Settimo
8th	Ottavo
9th	Nono
10th	Decimo

Once you've memorised these, the rest is a doddle. Here's how you structure any other ordinal number:

Number + "-esimo"

Here are some examples for you:

43rd = *Quarantatre* + *esimo* → ***Quarantatreesimo***

57th = *Cinquantasette* + *esimo* → ***Cinquantasettesimo***

82nd = *Ottantadue* + *esimo* → ***Ottantaduesimo***

Dates

Writing the date in different languages is something that sounds simple – and, for the most part, is. But there are a few little details and differences to bear in mind that will really have you speaking like a native. Here's an example of the date to highlight these key variations.

giovedì 4 aprile 2019

The first thing to note when writing the date in Italian is that they **DO NOT USE ORDINAL NUMBERS**. So, this actually makes it quite a lot easier than in English, and is also the same when you are saying the date aloud. Instead of the **FOURTH** of April, today is actually the **FOUR** April.

Secondly, neither the day of the week nor the month are capitalised – EVER. This goes for every time these words are used in any context (unless, obviously, they're at the beginning of a sentence).

Now for something that a lot of people struggle with: the year. Again, this is much easier in Italian than in English. Taking the year 1972, we can explain to you the differences between the Italian way of expressing this aloud, and the English way. In English, we would split the date into two separate numbers, and say this date as:

Nineteen seventy-two

But in Italian, we would take this at face value: i.e., treat it as one whole number. We would therefore say (as we learned earlier on in this guide):

Mille novecento settantadue

(One thousand, nine hundred and seventy-two)

And this is the same for any year or date.

Telling the Time

While we've got you thinking about numbers, we're going to talk you through how to express time in Italian which, again, has a few subtle differences from the English way of telling the time.

The simplest way to talk about the time in Italian is pretty much exactly the same as in English. **15:25** in English would be:

Three twenty-five

or

Twenty-five past three

Whereas, in Italian, you would simply say:

Tre e venticinque

(Three and twenty-five)

When you're feeling a little more old-school, and want to go analogue instead of digital, take a look at the following table:

Listen to track 121

Quarter past	E un quarto
Half past	E mezzo
Quarter to	Meno un quarto

You can also use '**meno**' for our equivalent of 'ten to' / 'five to' / 'twenty to' etc. For example, '**five to eleven**' would become:

Le undici meno cinque.

REMEMBER: time in Italian is always plural. So instead of saying:

It is ten 'o' clock

We would say:

Sono le dieci.

EXCEPT when it is: one 'o' clock, midday or midnight.

So that was our inclusive list of all things numerous. Hopefully now, when someone asks you for the date, time and number of cats you own, you'll be able to answer them seamlessly. While a lot of this requires a good memory and determination, you'll find that the regular patterns will help you as you're learning to count, tell the time and write the date in Italian.

To sum up...

Learning to count in Italian is a very important skill to master, as numbers are used in so many situations. Let's start with the basics:

- **1-10**: uno, due, tre, quattro, cinque, sei, sette, otto, nove, dieci
- **11-20**: undici, dodici, tredici, quattordici, quindici, sedici, diciassette, diciotto, diciannove, venti
- **20-29**: venti, ventuno, ventidue, ventitré, ventiquattro, venticinque, ventisei, ventisette, ventotto, ventinove

From here, you just apply the same principles: trenta (30), quaranta (40), cinquanta (50), sessanta (60), settanta (70), ottanta (80), novanta (90), cento (100), duecento (200), trecento (300), quattrocento (400), cinquecento (500), seicento (600), settecento (700), ottocento (800), novecento (900), mille (1000), duemila (2000), tremila (3000), quattromila (4000), cinquemila (5000), seimila (6000), settemila (7000), ottomila (8000), novemila (9000).

Italian ordinal numbers are primo, secondo, terzo, quarto, quinto, sesto, settimo, ottavo, nono, decimo. After '10th' all use the ending 'esimo'. Don't use ordinal numbers when writing the date in Italian, and note that the day of the week and the month are not capitalized.

Workbook Lesson 6. Numbers

Exercise 6.1: Complete the exercise by following the example:

Example: Quarantadue - 42

1. Ventuno - _____
2. Ottantaquattro - _____
3. Trentasette - _____
4. Cinquantanove - _____
5. Novantacinque - _____

Exercise 6.2: Complete the exercise by following the example:

Example: 19 - Diciannove

1. 76 - _____
2. 67 - _____
3. 12 - _____
4. 345 - _____
5. 876 - _____

Exercise 6.3: Complete the exercise with numbers:

1. Elisa studia ____ (4) ore al giorno. (Elisa studies for four hours a day.)
2. Devo prendere la medicina ogni ____ (8) ore. (I have to take the medicine every eight hours.)
3. Andiamo al supermercato ____ (2) volte alla settimana. (We go to the supermarket twice a week.)
4. Devi annaffiare la pianta ogni ____ (72) ore. (You have to water the plant every seventy-two hours.)
5. Paolo festeggia il suo compleanno ogni ____ (5) anni. (Paolo celebrates his birthday every 5 years.)

Exercise 6.4: Write the following numbers as words:

1. 13 chili. - _____
2. 68 anni. - _____
3. 46 chilometri. - _____
4. 19 giorni. - _____
5. 23 bambini. - _____

Exercise 6.5: Write the phone numbers as in the example:

Example: Luisa 3334456231 - tre tre tre quattro quattro cinque sei due tre uno

1. Roberta 3472190876 - _____
2. Maurizio 3358965456 - _____
3. Giacomo 3281232509 - _____
4. Andrea 3487751078 - _____
5. Antonella 3498802123 - _____

Answers:

Exercise 6.1:

1) 21 / 2) 84 / 3) 37 / 4) 59 / 5) 95

Exercise 6.2:

1. Settantasei / 2. Sessantasette / 3. Dodici / 4. Trecentoquarantacinque / 5. Ottocentosettantasei

Exercise 6.3:

1. Elisa studia quattro ore al giorno.

2. Devo prendere la medicina ogni otto ore.

3. Andiamo al supermercato due volte alla settimana.

4. Devi annaffiare la pianta ogni settantadue ore.

5. Paolo festeggia il suo compleanno ogni cinque anni.

Exercise 6.4:

1. Tredici chili. / 2. Sessantotto anni. / 3. Quarantasei chilometri. / 4. Diciannove giorni. / 5. Ventitré bambini.

Exercise 6.5:

1. Per la torta sono necessari cinquecentocinquanta grammi di farina.

2. Nella torre ci sono milleduecentotrentaquattro scalini.

3. Nel loro sito internet vendono un milione di prodotti.

4. Quest'anno mia nonna compie centotré anni.

5. Nella biblioteca ci sono settecentocinquantamila libri.

LESSON 7: COME FARE DOMANDE - HOW TO ASK QUESTIONS

A **question** is a sentence used to find out information, as opposed to sentences that make a statement, express an exclamation or deliver a command. Asking questions in Italian is simpler than in English and it is just a matter of intonation.

In this lesson, we will show you **how to ask questions in Italian**. Ready? Let's get right into it!

The Italian interrogative clauses

To ask a question in Italian, you just need to add a **question mark** at the end of the sentence and use the right intonation.

Look at the following examples:

Listen to track 123

Alessio è nato a settembre – Alessio was born in September

Alessio è nato a settembre? – Alessio was born in September?

As you can see, the sentence structure remains unchanged and we use the exact same words to ask a question. All you have to do is place a **question mark** at the end of the sentence and use a **rising intonation** of your voice. When asking a question, the pitch of your voice rises toward the end of the phrase, usually on the final word.

Unlike in English, there is no inversion of the subject and predicate. You can place the subject at the end of the phrase, but this is by no means always the case. For example:

Gli studenti si comportano bene – The students are well behaved

Gli studenti si comportano bene? / Si comportano bene gli studenti? – Are the students well behaved?

Different kinds of interrogative clauses in Italian

Listen to track 124

In Italian there are three kinds of interrogative clause:

1. **Simple interrogative clauses**, which are intended to have a specific answer. Polar questions, also called yes–no questions, are designed to have a *sì* (yes) or a *no* (no) as an answer.

Parla inglese? – Do you speak English?

Sei felice? – Are you happy?

Sei uscito ieri sera? – Did you go out last night?

2. **Alternative questions**, which give a choice of two or more answers.

Preferisci il panettone o il pandoro? – Do you prefer panettone or pandoro?

Veronica lavora in centro o in periferia? – Does Veronica work in the city or in the suburbs?

3. **Rhetorical questions**, which are posed only to make a point and are not supposed to be answered.

Non sembra anche a te che oggi sia una splendida giornata? – Doesn't today seem to you to be a wonderful day?

Italian question words

Listen to track 125

To ask questions that require more than a yes or no answer, you generally have to use a **question word**, a key piece of any language. The following are common Italian question words which never change their form:

Dove? – Where?

Come? – How?

Quando? – When?

Perché? – Why?

Chi? – Who?/Whom?

Che cosa? – What?

The following are question words which do sometimes change their form:

Quale(-i)? – Which?

Quanti(-e)? – How many?

Quanto(-a)? – How much?

In English, question words like *what*, *where* and *when* always come at the beginning of the sentence. Italian interrogatives usually come first in the sentence, but it is not compulsory. If you want to emphasize what you are asking about, you can put a pronoun or a noun first.

Here are some examples:

Listen to track 126

Tu chi sei? – Who are you?

Lei cosa ne pensa, dottoressa Mellini? – What do you think, Dr. Mellini?

Martina e Ilaria dove pensano di andare a quest'ora? – Where do Martina and Ilaria think they are going at this time?

Prepositions such as "di", "con", and "a" always precede the question words. Unlike in English, a question in Italian never ends with a preposition.

Di dove *sei?* – Where are you from?

Con chi *parlavi?* – Who were you talking to?

A che cosa *serve?* – What's it for?

Di chi *è questa borsa?* – Whose bag is this?

Italian interrogatives

Italian question words, also known as interrogatives, are pretty similar to English. Here is a list.

Listen to track 127

Chi? (who?/whom?)

Pronounced /kee/, *chi* means "who", is invariable and refers only to people, either singular or plural. Here are some examples:

Chi *parla?* – Who is speaking?

Chi *è quella ragazza?* – Who's that girl?

Vado al supermercato. **Chi** *vuole venire con me?* – I'm going to the supermarket. Who wants to come with me?

Listen to track 128

Cosa? / Che? / Che cosa? (what?)

Che, pronounced /keh/, and *cosa*, pronounced /koh-zah/, are abbreviated forms of the Italian phrase *che cosa (keh koh-zah)*, which means "what". *Che*, *cosa* and *che cosa* can be used on their own and are invariable, which means that they have the same form regardless of the number and gender of the following nouns. *Cosa* and *che* are interchangeable and more frequently used as they are shorter and easier to say.

Here are some sample sentences:

Che cosa *ha detto?* – What did you say?

Scusi, **che** *ore sono?* – Excuse me, what time is it?

Che *giorno è oggi?* – What day is it today?

Cosa *vuoi?* – What do you want?

Che cosa and *cosa* can be combined with the verb *essere* (to be) and become **che cos'** and **cos'** when followed by a vowel.

Che cos'era *che mi dovevi dire?* – What was it that you had to tell me?

Cos'è *questo?* – What is this?

Listen to track 129

Quando? (when?)

Pronounced /koo-ahn-doh/, *quando* means "when" and is useful for asking about times and dates. Have a look at these examples to get an idea how it works:

Quando *andiamo in vacanza?* – When are we going on holiday?

Quando *parte l'aereo?* – When is the plane leaving?

Quando *vai in Giappone?* – When are you going to Japan?

Listen to track 130

Dove? (where?)

Pronounced /doh-vay/, *dove* means "where" and, just like *cosa*, can be shortened to **dov'** when it is followed by a vowel.

Dove *abiti?* – Where do you live?

Dove *vai?* – Where are you going?

Dov'è *la stazione?* – Where is the train station?

Dov'eri *quando ti ho telefonato?* – Where were you when I called you?

Listen to track 131

Perché? (why?)

The Italian word *perché*, pronounced /pehr-keh/, is a little tricky, as it means both "why" and "because". You can usually tell which one it is by listening to the intonation and by the context the word is used in.

Here are some examples which use *perché* to mean "why":

Perché *sei qui?* – Why are you here?

Perché non sei andato a scuola? – Why didn't you go to school?

Perché non me l'hai detto? – Why didn't you tell me?

Perché non vieni? – Why don't you come?

Here are some examples of *perché* used to mean "because":

Oggi sono di buon umore **perché** *c'è il sole* – I am in a good mood today because it's a sunny day

Lucrezia non è venuta al cinema **perché** *aveva già visto quel film* – Lucrezia didn't come to the cinema because she had already seen that movie

Come mai (how come) is a synonym for *perché* and is a less direct way to ask "why". Asking *perché* (why) sounds like you are demanding justification, whereas *come mai* (how come) shows that you are interested in knowing the other person's reasons for doing or not doing something. *Come mai* invites a longer answer than *perché* would.

Listen to track 132

Come? (how?)

Pronounced /koh-meh/, *come* is the Italian word for "how". It is useful for asking about the state of things or the way something happened.

You might be familiar with it from the famous Italian greeting "come stai?", which translates as "how are you?".

Come lo sai? – How do you know?

Come si fa? – How do you do it?

Just like *cosa* and *dove*, *come* can be shortened to **com'** when it is followed by a vowel.

Com'è il tempo? – How's the weather? (What's the weather like?)

Com'era Giulia da bambina? – How was Giulia as a child?

Listen to track 133

Quale? (which?)

Pronounced /koo-ah-leh/, *quale* means "which" and agrees in gender and number with the nouns it goes with. Use it to ask for specific information about something or someone.

You use *quale* with singular nouns to ask "which" or "what".

Quale abito preferisci? – Which dress do you prefer?

Su **quale** *icona devo cliccare?* – Which icon should I click on?

Per **quale** *motivo?* – For what reason?

If the following word is *è* (is) or *era* (was), use *qual* without adding the apostrophe.

Qual *è l'autobus per il centro?* – Which is the bus to downtown?

Qual *è la tua più grande qualità?* – What's your greatest quality?

Quale has a plural form: *quali*. Use *quali* with plural nouns.

Quali *sono i tuoi hobby?* – Which are your hobbies?

Listen to track 134

Quanto? (How much?)

Pronounced /koo-ahn-toh/, *quanto* means "how much" and changes according to the gender and number of the nouns it goes with. You use the masculine form *quanto* as an adjective with masculine singular nouns and the feminine form *quanta*, pronounced /koo-ahn-tah/, with feminine singular nouns.

Quanto *tempo mi rimane?* – How much time do I have left?

Quanta *stoffa Le serve, signore?* – How much fabric do you need, sir?

Quanto *dura il volo per Glasgow?* – How long is the flight to Glasgow?

Quanto has a plural form: *quanti*. Use *quanti* as an adjective with masculine plural nouns and *quante* with feminine plural nouns.

Quanti *giorni mancano alla fine dell'anno?* – How many days are left until the end of the year?

Quante *notti vi fermate a Ravenna?* – How many nights are you staying in Ravenna?

Quanti *ne vuole, signora?* – How many do you need, Madam?

BEWARE: some common questions in Italian don't begin with the question word you might expect.

Listen to track 135

Come *ti chiami?* – What's your name?

Quanti *anni hai?* – How old are you?

Che *tempo fa oggi?* – What's the weather like today?

Feeling overwhelmed by all these **question words**? With practice, in no time at all you'll be asking questions in Italian like a pro.

Tag questions in Italian

Listen to track 136

Placed at the end of a sentence, a **question tag**, also known as question tail, turns a statement into a question and is used for checking information that we think we know is true. Italian **tag questions** basically correspond to English question phrases like "aren't you?", "isn't it?", "didn't you?", "don't they?" and so on.

Add the following phrases to the end of a statement and make your voice go up as you say them:

- *È vero?* (Is it right?)
- *Non è vero? / Nevvero?* (Isn't it right?)
- *Vero?* (Is it right?)
- *Giusto?* (Right?)
- *O sbaglio?* (Am I wrong?)
- *Sì?* (yes?)
- *No? / O no?* (No?)
- *Neh?* (Is that right?) [very frequently used in Piedmont and Lombardy]

Take a look at the following examples:

Tua cugina si chiama Marina, **giusto?** – Your cousin's name is Marina, isn't it?

Mi scriverai, **no?** – You will write to me, won't you?

Jessica è italiana, **o no?** – Jessica is Italian, isn't she?

Hai finito i compiti, **vero?** – You finished your homework, didn't you?

Vieni anche tu, **no?** – You're coming too, aren't you?

Il tempo è brutto oggi, **o sbaglio?** – The weather is bad today, isn't it?

Indirect questions in Italian

Listen to track 137

Questions such as "*cos'è successo?*" (what happened?) or "*dove vai?*" (where are you going?) are direct questions and can be phrased in a more roundabout way, in order to sound less direct and more polite. Look at the following examples:

Dimmi cos'è successo, per cortesia. – Tell me what happened, please.

Ti dispiace dirmi cos'è successo? – Would you mind telling me what happened?

This type of question is called an **indirect question**. Asking indirect questions in Italian is easy: all you have to do is add a phrase to the beginning of the direct question, for example you can add *"può dirmi"* (can you tell me) to the question *"cos'è successo?"* (what happened?).

Può dirmi cos'è successo, per favore? – Can you tell me what happened, please?

Here is a list of expressions that can be used to introduce an indirect question:

- Dimmi – Tell me

Dimmi *perché l'hai fatto* – Tell me why you did it

- Vorrei sapere – I'd like to know

Vorrei sapere *se c'è la taglia XS* – I'd like to know if the XS size is available

- Mi domando – I wonder

Mi domando *cosa pensano* – I wonder what they think

- Mi piacerebbe sapere – I'd like to know

Mi piacerebbe sapere *come vi siete conosciuti* – I'd like to know how you met

- Ti / Le / vi dispiace dirmi – Would you mind telling me

Ti dispiace dirmi *cosa sta succedendo?* – Would you mind telling me what's going on?

- Non capisco – I don't understand

Non capisco *cosa intendi dire* – I don't understand what you mean

- Mi potresti dire – Can you please tell me

Mi potresti dire *cos'è successo?* – Can you please tell me what happened?

To sum up...

Asking questions in Italian is simpler than in English. To ask a question in Italian, you just need to add a question mark at the end of the sentence and use a rising intonation of your voice.

To ask questions that require more than a yes or no answer, you have to use a question word. Italian question words are:

- **Dove?** (where?)
- **Come?** (how?)
- **Quando?** (when?)
- **Perché?** (why?) – **Come mai?** (how come?)
- **Chi?** (who?/whom?)
- **Cosa?/Che?/Che cosa?** (what?)
- **Quale?** (which?)
- **Quanto**? (how much?)

Note that *quale* (which?) agrees in gender and number with the nouns it goes with. *Quanto* (how much?) changes according to the gender and number of the nouns it goes with.

Workbook Lesson 7. How to Ask Questions

Exercise 7.1: Choose the correct answer:

1. You want to ask somebody his/her name. You should ask:

   a) Come ti chiami? (informale) / Come si chiama? (formale)

   b) Chi sei? (informale) / Chi è? (formale)

   c) Chi chiama tu? (informale) / Chi chiama lei? (formale)

2. You want to ask somebody where he/she is from. You should ask:
   a) Da dove sei / Da dov'è?

   b) Di dove sei? / Di dov'è?

   c) Di dove vieni? / Di dove viene?

3. You want to know what time it is. You should ask:
   a) Quante ore sono?   b) Quale ora è?   c) Che ore sono?

4. You want to know which bus is coming. You should ask:
   a) Quale autobus sta arrivando?

   b) Di quale autobus sta arrivando?

   c) Da quale autobus sta arrivando?

5. You want to know how much the ticket costs. You should ask:
   a) Quale costa il biglietto?

   b) Come costa il biglietto?

   c) Quanto costa il biglietto?

Exercise 7.2: Choose the correct translation:

1. Which is your favorite dish?
   a) Quale tuo piatto preferito?

   b) Che tuo piatto preferito?

   c) Qual è il tuo piatto preferito?

2. Which one is your hat?
   a) Qual è il tuo cappello? b) Quale cappello tuo? c) Chi cappello è tuo?

3. How old is your father?

a) Quanta età ha tuo padre? b) Che età tuo padre? c) Quanti anni ha tuo padre?

4. Where is your bag?

a) Di dov'è la tua borsa?   b) Dov'è la tua borsa?   c) Da dov'è la tua borsa?

5. How do you go home?

a) Come vai a casa?   b) Come andare a casa?   c) Come andavi a casa?

Exercise 7.3: Complete these questions with the right question words:

1. ____ orologi hai? (____ many watches do you have?)

2. ____ anni ha tua sorella? (____ old is your sister?)

3. ____ stiamo facendo? (____ are we doing?)

4. ____ non sei andato alla festa? (____ didn't you go to the party?)

5. ____ hai messo il mio libro? (____ did you put my book?)

Exercise 7.4: Choose the correct translation:

1. Why you don't like sushi?

a) Perché non piacere il sushi?

b) Perché non ti piace il sushi?

c) Perché non ti è piaciuto il sushi?

2. Who is your favorite singer?

a) Chi è il tuo cantante preferito?

b) Com'è il tuo cantante preferito?

c) Chi è stato il tuo cantante preferito?

3. How do you prepare pasta?

a) Come preparare la pasta?

b) Come si prepara la pasta?

c) Come prepari la pasta?

4. Is this your watch?

a) Qual è il tuo orologio?

b) Questo è il tuo orologio?

c) Com'è il tuo orologio?

5. Where is your umbrella?

   a) Dov'era il tuo ombrello?

   b) Dov'è andato il tuo ombrello?

   c) Dov'è il tuo ombrello?

Exercise 7.5: Translate the following sentences from English into Italian:

Italian	English
1. Where do you come from?	
2. When is your birthday?	
3. What do you think about it?	
4. How many books does she have?	
5. Why are they laughing?	

Answers:

Exercise 7.1:

1) Come ti chiami? (informale) / Come si chiama? (formale)

2) Di dove sei? / Di dov'è?

3) Che ore sono?

4) Quale autobus sta arrivando?

5) Quanto costa il biglietto?

Exercise 7.2:

1. Qual'è il tuo piatto preferito?

2. Qual è il tuo cappello?

3. Quanti anni ha tuo padre?

4. Dov'è la tua borsa?

5. Come vai a casa?

Exercise 7.3:

1. Quanti; 2. Quanti; 3. Cosa/Che; 4. Perché; 5. Dove

Exercise 7.4:

1) Perché non ti piace il sushi?

2) Chi è il tuo cantante preferito?

3) Come prepari la pasta?

4) Questo è il tuo orologio?

5) Dov'è il tuo ombrello?

Exercise 7.5:

1. Da dove vieni?

2. Quando è il tuo compleanno?

3. Cosa ne pensate?

4. Quanti libri ha?

5. Perché stanno ridendo?

LESSON 8: AGGETTIVI QUALIFICATIVI - REGULAR AND IRREGULAR ITALIAN QUALIFYING ADJECTIVES

Qualifying adjectives give information about people, animals, objects and situations, and define them in a better way. Adjectives in Italian do not work in quite the same way as they do in English.

In this lesson, you will find out all you need to know about Italian qualifying adjectives. Ready? Let's start!

Gendered nouns and Italian qualifying adjectives

Listen to track 138

Adjectives give more information about a noun. Italian has gendered nouns, which means that there are masculine and feminine nouns. **Italian adjectives** agree with the **gender** of the noun they are describing and, if you have a plural noun, you must also make the adjective plural. In other words, Italian adjectives change their form based on whether the word they refer to is masculine or feminine, singular or plural. This sounds scary, but after a while it becomes automatic.

Italian adjectives fit into three categories, depending on how they change to match a noun's **gender and number**. They can be regular, irregular and invariable.

Regular adjectives

Regular adjectives modify only their last letter, depending on gender and number. There are three groups of regular adjectives in Italian: those ending in **-o**, those ending in **-e** and those ending in **-a**.

1. Regular adjectives ending in -o

Adjectives ending in -o have four forms:

- masculine singular **-o**
- feminine singular **-a**
- masculine plural **-i**
- feminine plural **-e**

For example:

Un tipo sveglio e arguto (masculine singular) – A smart and witty guy

Una persona schietta e sincera (feminine singular) – A sincere and honest person

Dibattiti accesi (masculine plural) – Heated debates

Leggende metropolitane (feminine plural) – Urban legends

2. Regular adjectives ending in -e

Adjectives ending in **-e** are the same for the masculine and the feminine singular. In the plural, the **-e** changes to an **-i**, whether the noun is masculine or feminine.

For example:

*Un film **divertente*** – A funny movie

*Un'avventura **fugace*** – A short affair

*Gli alunni **intelligenti*** – Intelligent pupils

*Le nostre centraliniste **gentili*** – Our polite switchboard operators

Here is a list of the most common **Italian adjectives ending in -e**:

Listen to track 139

abile – able

amichevole – friendly

attraente – attractive

cortese – courteous

difficile – difficult

dolce – sweet

esuberante – exuberant

felice – happy

forte – strong

gentile – kind

grande – big, large, great

importante – important

intelligente – intelligent

interessante – interesting

intraprendente – enterprising

personale – personal

triste – sad

veloce – fast, speedy

ufficiale – official

utile – useful

3. Regular adjectives ending in -a

Listen to track 140

Adjectives ending in **-a** (-ista, -asta, -ita, -ida and -ota) are the same for the masculine and the feminine singular. In the plural, the **-a** changes to an **-i** if the noun is masculine, and to an **-e** if the noun is feminine.

Take a look at the following examples:

Un uomo ego**ista** – a selfish man

Una donna ego**ista** – a selfish woman

Uomini ego**isti** – selfish men

Donne ego**iste** – selfish women

Un uomo entusiast**a** – an enthusiastic man

Una donna entusiast**a** – an enthusiastic woman

Uomini entusiast**i** – enthusiastic men

Donne entusiast**e** – enthusiastic women

Un uomo ipocrit**a** – a hypocritical man

Una donna ipocrit**a** – a hypocritical woman

Uomini ipocrit**i** – hypocritical men

Donne ipocrit**e** – hypocritical women

Istinto omicid**a** – murderous instinct

Volontà omicid**a** – murderous will

Pensieri omicid**i** – homicidal thoughts

Fantasie omicid**e** – homicidal fantasies

Scherzo idiot**a** – silly joke

Domanda idiot**a** – stupid question

Scherzi idiot**i** – silly jokes

Domande idiot**e** – stupid questions

Irregular adjectives

Listen to track 141

Irregular adjectives have particular feminine and plural forms, and often modify more than just the last letter.

Feminine singular adjectives ending in **-cia** and **-gia** form the plural with **-ce** and **-ge** when a consonant comes before the suffix **cia/gia**.

saggia – sagge (wise)

marcia –marce (rotten)

Feminine singular adjectives ending in **-cia** and **-gia** form the plural with **-cie** and **-gie** when a vowel comes before the suffix cia/gia.

ligia – ligie (law-abiding)

sudicia – sudicie (dirty)

Italian adjectives ending in **-io** with the stress falling on the "i" form the masculine plural with the ending **-ii**. For example:

pio – pii (pious)

Adjectives ending in **-io** (not stressed) drop the -o in the plural. For example:

gaio – gai (cheerful)

serio – seri (serious)

Italian adjectives ending in **-co** with the accent on the penultimate syllable form the masculine plural with the ending **-chi**.

antico – antichi (ancient)

Multi-syllable adjectives ending in **-co** with the accent on the third last syllable form the masculine plural with the ending **-ci**.

simpatico – simpatici (nice)

statico – statici (static)

Here is a list of other irregular adjective endings:

-ca → -che   -   bianca –bianche

-cio → -ci   -   meticcio – meticci

-ga → -ghe   -   larga – larghe

-gio → -gi   -   grigio – grigi

-go → -ghi   -   largo – larghi

-**scia** → -sce   - liscia – lisce

-**scio** → -sci   - liscio –lisci

Invariable adjectives

Listen to track 142

Some Italian adjectives are invariable, which means that they have only one form. Among the commonest are:

- blu (blue), turchese (turquoise), rosa (pink), lilla (lilac), indaco (indigo), ocra (ocher), marrone (brown), nocciola (hazel), viola (purple) and beige (beige):

*Una camicia **rosa** / Due camicie **rosa***

- mathematical qualifiers pari (equal) impari (unequal) and dispari (odd):

*Un numero **pari** / I numeri **pari***

- compound adjectives formed by anti+noun, like antifurto (anti-theft), antincendio (anti-fire), antiurto (shockproof), antiruggine (anti-rust) and so on:

*Protezione **antincendio** / Protezioni **antincendio***

- adjectives taken from other languages, such as bordeaux (burgundy), snob (snobbish), trendy (trendy) and démodé (unfashionable):

*Accessorio **trendy** / Accessori **trendy***

- adverbial expressions used as adjectives, like perbene (respectable), dabbene (honest) and dappoco (insignificant):

*Una famiglia **perbene** / Due famiglie **perbene***

How to match one qualifying adjective to more than one noun

Listen to track 143

When a qualifying adjective is linked to more than one noun of different gender, it keeps its masculine ending. For example:

*In crociera ho conosciuto un gruppo di ragazzi e ragazze **bosniaci*** – On the cruise I met a group of Bosnian boys and girls

If all nouns are masculine, the adjective is masculine.

*Faccio volontariato in un rifugio per cani e gatti **abbandonati*** – I volunteer in a shelter for abandoned dogs and cats

If all nouns are feminine, the adjective is feminine.

*È vietato pubblicare foto e informazioni **inappropriate*** – It is forbidden to post inappropriate photos and information

Predicative and attributive Italian adjectives

Listen to track 144

There are two types of adjectives in Italian: predicative and attributive. According to the noun it is linked to, an adjective can be:

- **attributive**, when it is directly linked to the noun it is describing:

*Detesto le persone **false** e **ipocrite*** – I hate false and two-faced people

- **predicative**, when it uses a linking verb, like *essere* (to be) or *sembrare* (to seem), to describe a noun:

*Fabrizio è **subdolo** e **ipocrita*** – Fabrizio is sneaky and hypocritical

Italian adjective placement

Listen to track 145

One of the biggest differences between English and Italian is the placement of adjectives in a sentence. Most adjectives in Italian are **placed after the noun** to convey new information about them.

*La cucina **italiana** è apprezzata in tutto il mondo* – Italian cuisine is appreciated all over the world

*Milano è una metropoli **vivace** e **dinamica*** – Milan is a lively and dynamic city

There are adjectives that always go after the noun. They are those that indicate:

- nationality: *la nazionale **italiana*** – the Italian national football team
- color, shape, material: *il vino **rosso*** – the red wine
- place and position: *il gomito **sinistro*** – the left elbow
- belonging to a specific category: *un pittore **dadaista*** – a Dadaist painter
- a physical feature: *una donna **sordomuta*** – a deaf-mute woman

Adjectives with a describing function usually come before the noun. Here is a list:

Bello (good-looking, beautiful)

*La mamma di Anita è una **bella** donna* – Anita's mother is a beautiful woman

Bravo (good, capable)

*Cesare è un **bravo** ragazzo* – Cesare is a good boy

Brutto (ugly, bad)

*È un **brutto** affare* – It's a bad situation

Caro (dear)

*Giada è una mia **cara** amica* – Giada is a dear friend of mine

Cattivo (bad)

*Oggi sono di **cattivo** umore* – Today I'm in a bad mood

Giovane (young)

*I **giovani** imprenditori italiani* – Young Italian entrepreneurs

Lungo (long)

*Adoro fare **lunghe** passeggiate in mezzo alla natura* – I love taking long nature walks

Nuovo (new)

*Quello è il **nuovo** allenatore* – That's the new coach

Piccolo (small, little)

*Questo è un **piccolo** passo per l'uomo, un grande passo per l'umanità* (cit. Neil Armstrong) – That's one small step for a man, one giant leap for mankind

Stesso (same)

*Incontriamoci nello **stesso** posto dell'altra volta* – Let's meet in the same place as last time

Vecchio (old)

*Adalberto ha condiviso un **vecchio** aneddoto* – Adalberto shared an old anecdote

Vero (true)

Qual è il **vero** significato del tuo nome? – What's the true meaning of your name?

Bello (good-looking), buono (good), grande (big, large, great) and santo (saint, holy)

Listen to track 146

When used after a noun, **bello** (good-looking) is a regular adjective with four possible endings -o, -a, -i and -e. When it is used before a noun, it follows the rules of the definite article.

Bel

Use *bel* before masculine singular nouns starting with a consonant.

*Un **bel** r*agazzo

Bello

Use *bello* before masculine singular nouns that start with "s" followed by a consonant, "z", "ps", "pn", "gn", "y" and "x".

Bello sp*azio*

Bello z*aino*

Bello psicologo

Bello pneumatico

Bello gnomo

Bello yacht

Bello xilofono

When a masculine singular noun begins with a vowel, *bello* contracts into *bell'* (with an apostrophe).

Un bell'uomo

Un bell'esemplare

Bella

Use *bella* before feminine singular nouns starting with a consonant.

Bella domanda

*Una **bella giornata***

When a feminine singular noun begins with a vowel, *bella* contracts into *bell'* (with an apostrophe).

*Una **bell'automobile***

Bei

Use *bei* before masculine plural nouns beginning with a consonant.

Bei paesi

Begli

You use *begli* with masculine plural nouns starting with a vowel and with "z", "ps", "gn", "pn", "x", "y" or "s" followed by a consonant.

Begli occhi

Begli stivali

Begli zaini

Begli psicologi

Begli pneumatici

Begli gnomi

Begli yogurt

Begli xilofoni

Belle

Use *belle* before all feminine plural nouns.

Belle *passeggiate*

Belle *orchidee*

When used after a noun, **buono** (good) is a regular adjective with four possible endings -o, -a, -i and -e. When it is used before a singular noun, it follows the rules of the indefinite article.

Buon

Use *buon* before masculine singular nouns beginning with consonant or vowel.

Buon *anno!*

Un ***buon*** *profumo*

Buono

Use *buono* before masculine singular nouns that start with "s" followed by a consonant, "z", "ps", "pn", "gn", "y" and "x".

Buono *studio*

Buona

Use *buona* before feminine singular nouns starting with a consonant.

Buona *fortuna!*

When a feminine singular noun begins with a vowel, *buona* contracts into *buon'* (with an apostrophe).

Una ***buon'amica***

When it is used with plural nouns, it works like a regular adjective.

*Buon**i** consigli* (masculine plural)

*Buon**e** ragioni* (feminine plural)

When used after a noun, **grande** (big, large, great) is a regular adjective with three possible endings -e, -i and -e. It has an irregular form when it precedes the noun.

Gran

Use *gran* before masculine and feminine singular nouns beginning with a consonant.

Un ***gran*** *successo*

Una ***gran*** *rimonta*

Grand'

Use *grand'* before masculine and feminine singular nouns beginning with a vowel.

*Un **grand'a**mico*

*Una **grand'a**zienda*

Grande

Use *grande* before masculine and feminine singular nouns that start with "s" followed by a consonant, "z", "ps", "pn", "gn", "y" and "x".

*Un **grande sp**azio*

*Una **grande st**oria d'amore*

Grandi

Use *grandi* with feminine and masculine plural nouns.

Grandi *manovre*

Grandi *opere*

Grandi *amici*

Grandi *traguardi*

When used after a noun, **santo** (saint, holy) is a regular adjective with four possible endings -o, -a, -i and -e. It has an irregular form when it is used before a noun.

San

Use *san* before masculine nouns and names beginning with a consonant.

San *Giovanni*

San *Paolo*

Santo

Use *santo* before masculine nouns and names beginning with "z" and "s" followed by a consonant.

Santo *Stanislao*

Santa

Use *santa* before feminine nouns and names beginning with a consonant.

Santa *Chiara*

Santa *Teresa*

Sant'

Both *santo* and *santa* contract into *sant'* (with apostrophe) before nouns and names beginning with a vowel.

Sant'*Ignazio*

Sant'*Irene*

Santi

Use *santi* before more than one masculine noun or name.

Santi *Pietro e Paolo*

Sante

Use *Sante* before more than one feminine noun or name.

Sante *Melania e Paola*

Different meaning according to position

Some Italian adjectives have different meanings depending on their position in a sentence.

When you place *grande* after a noun it means *big, large*, whereas if you place it before a noun, it means *great*.

When you place the adjective *povero* after a noun it means *poor, penniless*. If you place it before a noun, it means *unlucky*.

When you place the adjective *stesso* before a noun, it means *same*. If you place it after a noun, it means *itself*.

To sum up...

Qualifying adjectives are usually placed after the noun to convey more information about it. They change their form based on whether the noun they are describing is masculine or feminine, singular or plural.

Italian qualifying adjectives can be regular, irregular and invariable. Regular adjectives modify only their last letter, depending on gender and number. Irregular adjectives have particular feminine and plural forms, and often modify more than just the last letter. Invariable adjectives have only one form.

Note that some Italian adjectives, such as *grande* (big, great), *povero* (poor, unlucky) and *stesso* (same, itself), have different meanings depending on their position in a sentence.

Workbook Lesson 8. Regular and Irregular Italian Qualifying Adjectives

Exercise 8.1: Complete each adjective to match its corresponding noun

Adjective	Noun
1. Una ragazza simpatic_	
2. Un cane rumoros_	
3. Degli amici sincer_	
4. Delle rose profumat_	
5. Degli scarponi pesant_	
6. Una strada tortuos_	

Exercise 8.2: Translate the following noun-adjective phrases into Italian

English	Italian
1. A pretty dress	
2. Two fast cars	
3. Some tasty cakes	
4. An amazing view	
5. A cute girl	
6. Three small boxes	

Exercise 8.3: Choose the right option

1. Una scelta difficile/difficila - _____
2. Un ragazzo audacio/audace - _____
3. Un padre presento/presente - _____
4. Dei fratelli idioti/idiota - _____
5. Una scoperta sconcertanta/sconcertante - _____

Exercise 8.4: Translate the following sentences into Italian

English	Italian
1. What's the name of that bright star?	
2. Dogs are loyal animals.	
3. Roses and lilies are pretty flowers.	
4. My new red car is very fast.	
5. She owns an expensive apartment.	

Exercise 8.5: Complete the following text

Il mio giocattolo preferito è una (old) bambola. Ha la faccia (round) e (plump), le mani (small) e un vestito ormai (dirty). Questo vestito (green) e (yellow) è strappato in più parti, e la mia mamma mi ha chiesto tante volte se volessi comprare una tutina (new) per la mia bambola, ma io ho sempre rifiutato le sue (generous) offerte. Nonostante le sue condizioni, per me è una (beautiful) bambola e un giocattolo che terrò sempre con me.

_____

_____

_____

_____

_____ .

Answers:

Exercise 8.1:

1. Una ragazza simpatica

2. Un cane rumoroso

3. Degli amici sinceri

4. Delle rose profumate

5. Degli scarponi pesanti

6. Una strada tortuosa

Exercise 8.2:

1. Un bel vestito/Un vestito bello

2. Due macchine veloci

3. Delle torte gustose

4. Una vista meravigliosa

5. Una ragazza carina

6. Tre scatole piccole

Exercise 8.3:

1. difficile; 2. audace; 3. presente; 4. idioti; 5. sconcertante

Exercise 8.4:

1. Come si chiama quella stella luminosa?

2. I cani sono animali fedeli.

3. Le rose e i gigli sono dei bei fiori.

4. La mia nuova macchina rossa è molto veloce.

5. Lei possiede un appartamento costoso.

Exercise 8.5:

Il mio giocattolo preferito è una (vecchia) bambola. Ha la faccia (rotonda) e (paffuta), le mani (piccole) e un vestito ormai (sudicio). Questo vestito (verde) e (giallo) è strappato in più parti, e la mia mamma mi ha chiesto tante volte se volessi comprare una tutina (nuova) per la mia bambola, ma io ho sempre rifiutato le sue (generose) offerte. Nonostante le sue condizioni, per me è una (bellissima) bambola e un giocattolo che terrò sempre con me.

LESSON 9: PRONOMI E AGGETTIVI POSSESSIVI – POSSESSIVE PRONOUNS AND ADJECTIVES

Possessive pronouns (*pronomi possessivi*) and possessive adjectives (*aggettivi possessivi*) are a must-know topic for all learners of Italian. Lucky for you, they are pretty simple and there aren't many irregularities.

In this lesson, we will show you how to use **possessive pronouns and adjectives** in Italian. Let's start!

Italian possessive adjectives

Listen to track 147

Possessive adjectives are words used with a specific noun to show to whom it belongs. They indicate possession or ownership, and correspond to "my", "your", "his", "her", "its", "our" and "their" in English.

Italian possessive adjectives agree in gender and number with the noun they refer to, and not with that of the possessor. Look at the following example:

*La **mia** amica Virginia vive a Udine* – My friend Virginia lives in Udine

We use "la mia" feminine singular because the friend Virginia is female, and not because the speaker is (or is not) female.

Each *aggettivo possessivo* has four forms, differing in their endings:

-o for the masculine singular

-a for the feminine singular

-i for the masculine plural

-e for the feminine plural

Here are all your options:

Masculine (singular)

mio – my

tuo – your

suo – his, her, its

Suo – your (polite)

nostro – our

vostro – your

loro – their

Feminine (singular)

mia – my

tua – your

sua – his, her, its

Sua – your (polite)

nostra – our

vostra – your

loro – their

Masculine (plural)

miei – my

tuoi – your

suoi – his, her, its

Suoi – your (polite)

nostri – our

vostri – your

loro – their

Feminine (plural)

mie – my

tue – your

sue – his, her, its

Sue – your (polite)

nostre – our

vostre – your

loro – their

Unlike in English, Italian possessive adjectives are generally preceded by the **definite article** (il, la, i, le). Take a look at the following examples:

Listen to track 148

Io (first person singular "I"): ***La mia*** *macchina è verde* (feminine singular) – My car is green

Tu (second person singular "you"): ***Il tuo*** *gatto ha tre anni* (masculine singular) – Your cat is 3 years old

Lui (third person singular "he"): *Mattia sta parlando con il suo allenatore* (masculine singular) – Mattia is talking to his coach

Lei (third person singular "she"): *Il suo fidanzato si chiama Lorenzo* (masculine singular) – Her partner is called Lorenzo

Lei (the formal way of saying "you" in Italian): *Ecco il Suo caffè*, signora (masculine singular) – Here is your coffee, Madam

Noi (first person plural "we"): *Le nostre speranze sono state deluse* (feminine plural) – All our hopes were disappointed

Voi (second person plural "y'all") *La vostra casa verrà pignorata e messa all'asta* (feminine singular) – Your property will be seized and auctioned

Loro (third person plural "they") *Le loro amiche sono tutte single* (feminine plural) – Their friends are all single

Loro (formal plural form) *Ecco i loro passaporti, signori* (masculine plural) – Here are your passports, gentlemen

The definite article is omitted in:

Listen to track 149

- exclamations and vocative expressions where the *aggettivo possessivo* follows the noun:

*Piacere **mio**!* – My pleasure!

*È colpa **tua**!* – It's your fault!

*Amici **miei**, buonanotte* – My dear friends, goodnight

- some idiomatic expressions such as:

Da parte mia / tua / sua… – On my / your / his… behalf

A casa mia / tua / sua… – To/at my / your / his… home/house

Per colpa mia / tua / sua… – Because of me / you / him…

In camera mia / tua / sua… - In my / your / his… bedroom

If you put the possessive adjective before the word **casa** (home, house), it will sound very strange to Italians.

*Federica è venuta a **casa mia** a studiare* – Federica came to my house to study

*Stasera veniamo a **casa tua**?* – Are we going to your house tonight?

The *aggettivo possessivo* may be placed after the noun it refers to in specific expressions, such as:

*Fatti gli affari **tuoi**!* – Mind your own business!

*Alle cose **mie** ci penso da me* – I take care of my stuff by myself

You can also use the **indefinite article** in front of the possessive adjective:

***Un mio** cliente* – One of my clients

***Una tua** amica* – A friend of yours

***Una sua** ex fidanzata* – One of his ex-girlfriends

***Un nostro** vicino di casa* – A neighbor of ours

***Una vostra** collega* – A colleague of yours

***Un loro** conoscente* – An acquaintance of theirs

Unlike in English, possessive adjectives aren't used with parts of the body in Italian. You usually use the definite article instead.

Eleonora si sta lavando i capelli – Eleonora is washing her hair

Mi fa male la gola – My throat hurts

Chiudi gli occhi – Close your eyes

Il nemico alzò le mani in segno di resa – The enemy raised his hands in surrender

Suo, sua, sue, suoi (his/her/its/your)

Listen to track 150

In English you say "his" to refer to something that belongs to a man, and "her" to refer to something that belongs to a woman. As mentioned previously, in Italian there is no such distinction. Instead of "his motorbike" or "her motorbike" you just say "*la sua* moto", regardless of whether the owner is a male or female. But it does change when the quantity changes.

*La **sua** moto* – his motorbike / her motorbike

*Le **sue** moto* – his motorbikes / her motorbikes

*Il **suo** cane* – his dog / her dog

*I **suoi** cani* – his dogs / her dogs

Suo, sua, suoi and *sue* are also used with *lei*, the formal way of saying "you" in Italian.

*Abbiamo ricevuto **la Sua** candidatura* – We received your application

Loro (their)

Listen to track 151

Loro, the Italian word for "their", doesn't change according to gender or quantity like all the others do. The female form is "lor**o**", the same as the masculine, not "lora".

So how do you know if you are talking about a masculine, feminine, singular or plural entity? Just pay attention to the article in front of the *aggettivo possessivo*. Take a look at the following examples:

*Hanno realizzato **il loro** sogno* – They have fulfilled their dream

*Non ho mai visto **i loro** vicini di casa* – I have never seen their neighbors

*Adoro **la loro** spontaneità!* – I love their spontaneity!

*Abbiamo seguito **le loro** indicazioni* – We followed their instructions

How to use possessive adjectives when talking about family members

To say *my mother, your wife, her grandma, his niece* and so on, use the **possessive adjective without the definite article**.

Listen to track 152

Mia madre – my mother

Tuo padre – your father

Suo figlio – her son

Nostra sorella – our sister

Vostro nipote – your nephew

For example:

*Arianna è in lite con **suo** fratello per questioni di eredità* – Arianna is having a dispute with her brother over inheritance

*Manuele è andato in vacanza con **mio** cugino* – Manuele went on vacation with my cousin

This applies to all family members in the singular, except for:

- mamma (mom): **la mia** mamma – my mom
- papà, babbo, papino (dad): *Nicolò e **il suo** papà* – Nicolò and his dad

The adjective **loro** (their) is always preceded by the definite article.

*Maddalena è **la loro** zia preferita* – Maddalena is their favorite aunt

*Corrado è **il loro** fratello minore* – Corrado is their younger brother

Note: if you describe a family member with an adjective, you always have to use the definite article with the *aggettivo possessivo*.

***La mia** adorata nipotina* – My beloved little niece

***La mia** sorella minore* – My younger sister

***Il tuo** fratello maggiore* – Your older brother

You do use the definite article with the possessive adjective when referring to family members in the plural.

***I miei** nonni* – My grandparents

*Giada e **le sue** sorelle* – Giada and her sisters

*Monica e **le sue** cognate* – Monica and her sisters-in-law

*Francesco e **le sue nuore*** – Francesco and his daughters-in-law

In Italian, *boyfriend, girlfriend, partner* and *fiancé* are not considered family. So, you must use the definite article along with the possessive adjective to refer to them.

***Il mio** ragazzo* – My boyfriend

***La mia** ragazza* – My girlfriend

***Il mio** fidanzato* – My fiancé

***La mia** fidanzata* – My fiancé

***Il mio** compagno* – My partner

***La mia** compagna* – My partner

Other possessive adjectives

Proprio (own)

Listen to track 153

Proprio expresses the idea of possession and ownership, and can be used to replace "suo" and "loro" to reinforce the sense of possession. It agrees in gender and number with the noun it goes with and is preceded by the definite article. Here are all your options:

Propri**o** (masculine singular)

Propri**a** (feminine singular)

Propr**i** (masculine plural)

Propri**e** (feminine plural)

*Raffaele ama **il proprio** lavoro* – Raffaele loves his (own) job

*Mauro non ha ancora trovato **la propria** strada nella vita* – Mauro has not yet found his way in life

*Irene e Margherita non credevano a**i propri** occhi* – Irene and Margherita couldn't believe their (own) eyes

*Ogni cultura ha **le proprie** usanze e tradizioni* – Every culture has its own customs and traditions

Altrui (others')

Listen to track 154

Altrui denotes an indefinite possessor and can be translated in English as *others* or *of others*. It is invariable, which means that it has the same form regardless of the gender and number of the following noun.

Have a look at the following examples:

*Chiara, devi imparare a rispettare le opinioni **altrui*** – Chiara, you must learn to respect other people's opinions

*È importante educare i bambini al rispetto delle cose **altrui*** – It is important to educate children to respect the things of others

Italian possessive pronouns

Listen to track 155

A **possessive pronoun** is a short word you use instead of a possessive adjective followed by a noun. The **Italian possessive pronouns** are exactly the same as possessive adjectives, and replace a noun so as to highlight it.

To turn a possessive adjective into a possessive pronoun, all you have to do is omit the noun. Have a look at these examples to get an idea of how it works:

il mio orologio – **il mio**

la mia maglietta – **la mia**

i miei orologi – **i miei**

le mie magliette – **le mie**

A *pronome possessivo* must agree with the noun it replaces in gender and number, and is always preceded by the definite article or a preposition.

Here are the **Italian possessive pronouns**:

Listen to track 156

Masculine (singular)

Il mio – mine

Il tuo – yours

Il suo – his, hers, its

Il Suo – yours (polite)

Il nostro – ours

Il vostro – yours

Il loro – theirs

Il proprio – own

L'altrui – others'

Listen to track 157

Feminine (singular)

La mia – mine

La tua – yours

La sua – his, hers, its

La Sua – yours (polite)

La nostra – ours

La vostra – yours

La loro – theirs

La propria – own

La altrui – others'

Listen to track 158

Masculine (plural)

I miei – mine

I tuoi – yours

I suoi – his, hers, its

I Suoi – yours (polite)

I nostri – ours

I vostri – yours

I loro – theirs

I propri – own
Gli altrui – others'

Listen to track 159

Feminine (plural)

Le mie – mine
Le tue – yours
Le sue – his, hers, its
Le Sue – yours (polite)
Le nostre – ours
Le vostre – yours
Le loro – theirs
Le proprie – own
Le altrui – others'

Listen to track 160

Take a look at the following examples:

*Questa bicicletta è **la mia*** – This bike is mine

*Mia nonna è più severa della **la sua*** – My grandma is stricter than hers

*A ciascuno **il suo*** – To each their own

*Prendiamo la mia macchina o **la tua**?* – Do you want to take my car or yours?

Using the Italian pronomi possessivi

Listen to track 161

The possessive pronouns are used to:

• talk about something that belongs to someone:

***Il suo** è stato un gesto molto nobile* – His was a very noble gesture

• refer to someone's parents:

*Barbara vive con **i suoi** (genitori)* – Barbara lives with her parents

*Cosa hanno detto **i tuoi** (genitori)?* – What did your parents say?

*Non potrò più contare sull'aiuto de**i miei** (genitori)* – I won't be able to count on my parents' help

- indicate friends and companions:

Anch'io sono dei vostri – I'm with you

Arrivano i nostri – Our buddies are arriving

- substitute the word *lettera/missiva* (letter) or *email* (e-mail) in correspondence and commercial language:

Spero che questa mia La trovi bene – I hope this finds you well

- refer to an opinion with the verb *dire* (to say):

Anch'io ho diritto di dire la mia – I have a right to say my opinion

- refer to tricks, pranks or nonsense with the verbs *combinare* (to combine), *dire* (to say) and *fare* (to make, to do):

Ne hai combinata una delle tue – You pulled a fast one

To sum up...

Listen to track 162

- Italian possessive adjectives *(aggettivi possessivi)* and possessive pronouns *(pronomi possessivi)* generally include a definite article, which is not translated into English.
- Use the *aggettivo possessivo* without the definite article when talking about a singular family member.

Mia sorella si chiama Alessia – My sister is called Alessia

- Use the *aggettivo possessivo* with the definite article when talking about family members in the plural.

I miei zii si sono trasferiti a Torino – My uncles moved to Turin

I suoi suoceri vivono in Inghilterra – Her in-laws live in England

- Italian possessive pronouns are the same as Italian possessive adjectives.
- Italian possessive pronouns are masculine or feminine, singular or plural, depending on what they refer to.

Workbook Lesson 9. Possessive Pronouns and Adjectives

Exercise 9.1: Complete the following sentences with the right possessive adjective:

1. Il ____ capo mi ha dato un giorno di riposo. (My boss gave me a day off.)

2. La ____ assistente si chiama Paola. (His assistant is called Paola.)

3. Le ____ zie non sono sposate. (Your aunts are not married.)

4. Com'è andata la ____ giornata? (How was your day?)

5. I ____ cani hanno il pelo corto. (Our dogs have short hair.)

Exercise 9.2: Complete the sentences as in the example:

Example: Di chi è questo bicchiere? È suo

1. È tuo questo telefono? È ____. (Is this your phone? It's mine.)
2. Di chi sono queste chiavi? Sono ____. (Whose keys are these? They are ours.)
3. È ____ questo biglietto? (Is this your ticket?)
4. Di chi sono queste scarpe? Sono ____. (Whose shoes are these? They are mine.)
5. Sono ____ questi libri? (Are these your books?)

Exercise 9.3: Complete these sentences with the right possessive adjective or pronoun:

1. Sto cercando un regalo per ____ padre. (I'm looking for a present for my father.)

2. La ____ scuola è vicino casa. (Her school is near home.)

3. Le ____ scuse non sono credibili. (Their excuses are not credible.)

4. La ____ penna è nera, la ____ è blu. (Your pen is black, mine is blue.)

5. I ____ amici non sono come i ____. (Their friends are not like mine.)

Exercise 9.4: Tick the right answer:

1. Le ____ scuse non sono accettabili. (Your apologies are not acceptable.)
   1) loro   2) mie   3) vostre

2. La ____ camicia è più grande della ____. (His shirt is bigger than mine.)
   1) sua, mia   2) suo, mia   3) mia, sua

3. Questo è il ____ cane? (Is this their dog?)
   1) suo   2) loro   3) nostro

4. Stasera venite a casa ____? (Are you coming to our house tonight?)
   1) nostra   2) loro   3) mia

5. Per colpa ____ non abbiamo vinto. (Because of him we didn't win.)
   1) loro   2) mia   3) sua

Exercise 9.5: Complete the following text:

____ mamma è professoressa di storia. I ____ alunni hanno tra i 14 e i 18 anni. Lei ama il ____ lavoro e va d'accordo con le ____ colleghe. La ____ scuola si trova vicino casa, ma lei prende la macchina di mio papà per andarci perché la ____ si è rotta. (My mom is a history teacher. Her students are between 14 and 18 years old. She loves her job and gets along with her colleagues. Her school is near our home, but she takes my dad's car to go there because hers broke down.)

_____

_____

_____

_____

_____

_____

_____

_____

_____.

Answers:

Exercise 9.1:

1. Il mio capo mi ha dato un giorno di riposo.

2. La sua assistente si chiama Paola.

3. Le vostre/tue zie non sono sposate.

4. Com'è andata la tua giornata?

5. Nostri cani hanno il pelo corto.

Exercise 9.2:

1. È tuo questo telefono? È mio.

2. Di chi sono queste chiavi? Sono nostre.

3. È vostro/tuo questo biglietto?

4. Di chi sono queste scarpe? Sono mie.

5. Sono vostri/tuoi questi libri?

Exercise 9.3:

1. mio; 2. sua; 3. loro; 4. tua, mia; 5. loro, miei

Exercise 9.4:

1) vostre; 2) sua, mia; 3) loro; 4) nostra; 5) sua

Exercise 9.5:

Mia mamma è professoressa di storia. I suoi alunni hanno tra i 14 e i 18 anni. Lei ama il suo lavoro e va d'accordo con le sue colleghe. La sua scuola si trova vicino casa, ma lei prende la macchina di mio papà per andarci perché la sua si è rotta.

LESSON 10: AGGETTIVI E PRONOMI DIMOSTRATIVI

Demonstrative adjectives and pronouns (*aggettivi* and *pronomi dimostrativi*) are essential in any kind of communication, so it is crucial to master them.

In this lesson, we will show you how to use the Italian *aggettivi* and *pronomi dimostrativi*. Let's get started!

Italian demonstrative adjectives

Demonstrative adjectives (*aggettivi dimostrativi*) determine the position in space or time of something or someone with respect to the person who speaks or writes. They agree in gender and number with the noun they refer to. As in English, Italian *aggettivi dimostrativi* go before the noun.

Each *aggettivo dimostrativo* has four forms, with different endings:

- **-o** for the masculine singular;
- **-a** for the feminine singular;
- **-i** for the masculine plural;
- **-e** for the feminine plural.

Here are all your options:

Listen to track 163

Masculine (singular)

Questo – this

Quello – that

Masculine (plural)

Questi – these

Quei, quegli – those

Feminine (singular)

Questa – this

Quella – that

Feminine (plural)

Queste – these

Quelle – those

Let's look at each one closely.

Questo (this)

Listen to track 164

Questo is used to indicate that someone or something is close to both the speaker and the listener, and corresponds by and large to "this" in English. It is applied to anything which the speakers view as close to them in space or time.

Use *questo* with masculine singular nouns, *questa* with feminine singular nouns, *questi* with masculine plural nouns and *queste* with feminine plural nouns.

Queste *crespelle sono deliziose* – These crepes are delicious (I am talking about the crepes that are close to me to the people who are listening to me)

Nessuno di ***questi*** *divieti è entrato in vigore* – None of these bans have taken effect

Questo *pomeriggio vado in palestra* – I'm going to the gym this afternoon

Non capisco perché Alice abbia avuto ***questa*** *reazione* – I don't understand why Alice had this reaction

In informal speech, *questo, questa, questi* and *queste* are frequently replaced by their shortened forms *'sto, 'sta, 'sti* and *'ste*. Don't use them in formal discourse and writing.

Che è ***'sta*** *roba?* – What is this stuff?

Chi ha combinato ***'sto*** *disastro?* – Who on earth did this?

Quello (that)

Quello corresponds to "that" in English and indicates beings or objects far away from both the speaker and the listener. Like the masculine definite article, *quello* has several different forms.

Listen to track 165

Quel

You use *quel* with masculine singular nouns starting with a consonant.

Quel *colore* – that color
Quel *viaggio* – that trip
Quel *bracciale* – that bracelet

Listen to track 166

Quello

You use *quello* with masculine singular nouns that start with "s" followed by a consonant, "z", "ps", "pn", "gn", "y" and "x". Look at the following examples:

Quello strumento – that tool

Quello zaino – that backpack

Quello psicologo – that psychologist

Quello pneumatico – that tire

Quello gnomo – that gnome

Quello yacht – that yacht

Quello xilofono – that xylophone

When a masculine singular noun begins with a vowel, *quello* contracts into *quell'* (with an apostrophe).

Quell'orologio – that watch

Quell'aereoplano – that airplane

Listen to track 167

Quella

You use *quella* with feminine singular nouns starting with a consonant.

Quella relazione – that relationship

Quella domanda – that question

When a feminine singular noun begins with a vowel, *quella* contracts into *quell'* (with an apostrophe).

Quell'estate – that summer

Quell'informazione – that information

Listen to track 168

Quei

You use *quei* with masculine plural nouns beginning with a consonant.

Quei fiumi – those rivers

Quei paesi – those countries

Listen to track 169

Quegli

You use *quegli* with masculine plural nouns starting with a vowel and with "z", "ps", "gn", "pn", "x", "y" or "s" followed by a consonant.

***Quegli* o**spedali* – those hospitals

***Quegli* st**ivali* – those boots

***Quegli* z**aini* – those backpacks

***Quegli* ps**icologi* – those psychologists

***Quegli* pn**eumatici* – those tires

***Quegli* gn**omi* – those gnomes

***Quegli* y**ogurt* – those yogurts

***Quegli* x**ilofoni* – those xylophones

Listen to track 170

Quelle

You use *quelle* with all feminine plural nouns.

***Quelle* *navi* – those boats

***Quelle* *chiavi* – those keys

***Quelle* *affermazioni* – those statements

How to use the Italian aggettivi dimostrativi

Listen to track 171

If there is an *aggettivo dimostrativo* in a sentence, you have to:

- place possessive adjectives between the demonstrative adjective and the noun

*Adoro **quel suo** accento francese* – I love her French accent

- place qualifying adjectives after the noun

*Ti piace **questa** gonna plissettata?* – Do you like this pleated skirt?

As mentioned previously, when the *aggettivi dimostrativi* precede a noun starting with a vowel, all singular forms drop their vowel endings and replace them with an apostrophe.

***Quest'*albero* – this tree

***Quell'*albero* – that tree

Quest'*ipotesi* – this hypothesis

Quell'*ipotesi* – that hypothesis

Other demonstrative adjectives

Listen to track 172

Take a look at some other demonstrative adjectives in Italian.

Codesto (that)

Codesto, sometimes also *cotesto*, indicates something or someone far away from the speaker but near the listener. Still used in Tuscany and in commercial, administrative and bureaucratic language, *codesto* is falling into disuse. It is now generally considered archaic and is being replaced by *quello*.

Codesto agrees in number and gender with the noun it refers to.

Dammi **codesti** *libri, per favore* – Give me those books, please

Si prega di rivolgersi a **codesto** *Ministero* – Please contact that Department

Listen to track 173

Stesso, medesimo (same)

Stesso and *medesimo* determine equality among people or things, and mean "same" or "identical". They agree in gender and number with the noun they refer to.

Gianluca dice sempre le **stesse** *cose* – Gianluca always says the same things

Prenderemo lo **stesso** *treno* – We will take the same train

Emanuele, Morena e Lorenzo abitano nel **medesimo** *condominio* – Emanuele, Morena and Lorenzo live in the same apartment building

BEWARE: *stesso* and *medesimo* are often used to emphasize the noun or pronoun they refer to, in order to underline its identity. In this form, they take the meaning of *perfino* (even), *proprio* (himself, herself), *lui/lei in persona* (he/she in person). For example:

Gloria **stessa** *si è accorta di aver sbagliato* – Gloria herself realized she was wrong

L'hanno visto loro **stessi** – They saw it themselves

Lei **medesimo** *me lo disse* – You told me, sir

Tale (such)

Listen to track 174

Tale is an adjective and usually precedes the noun. It means "such (a)".

Tali *sostanze nuocciono gravemente alla salute* – Such substances are harmful to health

Italian demonstrative pronouns

In English, the **demonstrative pronouns** (*pronomi dimostrativi*) are *this, these, that* and *those*. Used instead of a noun to point out people or objects, the *pronome dimostrativo* must agree in gender and number with the antecedent noun it replaces.

Here are the **Italian demonstrative pronouns:**

Listen to track 175

Masculine (singular)

Questo – this, this one

Quello – that, that one

Feminine (singular)

Questa – this, this one

Quella – that, that one

Masculine (plural)

Questi – these, these ones

Quelli – those, those ones

Feminine (plural)

Queste – these, these ones

Quelle – those, those ones

The Italian *pronomi dimostrativi* can be used as subjects, objects or indirect objects when accompanied by a preposition.

Listen to track 176

'This one' and 'these ones' in Italian

Questo is used to indicate something or someone physically or mentally close to the speaker. Use *questo* to replace masculine singular nouns, *questa* to replace feminine singular nouns, *questi* to replace masculine plural nouns and *queste* to replace feminine plural nouns.

Look at the following examples:

*Secondo te l'unica cosa da fare è **questa**?* – Is this the only thing left to do?

*Non so se **questo** possa essere considerato un problema* – I don't know if this can be considered a problem

***Questi** sono i colori di tendenza di questa stagione* – These are the trendy colors this season

***Queste** sono questioni che non mi riguardano* – These are matters that do not concern me in any way

When you want to say *this one*, don't translate *one*. Just use *questo* if what you are referring to is masculine, *questa* if it is feminine and so on.

*Qual è la tua cravatta? **Questa*** – Which one is your tie? This one

In colloquial speech, *questo* and *questa* are often used to mean "this man" and "this woman", and are often reinforced by the adverbs of place **qui** (here) or **qua** (here).

*Chi diavolo è **quello**?* – Who on earth is that man?

*Ma chi crede di essere **questa qui**?* – Who does she think she is?

Listen to track 177

Questa often appears in ironic or humorous exclamations:

***Questa** è bella!* – That's funny!

*Ci mancava anche **questa**!* – That was all we needed! / That's just great!

Listen to track 178

Questo is often used to refer to a previous proposition, assertion or question. For example:

Ognuno ha I suoi difetti.

***Questo** è vero.* – We all have our faults. That's true.

'That one' and 'those ones' in Italian

Listen to track 179

Quello indicates someone or something far away from both the speaker and the listener. Use *quello* to replace masculine singular nouns, *quella* to replace feminine singular nouns, *quelli* to replace masculine plural nouns and *quelle* to replace feminine plural nouns.

Here are some examples:

*Mia sorella è **quella** bionda, non **quella** mora* – My sister is the blonde one, not the brunette one

*In questa foto, mio nipote è **quello** con la maglietta blu* – In this photo, my nephew is the one with the blue T-shirt

***Quelli** sì che erano bei tempi!* – Those sure were good times!

*Chi cade e si rialza è più forte di **quelli** che non ci provano nemmeno* – The one who falls and gets up is stronger than those who never tried

In informal speech, *quello* and *quella* are often used to mean "that man" and "that woman".

Note: using *quello* and *quella* suggests a negative attitude towards the person, and the effect may sound slightly discourteous, especially when reinforced by the adverbs of place **lì** (there) or **là** (there).

*Chi è **quella**?* – Who's that woman?

*Non fidarti di **quello** là* – Don't trust that guy

*Ma chi crede di essere **quello** lì?* – Who does he think he is?

It is easy to confuse demonstrative adjectives and pronouns. Remember that *aggettivi dimostrativi* add a feature to the noun they refer to, whereas *pronomi dimostrativi* replace another element of the sentence.

Other demonstrative pronouns

Listen to track 180

Costui/costei/costoro (this person, these people)

A more formal way to refer to people near the speaker is to use *costui, costei* and *costoro* instead of *questo, questa* and *questi(-e)*.

Note: *costui* may have a pejorative ring when it is used to point to a person. In this form, it takes the meaning of "that person over there".

*Ma chi si crede di essere **costui**?* – Who does he think he is?

Costei mi detesta e non capisco perché – She hates me and I don't understand why

Costoro rischiano il licenziamento – They risk dismissal

Colui/colei/coloro che (the one who/those who)

A more formal way to refer to people far from both speaker and listener is to use *colui*, *colei* and *coloro* instead of *quello*, *quella* and *quelli(-e)*.

*Lo scettico è **colui** che non crede mai a nulla* – The skeptic is someone who never believes in anything

***Colei** che infranse le regole fu immediatamente scoperta* – The person who broke the rules was immediately identified

*Abbiamo inviato un'email a tutti **coloro** che parteciperanno all'evento* – We sent an email to all those who will take part in the event

Note: *costui, costei, costoro, colui, colei* and *coloro* refer only to human beings and are used in formal and written language.

Listen to track 181

Lo stesso, il medesimo (the same)

Lo stesso is the Italian word for "the same", "the same person" and "the same thing".

*Fai quello che vuoi, tanto per me è **lo stesso*** – Do what you want, it's all the same to me anyway

*La preside è **la stessa** di qualche anno fa* – The principal is the same one as a few years ago

Note: *il medesimo* is more formal than *lo stesso*.

*L'indirizzo è **il medesimo** che Le ha dato la signora Paolini* – The address is the same one that Ms. Paolini gave you

Ciò (this/that thing)

Ciò is a neuter and indeclinable pronoun, and refers to events and ideas. It can be used instead of *questo* (this) and *quello* (that).

*Fate **ciò** che vi piace* – Do what you like

*Vorrei spiegarti **ciò** di cui ha parlato ieri il direttore* – I'd like to explain to you what the manager talked about yesterday

To sum up...

- Demonstrative adjectives point out the position of specific people or objects in time or space.
- Use *questo* or *questa* for "this".
- Use *questi* or *queste* for "these".
- *Questo, questa, questi* and *queste* refer to elements that are close to both the speaker and the listener.
- Use *quello* or quella for "that".
- Use *quei/quegli* o *quelle* for "those".
- *Quello* behaves like the masculine definite article "il".
- *Quello, quella, quei/quegli* and *quelle* refer to elements that are far away from both the speaker and the listener.
- The Italian demonstrative pronouns are *questo* and *quello*.
- *Questo* and *quello* have masculine, feminine, singular and plural forms.

Workbook Lesson 10. Demonstrative Adjectives and Pronouns

Exercise 10.1: Fill in the gaps in the tables

This	Singular	Plural
Masculine	Questo	
Feminine		
That	Singular	Plural
Masculine		
Feminine		Quelle

Exercise 10.2: Translate the following sentences into Italian

English	Italian
1. That's my bag.	
2. This is our little sister.	
3. My mom made these cookies.	
4. Those trousers are very pretty!	
5. They are cutting that tree.	
6. I wanna visit that beach.	

Exercise 10.3: Complete these sentences with the right word

1. Ho deciso di comprare _____ maglia laggiù.

2. _____ pacco qui è arrivato ieri.

3. _____ sedute lì in fondo sono le mie amiche.

4. _____ panino è davvero ottimo!

5. _____ casa in fondo alla via è molto costosa.

Exercise 10.4: Underline demonstrative adjectives once, and demonstrative pronouns twice

1. Non voglio mettere quelle scarpe: preferisco queste!

2. In quel cortile crescono erbacce ovunque, mentre questo è molto curato.

3. Quella è la mia borsa: la metto sempre allo stesso posto e non posso sbagliare!

4. Quell'albero laggiù è un sempreverde mentre questo è a foglie caduche.

5. Quella soluzione non mi convince: sono molto meglio questa o quella.

6. Questa volta sarò molto più attento di quella in cui caddi nella piscina.

Exercise 10.5: Translate the following sentences

English	Italian
I wanted that shirt, not this one.	
This idea is better than that one.	
Those guys are a bit weird. I don't trust people like them.	
I baked these cookies myself, but the ones I saw at the store look better.	
I chose these shoes, not those ones.	
I prefer this sport, not that one.	

Answers:

Exercise 10.1:

This	Singular	Plural
Masculine	Questo	Questi
Feminine	Masculine	Questo
That	Singular	Plural
Masculine	Quello	Quelli
Feminine	Quella	Quelle

Exercise 10.2:

1. Quella è la mia borsa.
2. Questa è nostra sorella minore.
3. La mia mamma ha fatto questi biscotti.
4. Quei pantaloni sono davvero belli!
5. Stanno tagliando quell'albero.
6. Voglio visitare quella spiaggia.

Exercise 10.3:

1. quella; 2. Questo; 3. Quelle 4. quel; 5. quella

Exercise 10.4:

1. Non voglio mettere quelle scarpe: preferisco queste!
2. In quel cortile crescono erbacce ovunque, mentre questo è molto curato.
3. Quella è la mia borsa: la metto sempre allo stesso posto e non posso sbagliare!
4. Quell'albero laggiù è un sempreverde mentre questo è a foglie caduche.
5. Quella soluzione non mi convince: sono molto meglio questa o quella.
6. Questa volta sarò molto più attento di quella in cui caddi nella piscina.

Exercise 10.5:

1. Volevo quella maglia, non questa.
2. Quest'idea è meglio di quella.
3. Quei ragazzi sono un po' strani. Non mi fido di quelli come loro.
4. Ho cucinato questi biscotti io stessa, ma quelli che ho visto al negozio sembrano più buoni.
5. Ho scelto queste scarpe, non quelle là.
6. Preferisco questo sport, non quello.

LESSON 11. DIRECT AND INDIRECT OBJECT PRONOUNS

Pretty useful in conversations, **Italian direct and indirect object pronouns** have been giving English native speakers hell since forever. Don't worry, they are not as scary as they sound! Lots of practice usually helps.

With this book we aim to show you how to use Italian direct and indirect object pronouns. Sounds good? Let's start!

Italian direct object pronouns

Always paired with transitive verbs, **direct object pronouns** (*pronomi diretti*) get acted upon by the verb, and answer the questions *what?* or *whom?*. In other words, they directly receive the action of the verb in question, and replace the name of a person or object.

In Italian, there are two types of direct object pronouns: those that go before the verb, also known as 'unstressed', and those that go after the verb, which are also called 'stressed'. Depending on their position before or after the verb, unstressed and stressed direct object pronouns have slightly different forms.

Unstressed direct object pronouns

Here are the **Italian unstressed direct object pronouns**:

Listen to track 182

mi – me (first person singular)

ti – you (second person singular)

lo – him (third person masculine singular)

la, La– her (third person feminine singular), you (polite singular)

ci – us (first person plural)

vi – you (second person plural)

li – them (third person masculine plural)

le – them (third person feminine plural)

Unlike English, you usually put them **before the verb** that's being conjugated. Let's look at a few examples:

Mi vedi? Sì, ti vedo – Can you see me? Yes, I see you

Ti richiamo più tardi – I'll call you back later

Lo sapevo! – I knew it!

Hai visto la mia agenda? La cerco da un'ora! – Have you seen my personal organizer? I've been looking for it for an hour!

Ci vediamo! – See you later!

Vi trovo in splendida forma – You look great!

Se avessi maggiori profitti, li investirei in quel progetto – If I had more profit, I'd invest it in that project

Le vado a prendere io in aeroporto domani – I'll pick them up at the airport tomorrow

As you can see, the Italian direct object pronouns *lo* (him), *la* (her), *li* (them) and *le* (them) can replace both people and inanimate objects. *Li* and *le* are the plural counterparts to *lo* and *la*.

Listen to track 183

When **non** (not) is used to show the negative, it goes before the pronoun. For example:

Conosci Raffaele? No, non lo conosco – Do you know Raffaele? No, I don't know him

Perché non li inviti? – Why don't you invite them?

The unstressed direct object pronouns *mi* (me), *ti* (you), *lo* (him) and *la* (her) can be shortened to *m'*, *t'* and *l'* before a vowel or before an "h". Take a look at the following examples:

Il bacio è un apostrofo rosa tra le parole t'amo (cit. Edmond Rostand) – Literally: A kiss is a pink apostrophe between the words I love you / English version: A kiss is the pink exclamation mark that comes after "I love you!"

Hai visto Marzia? No, non l'ho vista – Have you seen Marzia? No, I haven't seen **her**

Hai visto Alberto? Sì, l'ho visto – Have you seen Alberto? Yes, I've seen **him**

As you might have noticed, when using an unstressed direct object pronoun with a compound verb, like the *passato prossimo*, the past participle matches it in gender and number.

When you are using the **gerund** (*gerundio*) or the **imperative** (*imperativo*) to tell someone to do or not to do something, the pronoun comes after the verb and is joined onto it. Have a look at these examples:

Listen to track 184

Lasciami stare! – Leave me alone! (imperative)

Eravamo tutti preoccupati per Floriana, vedendola così giù di morale – We were all very worried about Floriana, when seeing her so upset (gerund)

Aiutalo! – Help him! (imperative)

Dobbiamo chiamare un'ambulanza? Sì, chiamatela subito – Should we call an ambulance? Yes, call it right away (imperative)

When you are using an unstressed direct object pronoun with the infinitive (*infinito*), it is joined onto the verb. You just have to take off the final "**e**" of the infinitive. For example:

Andrea vorrebbe incontrarti – Andrea would like to meet you

Venite a trovarci! – Come visit us!

With the **modal verbs** *potere* (to can, to be able to), *volere* (to want), *dovere* (to must, to have to) and *sapere* (to know), the *pronomi diretti* can either precede the conjugated verb or be joined onto the end of the infinitive.

Listen to track 185

*Non **ti** posso aiutare / Non posso aiutarti* – I can't help you

*Non **ti** volevo ferire / Non volevo ferirti* – I didn't want to hurt you

Le dovresti chiedere scusa / Dovresti chiederle scusa – You should apologize to her

*Nel corso delle prossime ore **vi** sapremo dare più dettagli in merito / Nel corso delle prossime ore sapremo darvi più dettagli in merito* – In the next few hours we will be able to give you more details on this

With short verbs, like *fare* (to do, to make), *dare* (to give) and *dire* (to say, to tell), remember to double the consonant the direct object pronoun starts with.

Fallo in fretta – Do it quickly

Dimmi la verità! – Tell me the truth!

Dalle un bacio – Give her a kiss

Direct object pronouns can be attached to **ecco** (here) to express the phrases "here I am", "here you are", and so on.

*Dov'è Enrico? **Eccolo!*** – Where is Enrico? Here he is!

*Dove sono i miei stivali? **Eccoli!*** – Where are my boots? Here they are!

Stressed direct object pronouns

Listen to track 186

Here are the **Italian stressed direct object pronouns**:

me – me (first person singular)

te – you (second person singular)

lui – him (third person masculine singular)

lei/Lei – her (third person feminine singular), you (polite singular)

noi – us (first person plural)

voi – you (second person plural)

loro – them (third person plural)

As you can see, the **stressed direct object pronouns** are exactly the same as the subject pronouns, except that *me* (me) is used instead of *io* (I) and *te* (you) is used instead of *tu* (you).

Stressed direct object pronouns generally go **after the verb**. You use them:

- to emphasize that you mean a specific person and not somebody else:

*Amo solo **te*** – I love only you

*Francesca non guardava **me**, guardava **lui*** – Francesca wasn't looking at me, she was looking at him

- after a preposition:

*Possiamo venire con **voi**?* – Can we come with you?

*C'è posta per **te*** – You've got mail

- in comparisons:

*Ambrogio è molto più alto di **me*** – Ambrogio is much taller than me

*La signora Franzini è più anziana di **te*** – Mrs. Franzini is older than you

Italian indirect object pronouns

Listen to track 187

Indirect object pronouns (*pronomi indiretti*) answer the questions *to whom?* and *to what?,* and are the receiver of the verb's action. You use them when you give something to someone, tell somebody something, and so on. Take a look at the following examples:

Ieri era il compleanno di Patrizia. Abbiamo regalato un libro di cucina a Patrizia – It was Patrizia's birthday yesterday. We gave Patrizia a cookbook

Ieri era il compleanno di Patrizia. **Le** *abbiamo regalato un libro di cucina* – It was Patrizia's birthday yesterday. We gave her a cookbook

In the above examples, the cookbook is the direct object and the indirect object is Patrizia, because she is the person we bought the cookbook for. **Le** (her) is an indirect object pronoun, and you use it to avoid repeating the name Patrizia over and over again. As you can see, using an indirect object pronoun in place of a noun makes the conversation more fluid and smooth.

Like direct object pronouns, there are unstressed and stressed indirect object pronouns, which go before and after the verb respectively.

Unstressed indirect object pronouns

Here are the **Italian unstressed indirect object pronouns**:

Listen to track 188

mi – to me, me (first person singular)

ti – to you, you (second person singular)

gli – to him, him (third person masculine singular)

le, Le – to her, her (third person feminine singular); to you, you (polite singular)

ci – to us, us (first person plural)

vi – to you, you (second person plural)

gli, loro – to them, them (third person plural)

Not so bad, right? The differences between unstressed direct and indirect pronouns are in:

lo / gli

la / le

li/le / gli/loro

Listen to track 189

Check out these unstressed indirect object pronouns:

Mi *dai una mano, per favore?* – Would you give me a hand, please?

Mi *puoi prestare la tua penna?* – Can I borrow your pen?

Ti *posso fare una domanda?* – May I ask you a question?

Ti faremo sapere – We'll let you know

Le conviene fare inversione a U, signor Barzini – You should make a U-turn, Mr. Barzini

Ci piacciono i cani – We like dogs

Le ho confidato tutti i miei segreti – I confided all my secrets to her

Dopo il primo appuntamento Riccardo non le ha più telefonato – After their first date, Riccardo didn't call her again

Gli ho detto la verità – I told him the truth

Gli farò un bel regalo a Natale / Farò loro un bel regalo a Natale – I'll give them a nice Christmas present

As you can see, indirect object pronouns don't shorten before a vowel or an "h".

Listen to track 190

Indirect object pronouns are usually paired with verbs that have to do with:

- **giving**, like *dare* (to give), *offrire* (to offer), *mandare* (to send), *portare* (to bring), *consegnare* (to deliver), *restituire* (to give back, to return) and *prestare* (to lend);

Vittorio mi ha offerto un caffè – Vittorio offered me a cup of coffee

- **communication**, like *parlare* (to talk, to speak), *dire* (to say), *chiedere* (to ask), *rispondere* (to answer), *scrivere* (to write), *insegnare* (to teach), *spiegare* (to explain) and *consigliare* (to suggest):

Ti consiglio di rivolgerti a un commercialista – I advise you to speak to an accountant

Note: when a sentence contains a verb in the **infinitive**, the final "e" is dropped and the indirect object pronoun is attached to the end of it. For example:

Devo parlargli urgentemente – I need to talk to him urgently

Listen to track 191
Stressed indirect object pronouns

Here are the **stressed indirect object pronouns**:

a me – (to) me (first person singular)

a te – (to) you (second person singular)

a lui – (to) him (third person masculine singular)

a lei, a Lei – (to) her (third person feminine singular), you (polite singular)

a noi – (to) us (first person plural)

a voi– (to) you (second person plural)

a loro – (to) them (third person plural)

Easy, right? Note: each of these includes the preposition *a* (to). In Italian, *a* (to) is always used before a stressed indirect object pronoun, whereas in English the word "to" can be omitted.

You use stressed indirect object pronouns to emphasize that you mean a particular person and not somebody else. For example:

*Alessandra ha consegnato l'invito **a me**, non a Beatrice* – Alessandra gave the invitation to me, not to Beatrice

Using direct and indirect object pronouns together

Italian direct and indirect object pronouns may be used in the same sentence or even in the same word. The indirect object pronoun usually goes before the direct object pronoun, and changes its form as follows:

Listen to track 192

mi → **me**

ti → **te**

ci → **ce**

vi → **ve**

For example:

***Me** l'avevi promesso* – You promised it to me

***Te** li farò avere entro giovedì* – You'll have them by Thursday

When you need to use *gli* (them, him) and *le* (her) with *lo, la, li* and *le*, add the letter "e" to ***gli*** and attach it to the appropriate direct object pronoun as follows:

gli / le + lo → **glielo**

gli / le + la → **gliela**

gli / le + li → **glieli**

gli / le + le→ **gliele**

Take a look at these examples to get an idea of how it works:

***Glielo** avevi promesso* – You promised it to him

Glieli puoi inviare? – Can you send them to her?

Glielo dirò domani – I'll tell them tomorrow

When using the infinitive, direct and indirect object pronouns join together and are attached to the verb. The final "e" of the infinitive is dropped. For example:

Non vuole dirmelo – He doesn't want to tell me

Non ho ricevuto la mail, potresti rimandarmela? – I didn't receive the email, could you send it to me again?

All done for now! Read the explanations again and again, and practice as much as you can until you get the hang of it. Real conversation practice is the key to mastering Italian direct and indirect object pronouns.

To sum up...

Direct object pronouns are acted upon by the verb, and answer the questions *what?* or *whom?* Always paired with transitive verbs, they are directly involved in or affected by the action described by the verb in question, and replace the name of a person or object. In Italian, there are two types of direct object pronouns:

- those that go before the verb, also known as 'unstressed': **mi, ti, lo, la, La, ci, vi, li, le**.
- those that go after the verb, which are also called 'stressed': **me, te, lui, lei, Lei, noi, voi, loro**.

Indirect object pronouns answer the questions *to whom?* and *to what?* and are the receiver of the verb's action. There are unstressed (**mi, ti, gli, le, Le, ci, vi, gli, loro**) and stressed (**a me, a te, a lui, a lei, a Lei, a noi, a voi, a loro**) indirect object pronouns, which go before and after the verb respectively.

Workbook Lesson 11. Direct and Indirect Object Pronouns

Exercise 11.1: Choose the right option

1. Non _ ho fatto apposta! (Lo, la, gli)

2. Ho visto le mie amiche ieri, ma oggi non _ ho viste. (gli, mi, le)

3. Luigi? Non credo di conoscer_. (la, lo, mi)

4. Spiegate_ meglio, non capisco cosa volete dire. (la, ti, vi)

5. Io mangio quasi ogni cosa, ma la lattuga proprio non _ sopporto. (ci, mi, la)

6. A volte, quando parlo con Matteo, non so se _ capisce. (Vi, mi, ci)

Exercise 11.2: Underline all the direct and indirect object pronouns in the text

Ho incontrato Marco e Francesca l'altro giorno: quando gli ho parlato mi sono sembrati tutti e due molto preoccupati. La loro figlia infatti è in vacanza in India e non gli telefonava da una settimana: sicuramente non le era successo niente di male, ma di solito chiamava ogni tre giorni. Francesca voleva telefonare all'ambasciata, ma io le ho detto che era ancora troppo presto per fare cose di questo tipo. Mi è dispiaciuto vederli così perché gli voglio molto bene.

Per fortuna ieri mattina Marco mi ha detto che la figlia, finalmente, gli ha telefonato. Come immaginavo non le era successo niente di grave: semplicemente le si era rotto il telefonino.

Exercise 11.3: Replace the noun with a pronoun

Noun	Pronoun
1. Ho visto **quel film**.	
2. I bambini adorano **le caramelle**.	
3. La mia gatta guarda sempre **il mio cane**.	
4. Non ho visto **né te né Marta** ieri.	
5. Non voglio incontrare **Luca e Paolo** domani.	
6. **A noi** fa piacere vedervi.	

Exercise 11.4: Translate the following sentences into Italian

English	Italian
1. You told me you'd come!	
2. I'll show him how to do that.	
3. Who's gonna ask the teacher? They'll ask her.	
4. Don't ask me, I don't know!	
5. I told you all that!	

Exercise 11.5: Link the sentences to make a conversation. Pay attention to the pronouns!

1) Hai mangiato la pizza a Napoli?	A) Certo che ti amo!
2) Avete visto il film di Sorrentino?	B) Non lo so. Non ho l'orologio.
3) Che ore sono?	C) Purtroppo, non ho potuto mangiarla. Avevo fretta.
4) Mi ami, amore?	D) Sì, le ho comprate ieri in saldo.
5) Hai comprato le scarpe nuove?	E) Non l'ho ancora visto.

Answers:

Exercise 11.1:

1) Lo; 2) le; 3) lo; 4) vi; 5) la; 6) mi

Exercise 11.2:

Ho incontrato Marco e Francesca l'altro giorno: quando <u>gli</u> ho parlato <u>mi</u> sono sembrati tutti e due molto preoccupati. La loro figlia infatti è in vacanza in India e non <u>gli</u> telefonava da una settimana: sicuramente non <u>le</u> era successo niente di male, ma di solito chiamava ogni tre giorni. Francesca voleva telefonare all'ambasciata, ma io <u>le</u> ho detto che era ancora troppo presto per fare cose di questo tipo. <u>Mi</u> è dispiaciuto vederli così perché <u>gli</u> voglio molto bene.

Per fortuna ieri mattina Marco mi ha detto che la figlia, finalmente, <u>gli</u> ha telefonato. Come immaginavo non <u>le</u> era successo niente di grave: semplicemente <u>le</u> si era rotto il telefonino.

Exercise 11.3:

1. Lo ho visto.; 2. I bambini le adorano.

3. La mia gatta lo guarda sempre.

4. Non vi ho visto ieri.

5. Non li voglio incontrare domani.

6. Ci fa piacere vedervi.

Exercise 11.4:

1. Mi avevi detto che saresti venuto!

2. Gli faccio vedere come si fa.

3. Chi lo chiede all'insegnante? Glielo chiederanno loro.

4. Non chiederlo a me, non lo so!

5. Ve lo avevo detto!

Exercise 11.5: 1-C; 2-E; 3-B; 4-A; 5-D

LESSON 12. "C'È" AND "CI SONO" (THERE IS, THERE ARE)

Today's language lesson is about how to use *c'è* (there is) and *ci sono* (there are). Learning how to use these useful phrases is a big step towards fluency. Let's get right into it!

"There is" and "there are" in Italian

There is (*c'è*) and there are (*ci sono*) are very common expressions used to indicate the **existence** or the **presence** of people, animals and objects in a certain place.

Listen to track 193

C'è – There is

C'è (there is) refers to something singular and is used to indicate the existence or presence of **one** element. *C'è* is the short form of *ci è*. Here are some examples:

C'è troppo zucchero nel mio caffè – There is too much sugar in my coffee

Non c'è fretta – There is no hurry

If we open it up, we find two words:

Ci + è = there + third person singular of the verb *essere* (to be).

Note: in this case, *ci* doesn't mean *us* or *to us*. It means *there*.

You use *c'è* with singular items or collective nouns, and *ci sono* with countable items in the plural.

C'è del formaggio in frigo? No, non c'è – Is there any cheese in the fridge? No, there isn't

Se hai fame, c'è della frutta in cucina – If you're hungry, there's some fruit in the kitchen

C'è can also be translated as "**is here**". Italian uses *ci* to mean *there* and *here* interchangeably for the most part. For example:

Non c'è nessuno – Nobody is here

Non piangere, c'è la mamma! – Don't cry, mom is here!

If you want to distinguish between *here* and *there*, you can use *qui/qua* (here) and *lì/là* (there).

Non c'è nessuno qui – There's nobody here

C'è qui la mamma – Mom is here

As mentioned previously, *c'è* indicates not only the presence, but also the existence of someone. The phrase "*non c'è più*" (literally: there is no more) is a softer way to say that someone has died.

*Mio zio purtroppo **non c'è più*** – My uncle has passed away

Ci sono – There are

Listen to track 194

Ci sono (there are) is used to indicate the presence or existence of **two or more** elements. For example:

*Non **ci sono** più le mezze stagioni* – There are no more middle seasons

***Ci sono** tre sedie* – There are three chairs

***Ci sono** giorni in cui il tempo sembra non passare mai* – There are days when time seems to be passing so slowly

***Ci sono** quindici alunni in quella classe* – There are fifteen students in that class

 "There are" in Italian is formed by *ci* (there) and **sono**, the third person plural of the verb *essere* (to be). You use *ci sono* with countable items in the plural:

Ci sono** delle patate? Sì, **ci sono – Are there any potatoes? Yes, there are

Interrogative and negative forms

As you can see from the above examples, *c'è* and *ci sono* can be used not only in affirmative sentences, but also in **interrogative** and **negative** ones.

In the interrogative form, you only need to change the intonation of your voice. Unlike in English, statements and questions in Italian have the same word order. It is the inflection (or implied punctuation) that tells you whether it is a statement or a question. For example:

Listen to track 195

*Scusi, **c'è** Noemi?* – Excuse me, is Noemi there? (When asking for someone on the phone, Italians use *c'è*)

***Ci sono** novità?* – What's new?

C'è un telefono in camera?** Certo che **c'è – Is there a telephone in the room? Of course there is

C'è un dizionario inglese-italiano in biblioteca? – Is there an English-Italian dictionary in the library?

You have probably already heard the popular expression *che c'è?* (literally: what is there?), which is the Italian equivalent of *what's the matter?* or *what's up?*.

Che c'è, *Camilla? Ti vedo giù di morale* – What's up, Camilla? You look upset

To express **negation**, you just need to put the particle **non** (not) before *c'è* and *ci sono*.

Non **c'è** *bisogno di gridare* – There's no need to shout

Su questo non **ci sono** *dubbi* – There's no doubt about that

Different tenses and moods

Listen to track 196

C'è and *ci sono* can be conjugated in all the Italian tenses and moods. It's super easy. All you have to do is conjugate the verb *essere* (to be) in the right way.

Present tense

C'è (ci è) = There is

Ci sono = There are

Here are some examples of these phrases being used in the present tense:

C'è *qualcosa che non va?* – What's wrong?

Chi **c'è** **c'è**, *chi* **non c'è** **non c'è** – Literally: whoever is there is there, whoever isn't there, isn't there / If you are with me you are with me, if you are not, you are not

C'è *tanta gente* – There are a lot of people (BEWARE: *people* in English is plural, while the Italian *gente* is singular)

Ci sono *dei pomodori maturi nell'orto* – There are some ripe tomatoes in the garden

Past tense

Imperfect (*imperfetto*)

Listen to track 197

C'era (ci era) – There was

C'erano – There were

Let's look at a few examples:

C'era *una strana atmosfera quella sera* – There was a strange atmosphere that night

C'erano dieci persone – There were ten of them

Present perfect (*passato prossimo*)

Listen to track 198

C'è stato (ci è stato) – There was, there has been

Ci sono stati – There were, there have been

Here are some examples of these phrases being used in the *passato prossimo*:

*Non **c'è stato** bisogno di intervenire* – There was no need to intervene

*Fortunatamente non **ci sono state** polemiche* – Fortunately, there has been no controversy

Remote past tense (*passato remoto*)

Listen to track 199

Ci fu – there was

Ci furono – there were

Have a look at the following examples:

Ci fu un'ovazione – There was an ovation

*Qualche anno fa, **ci furono** dei problemi simili* – A few years ago, there were similar problems

Past perfect (*trapassato prossimo*)

Listen to track 200

C'era stato (ci era stato) – there had been (singular)

C'erano stati (ci erano stati) – there had been (plural)

Here are some examples of these phrases being used in the *trapassato prossimo*:

*La questione avrebbe già dovuto essere discussa durante la scorsa seduta, ma non **c'era stato** abbastanza tempo* – The question should have been discussed already during the last session, but there was not enough time

*Cinzia sarebbe dovuta arrivare a Bologna in serata, ma **c'erano stati** dei disguidi* – Cinzia was supposed to arrive in Bologna in the evening, but there were some mistakes

Future tense

Simple future tense (*futuro semplice*)

Listen to track 201

Ci sarà – There will be (singular)

Ci saranno – There will be (plural)

For example:

Ci sarà un modo per raggiungere un accordo – There will be a way to reach an agreement

Ci saranno sei persone a cena da noi stasera – There will be six people for dinner tonight

Future perfect tense (*futuro anteriore*)

Ci sarà stato – There will have been (singular)

Ci saranno stati – There will have been (plural)

Let's look at a few examples:

*Probabilmente **ci sarà stato** un fraintendimento*– There must have been a misunderstanding

Ci saranno state non più di trenta persone in platea – There must have been no more than thirty people in the audience

"C'è" and "ci sono" in the subjunctive mood

Present subjunctive (*congiuntivo presente*)

Listen to track 202

(che) **ci sia** – (that) there is (singular)

(che) **ci siano** – (that) there are (plural)

Here are some examples of these phrases being used in the *congiuntivo presente:*

*Spero **che ci sia** qualcuno in grado di aiutarti* – I hope there is someone who can help you

*Speriamo **che ci siano** i presupposti per qualcosa di interessante* – We hope that there are the conditions for something interesting to happen

Imperfect subjunctive (*congiuntivo imperfetto*)

Listen to track 203

(che) **ci fosse** – (that) there was (singular)

(che) **ci fossero** – (that) there were (plural)

Take a look at the following examples:

Mi aspettavo **che ci fosse** *più partecipazione* – I expected there to be more participation

Non pensavo **che ci fossero** *ancora pregiudizi verso gli stranieri* – I didn't think that there were still prejudices against foreigners

Past subjunctive (*congiuntivo passato*)

Listen to track 204

(che) **ci sia stato** – (that) there has been (singular)

(che) **ci siano stati** – (that) there have been (plural)

For example:

Siamo contenti **che ci sia stata** *la possibilità di collaborare a questo progetto* – We are happy that there has been the opportunity to collaborate on this project

Voi pensate **che ci siano state** *delle scorrettezze, ma non è così* – You think there have been some mistakes, but it is not so

Pluperfect subjunctive (*congiuntivo trapassato*)

Listen to track 205

(che) **ci fosse stato** – (that) there had been (singular)

(che) **ci fossero stati** – (that) there had been (plural)

Here are some examples of these phrases being used in the *congiuntivo trapassato:*

Molti abitanti hanno pensato **che ci fosse stata** *una scossa di terremoto, ma invece era crollata una palazzina* – Many residents thought there had been an earthquake in the area, but actually a building had collapsed

Sostenevano **che ci fossero state** *palesi irregolarità nella gestione dei fondi statali* – They claimed that there had been blatant irregularities in the management of state funds

"C'è" and "ci sono" in the conditional mood

Listen to track 206

Present conditional tense (*condizionale presente*)

Ci sarebbe – There would be (singular)

Ci sarebbero – There would be (plural)

For example:

Se anche fosse così, non **ci sarebbe** *niente di male* – If that was the case, there would be nothing wrong with it

Se tutti rispettassero il codice della strada, **ci sarebbero** *meno incidenti* – If everyone followed the traffic rules, there would be fewer accidents

Perfect conditional (*condizionale passato*)

Listen to track 207

Ci sarebbe stato – There would have been (singular)

Ci sarebbero stati – There would have been (plural)

Take a look at the following examples:

Avevo saputo che alla festa **ci sarebbe stata** *anche Elena* – I heard that Elena would have been at the party

Immaginavo che **ci sarebbero state** *altre sorprese nei giorni a seguire* – I imagined that there would have been other surprises in the following days

Ecco – Here is

Listen to track 208

C'è and *ci sono* should not be confused with **ecco**, which is invariable and is used to draw attention to someone or something. With *c'è* and *ci sono* we simply state the existence or presence of someone or something.

Ecco gli sposi! – Here are the bride and groom!

Eccoti il dizionario inglese-italiano! – Here is the English-Italian dictionary!

Eccola! – Here she is, here she comes

Ecco il fascicolo che avevi richiesto – Here is the file you requested

To sum up...

- *C'è* corresponds pretty neatly to the English phrase *there is*.
- *Ci sono* corresponds pretty neatly to the English phrase *there are*.
- *C'è* is used when the following word is singular.
- *Ci sono* is used when the following word is plural.
- You can use these useful phrases in different moods and tenses, by simply conjugating the verb *essere* (to be) accordingly.

Practice a little every day and learning how to use *there is* and *there are* in Italian will be a breeze. The use of *c'è* and *ci sono* is pretty easy when you get the hang of it!

Workbook Lesson 12. There is and There are

Exercise 12.1: Translate the following sentences

English	Italian
1. There's a cat on the table.	
2. There are three dogs outside, barking.	
3. Are there any beers in the fridge?	
4. There's a high chance of rain today.	
5. I wanted to go to the amusement park today, but there are no tickets.	
6. Is Marco there?	

Exercise 12.2: Choose the right option

1. Ho aperto il frigo per cercare del cibo, ma (c'è/non c'è) niente!

2. (Ci sono/Non ci sono) dubbi che sia stato lui, l'ho visto io.

3. Fai pure con calma, (c'è/non c'è) fretta!

4. Oggi fa proprio caldo, (ci sono/non ci sono) 40 gradi!

5. Smettila di piangere, (c'è/non c'è) pericolo!

Exercise 12.3: Complete the following sentences

1. _____ tre gatti qui!

2. Non _____ posto per tutti.

3. _____ del latte?

4. In questo mese _____ trenta giorni.

5. Purtroppo non _____ biscotti per la colazione.

6. Non _____ neppure del caffè. Vado a comprarlo!

Exercise 12.4: Complete with "C'è" or "C'era"

1. Qui non _____ niente!

2. Sono andata al supermercato, ma non _____ niente di quello che mi serviva.

3. Anche se ieri _____ caldo, oggi ____ parecchio freddo!

4. Nel cestino _____ una mela, dov'è adesso?

5. Qui dove _____ il parco, l'anno scorso _____ un parcheggio.

Exercise 12.5: Complete with "ci sono" or "c'erano"

1. Oggi _____ 30 gradi, eppure ieri era freddissimo!

2. Sono andata a comprare dei libri, ma non _____ quelli che volevo.

3. Non _____ dubbi che avrebbe vinto lui!

4. _____ delle persone alla porta.

5. In classe mia _____ 32 studenti.

Answers:

Exercise 12.1:

1. C'è un gatto sul tavolo.

2. Fuori ci sono tre cani che abbaiano.

3. Ci sono delle birre in frigo?

4. Oggi c'è un'alta possibilità di pioggia.

5. Oggi volevo andare al parco divertimenti, ma non ci sono biglietti.

6. C'è Marco?

Exercise 12.2:

1. non c'è; 2. Non ci sono; 3. non c'è 4. ci sono; 5. non c'è

Exercise 12.4:

1. Ci sono; 2. C'è; 3. C'è 4. Ci sono; 5. Ci sono; 6. C'è

Exercise 12.7:

1. Qui non c'è niente!

2. Sono andata al supermercato, ma non c'era niente di quello che mi serviva.

3. Anche se ieri c'era caldo, oggi c'è parecchio freddo!

4. Nel cestino c'era una mela, dov'è adesso?

5. Qui dove c'è il parco, l'anno scorso c'era un parcheggio.

Exercise 12.8:

1. Oggi ci sono 30 gradi, eppure ieri era freddissimo!

2. Sono andata a comprare dei libri, ma non c'erano quelli che volevo.

3. Non c'erano dubbi che avrebbe vinto lui!

4. Ci sono delle persone alla porta.

5. In classe mia ci sono 32 studenti.

LESSON 13. PREPOSITIONS

Crucial for fluency, prepositions (*preposizioni*) are an essential part of the Italian language. It is nearly impossible to say a single sentence without one of these little yet extremely useful words. Let's dive in and figure out **how to use Italian prepositions**.

What's a preposition?

A preposition is a little word that forms the connections between different elements in a sentence. Italian *preposizioni* can be followed by a noun, a pronoun or an infinitive verb, and show how the words in a phrase or sentence are related.

Learning how to use **prepositions in Italian** isn't overly difficult but it can be confusing at times. Italian prepositions can actually have different meanings and uses depending on the context, and most of the time there isn't an exact one-to-one correlation with English prepositions.

Another important aspect to keep in mind is that, in English, you can separate a preposition from its noun and put it at the end of a sentence, while in Italian prepositions always go in front of another word. For example:

Listen to track 209

***Con** chi sei andato al concerto?* – Who did you go to the concert with?

Italian *preposizioni* can be **simple** or **articulated**. Let's start with simple prepositions.

Italian simple prepositions

Simple prepositions (*preposizioni semplici*) are the basic prepositions in Italian. Here they are:

Listen to track 210

Di (of, about, from, by, than)

A (at, to, in, on)

Da (from, by, as, since, for)

In (in, at, by)

Con (with)

Su (on, above, over, about, out of)

Per (for, to, in order to, because)

Tra/Fra (between, among, within, in)

We will take you through each of these little words one-by-one. Let's start from the top.

Listen to track 211

1. Di (of, about, from, by, than)

Di is to be used:

- to say where someone is from:

*Sono **di** Milano* – I'm from Milan

- in comparisons:

*Samuele è più alto **di** me* – Samuele is taller than me

- to show possession of something:

*Questo libro è **di** Alessandra* – This is Alessandra's book

- to talk about age:

*Sonia ha una sorella **di** 12 anni* – Sonia has a 12-year-old sister

- to indicate the material something is made from:

*Ho comprato una camicia **di** seta* – I bought a silk shirt

*La nonna mi ha regalato una collana **d'**argento* – Grandma gave me a silver necklace

- to indicate the subject someone is talking about:

*Roberto parla sempre **di** politica* – Roberto always talks about politics

2. A (at, to, in, on)

Listen to track 212

You can translate *a* into English as "to", "at", "on" or "in". It is used to:

- talk about going to a place, city or small island:

*Mi piacerebbe andare **a** Capri* – I'd like to go to Capri

*Siamo andati in vacanza **a** Varazze* – We went on holiday to Varazze

*Devo andare **all'**aeroporto* – I have to go to the airport

- talk about being at a place:

*Martina è stata **a** casa tutto il giorno* – Martina has been at home all day

*Quando mio figlio è **all'**asilo, posso dedicarmi alla mia attività* – When my son is in the kindergarten, I can work on my business

- talk about time:

*Ho una riunione **a** mezzogiorno* – I have a meeting at noon

- indicate the receiver of something:

*Ho mandato un messaggio vocale **a** Gabriella* – I sent a voice message to Gabriella

- describe movement:

*Aurora va **a** scuola **a** piedi ogni giorno* – Aurora goes to school on foot every day

*Andiamo **a** pescare!* – Let's go fishing!

Use ***a*** with festivities, like *a Natale* (at Christmas), *a Pasqua* (at Easter) and *a Ferragosto* (on Assumption Day).

Remember that, when the Italian preposition *a* is followed by a word starting with the letter *a*, it changes to *ad* for phonetic reasons. For example:

*Ho dato un bacio **ad** Antonella* – I gave Antonella a kiss

3. Da (from, by, as, since, for)

Listen to track 213

Da is to be used to:

- indicate someone's origin:

*Mohammad viene **da** Islamabad, in Pakistan* – Mohammad comes from Islamabad, in Pakistan

- indicate the amount of time since something started:

*Vivo a Milano **da** otto anni* – I have been living in Milan for eight years (I still live in Milan)

*Vivo a Milano **da** quando sono nato* – I have been living in Milan since I was born (I still live in Milan)

- indicate by whom something was done:

*Carlotta è stata soccorsa **da** un passante* – Carlotta was rescued by a passer-by

- indicate the value or worth of something:

*Ho visto una villa **da** un milione di euro in vendita a metà prezzo* – I saw a villa worth one million euros on sale for half price

- explain what an object is used for:

*Ti piace il mio costume **da** bagno?* – Do you like my swimsuit (suit for swimming)?

You can use the preposition of place *da* with shops or people's names to say that you are going there. For example:

*Vado **da** Letizia* – I'm going to Letizia's house

*Vado **dal** giornalaio* – I'm going to the paper shop

4. In (in, at, by)

Listen to track 214

In is to be used to talk about:

- being in or going to a country, continent, region or province:

*Bianca vive **in** Liguria* – Bianca lives in Liguria

*Daniele si è trasferito **in** Lussemburgo* – Daniele moved to Luxembourg

- a place where someone is going:

*Marta sta andando **in** palestra* – Marta is going to the gym

- periods of the year, like seasons:

***In** inverno nevica spesso* – It often snows in winter

- means of transport:

*Siamo andati a Roma **in** aereo* – We went to Rome by plane

5. Con (with)

Listen to track 215

Con corresponds pretty neatly to the English word *with*, and is used to talk about being with someone.

*Ieri sono andata al cinema **con** Loredana* – Yesterday I went to the cinema with Loredana

6. Su (on, above, over, about, out of)

Listen to track 216

Su can be translated as "on", "about", "over" or "above", and refers to:

- a topic:

*Si è diplomato con una tesi **su** Edward Hopper* – He graduated with a thesis on Edward Hopper

- ratios:

*In un caso **su** tre* – In a case out of three

- the position of something which is higher or on top of something else:

*Il mio dizionario inglese-italiano è **sullo** scaffale* – My English-Italian dictionary is on the shelf

7. Per (for, to, in order to, because)

Listen to track 217

Per is used to talk about:

- a reason, purpose or cause:

*Cecilia lavora occasionalmente come babysitter **per** guadagnare qualche soldo* – Cecilia occasionally works as a babysitter to earn some money

- a length of time:

*Gabriele ha lavorato in un call center **per** cinque anni* – Gabriele worked in a call center for five years (he doesn't work there anymore)

- price:

*Ho comprato due chili di patate **per** un euro* - I bought two kilos of potatoes for one euro

- the receiver of a benefit:

*C'è una sorpresa **per** te* – There's a surprise for you

The preposition of place *per* is used with the verbs of movement *partire* (to leave) and *passare* (to go through). For example:

*Quando partite **per** Genova?* – When are you leaving for Genoa?

*La prossima volta che vado a Venezia passerò **per** Verona* – The next time I go to Venice, I shall go through Verona

8. Tra/fra (between, among, within, in)

Listen to track 218

Tra and *fra* have exactly the same meaning. Which one to use one is just a stylistic choice governed by personal preference. *Tra/fra* is used to refer to:

- a time in the future:

*Mi sposo **tra** un mese* – I'm getting married in a month

- space between two places, objects or people:

*La scuola si trova **tra** l'ufficio postale e la farmacia* – The school is located between the post office and the drugstore

- comparisons:

***Tra** tutte le compagne di classe, Veronica è la più carina* – Among all the classmates, Veronica is the prettiest

Italian articulated prepositions

When the prepositions ***di, a, da, in*** and ***su*** are followed by the definite article, they combine with it to make one word.

Listen to track 219

Di

di + il = **del** + masculine singular noun beginning with a consonant

di + lo = **dello** + masculine singular noun beginning with "z", "ps", "gn", "pn", "x", "y" or "s" followed by a consonant

di + la = **della** + feminine singular noun beginning with a consonant

di + l' = **dell'** + masculine or feminine singular noun beginning with a vowel

di + i = **dei** + masculine plural nouns starting with a consonant

di + gli = **degli** + masculine plural nouns that start with a vowel and with "z", "ps", "gn", "pn", "x", "y" or "s" followed by a consonant

di + le = **delle** + feminine plural nouns

Listen to track 220

A

a + il = **al** + masculine singular noun beginning with a consonant

a + lo = **allo** + masculine singular noun beginning with "z", "ps", "gn", "pn", "x", "y" or "s" followed by a consonant

a + la = **alla** + feminine singular noun beginning with a consonant

a + l' = **all'** + masculine or feminine singular noun beginning with a vowel

a + i = **ai** + masculine plural nouns starting with a consonant

a + gli = **agli** + masculine plural nouns that start with a vowel and with "z", "ps", "gn", "pn", "x", "y" or "s" followed by a consonant

a + le = **alle** + feminine plural nouns

Listen to track 221

Da

da + il = **dal** + masculine singular noun beginning with a consonant

da +lo = **dallo** + masculine singular noun beginning with "z", "ps", "gn", "pn", "x", "y" or "s" followed by a consonant

da + la = **dalla** + feminine singular noun beginning with a consonant

da + l' = **dall'** + masculine or feminine singular nouns beginning with a vowel

da + i = **dai** + masculine plural nouns starting with a consonant

da + gli = **dagli** + masculine plural nouns that start with a vowel and with "z", "ps", "gn", "pn", "x", "y" or "s" followed by a consonant

da + le = **dale** + feminine plural nouns

Listen to track 222

In

in + il = **nel** + masculine singular noun beginning with a consonant

*Hai sempre desiderato vivere **nello** spazio.* - You've always wanted a life in space.

in + lo = **nello** + masculine singular noun beginning with "z", "ps", "gn", "pn", "x", "y" or "s" followed by a consonant

in + la = **nella** + feminine singular noun beginning with a consonant

in + l' = **nell'** + masculine or feminine singular noun beginning with a vowel

in + i = **nei** + masculine plural nouns starting with a consonant

*Ho visto quella foto **nei** notiziari **negli** ultimi giorni.* - I seen that picture in the news the last couple of days.

in + gli = **negli** + masculine plural nouns that start with a vowel and with "z", "ps", "gn", "pn", "x", "y" or "s" followed by a consonant

in + le = **nelle** + feminine plural nouns

*La compravendita **nelle** strade è illegale.* - It's illegal to buy or sell anything on the street.

Listen to track 223

Su

su + il = **sul** + masculine singular noun beginning with a consonant

*Ho lasciato le chiavi **sul** tavolo.* – I left the keys on the table.

su + lo = **sullo** + masculine singular noun beginning with "z", "ps", "gn", "pn", "x", "y" or "s" followed by a consonant

su + la = **sulla** + feminine singular noun beginning with a consonant

su + l' = **sull'** + masculine or feminine singular noun beginning with a vowel

su + i = **sui** + masculine plural nouns starting with a consonant

su + gli = **sugli** + masculine plural nouns that start with a vowel and with "z", "ps", "gn", "pn", "x", "y" or "s" followed by a consonant

*Di recente ho riflettuto molto **sugli** ultimi pensieri.* - I've been thinking a lot about last thoughts recently.

su + le = **sulle** + feminine plural nouns

*La terremo aggiornata **sulle** sue condizioni.* - We'll keep you updated on his condition.

Listen to track 224

Con

The Italian preposition *con* combines with the article only when followed by *il* and *i*.

con + il = **col** + masculine singular noun beginning with a consonant

*Puoi parlarne domattina **col** tuo medico.* - You can discuss it in the morning with your doctor.

con + lo = con lo

con + l' = con l'

*Ero al telefono **con** l'anatomopatologo* - I was on the phone with the pathologist.

con + la = con la

con + i = **coi** + masculine plural nouns starting with a consonant

*Ero ossessionato **coi** robot da ragazzino.* - I was obsessed with robots as a kid.

con + gli = con gli

con + le = con le

Per and **tra/fra** are invariable and don't change form when followed by a definite article. The two words remain separate.

Listen to track 225

Articulated prepositions are used when the following noun requires an article.

*Ci vediamo **alle** ore 19:30* – We'll see each other at 7:30pm

Note: articulated prepositions can be used before names of continents, countries, regions, rivers, lakes and mountains, but not before cities and people's names.

***Dagli** Appennini **alle** Ande* – From the Apennines to the Andes

*Massimiliano torna **dalla** Finlandia venerdì prossimo* – Massimiliano is coming back from Finland next Friday

To sum up...

- A preposition (*preposizione*) is a part of speech that links elements in a sentence and establishes connections between them.
- Italian prepositions are always used in front of another word.
- Italian simple prepositions are *di, a, da, in, con, su, per, tra/fra*.
- *Di, a, da, in* and *su* combine with a following definite article to make one word.
- *Con* combines only with *il* and *i*.

Practice a little every day and expose yourself to lots of Italian reading and listening content, and learning **how to use prepositions in Italian** will be easier than you might think. The more you practice them, the easier they become.

Workbook Lesson 13. Prepositions

Exercise 13.1: Choose the right option

1. Dove deve andare Roberta? Questa mattina va _____ Firenze. (per/a/da)
2. Come andrai a Milano? Andrò _____ treno. (su/con/in)
3. Come vanno a lavoro i tuoi genitori?
   Generalmente _____ piedi, è vicino. (tra/su/a)
4. Fate tardi? No, arriviamo _____ dieci minuti. (per/di/tra)
5. Dove ci incontriamo?
   Nella piazzetta _____ la chiesa e il comune. (tra/su/di)

Exercise 13.2: Translate the following sentences

English	Italian
1. This is Marta's book.	
2. Are you going to Milan next week?	

3. You can count on me!	
4. I am from Venice.	
5. I'll go with Andrea.	
6. My house is located between the school and the mall.	

Exercise 13.3: Complete with the missing prepositions

1. Ammetto _____ avere sbagliato.

2. Ho deciso _____ partire.

3. _____ cosa serve quella macchina?

4. Lavoro solo _____ i soldi.

5. Ci devo pensare un po' _____.

Exercise 13.4: Underline the prepositions in this text.

Ciao, mi chiamo Carlo e ho 18 anni. Oggi vorrei parlarvi della mia tipica giornata. Mi alzo sempre alle 7:00 e faccio una buona colazione con tè e biscotti. Dopo aver incontrato il mio amico Marco prendo alle 7:40 l'autobus che mi porta a scuola. Mi piace molto la mia scuola perché ho molte materie che riguardano il mondo dell'informatica! Ogni giorno ho 6 ore di lezione, tranne il sabato in cui ne ho 5. Quando torno a casa studio e faccio i compiti, ma mi diverto anche giocando al computer e suonando la mia chitarra. Ceno alle 19:00 con la mia famiglia, composta da mia mamma, mio papà e i miei tre fratelli. Alle 22:30 circa vado a letto a leggere alcuni libri prima di dormire.

Exercise 13.5: Complete with the right articulated prepositions

1. Le lezioni iniziano (a)_____ 8.10.

2. (in)_____ zaini (di)_____ragazzi c'è di tutto.

3. Le ragazze (di)_____ terze, sono attente (con)_____insegnanti.

4. Ho incontrato Omar (su)_____ scale.

5. I diari (di) _____ mie amiche sono (su) _____ banchi.

6. (in)_____momenti liberi mi piace leggere.

Answers:

Exercise 13.1:

1) a; 2) in; 3) a tra 4) tra; 5) con

Exercise 13.2:

1. Questo è il libro di Marta.

2. Andrai a Milano la settimana prossima?

3. Puoi contare su di me!

4. Io vengo da Venezia.

5. Andrò con Andrea.

6. La mia casa si trova tra la scuola e il centro commerciale.

Exercise 13.3:

1) di; 2) di; 3) a; 4) per; 5) su

Exercise 13.4:

Ciao, mi chiamo Carlo e ho 18 anni. Oggi vorrei parlarvi della mia tipica giornata. Mi alzo sempre alle 7:00 e faccio una buona colazione con tè e biscotti. Dopo aver incontrato il mio amico Marco prendo alle 7:40 l'autobus che mi porta a scuola. Mi piace molto la mia scuola perché ho molte materie che riguardano il mondo dell'informatica! Ogni giorno ho 6 ore di lezione, tranne il sabato in cui ne ho 5. Quando torno a casa studio e faccio i compiti, ma mi diverto anche giocando al computer e suonando la mia chitarra. Ceno alle 19:00 con la mia famiglia, composta da mia mamma, mio papà e i miei tre fratelli. Alle 22:30 circa vado a letto a leggere alcuni libri prima di dormire.

Exercise 13.9:

1. alle; 2. Negli, Negli; 3. delle, con gli; 4. sulle; 5. sulle, sui; 6. sui

LESSON 14. NEGATION

Learning how to change affirmative sentences into negative ones is an important step in your learning journey. Ready to find out how to use **negatives in Italian**? Read on for a quick and easy guide on how to say 'no' in Italian.

How to form negative sentences in Italian

In Italian, to turn an affirmative sentence into a negative one all you have to do is place the particle *non* (not) in front of the main verb. That's it. *Non* (not) is the only word you need to use to make a statement or a question negative. Take a look at the following examples:

Listen to track 226

Vivo in Italia – I live in Italy → ***Non** vivo in Italia* – I don't live in Italy

Dalila parla italiano – Dalila speaks Italian → *Dalila **non** parla italiano* – Dalila doesn't speak Italian

La lezione è finita – The lesson is over → *La lezione **non** è finita* – The lesson isn't over

Lo so – I know → ***Non** lo so* – I don't know

Easy, right?

As you can see, a negative sentence in Italian is formed by:

(Subject/personal pronoun) + **non** + verb + rest of the sentence

In negative sentences, Italian doesn't use extra phrases or words like *don't, doesn't* and so on. Never use the transitive verb **fare** (to do, to make) to translate *don't, doesn't* and *didn't*.

Italian double negatives

In English, the grammar rule is to only use one negative word in a sentence, while in Italian this is not the case. Italians do use double negatives, and even triple or quadruple negatives. Let's see how to use them.

First let's look at some common **negative expressions**. You already know *non* (not), and here are some more:

Listen to track 227

- **Non... niente / nulla** – nothing, anything
- **Non... nessuno** – nobody, no one, anybody, anyone
- **Non... nessuno / nessun / nessuna + noun** – no or not... any
- **Non ... mai** – never
- **Non... neanche, nemmeno, neppure** – not even, neither
- **Non... né... né** – neither ... nor

You can use the Italian word *non* (not) in front of any of these negative expressions. Let's look at a few examples of how these phrases can be used in Italian:

Listen to track 228

Non posso farci **nulla** – I can't do anything about it

Non ho **niente** *da dirti* – I have nothing to say to you

Non abbiamo **nulla** *da rimproverarci* – We have nothing to reproach ourselves for

Non ho fatto **niente** *di male* – I didn't do anything wrong

Al momento **non** *c'è* **nessuno** *che possa prendere il suo posto* – At the moment there is no one who can replace him

Non c'è **nessun bisogno** *di informarli* – There's no need to inform them / There isn't any need to inform them

Non sono **mai** *stata in Nuova Zelanda* (remember to put *mai* between the two parts of the *passato prossimo*) – I've never been to New Zealand

Giorgio **non** *mi ha degnato* **neanche** *di uno sguardo* – Giorgio didn't even glance at me

Diletta **non** *mi ha* **nemmeno** *salutato* – Diletta didn't even say hi to me

Tiziana **non** *mi ha* **neppure** *risposto* – Tiziana didn't even answer me

Non ho saputo rispondere **né** *sì* **né** *no* – I couldn't say either yes or no

As you can see, the negative word *non* (not) is frequently the first word in a sentence.

Here are some other common expressions:

Listen to track 229

- **Non... ancora** – not yet

Chiara **non** *ha* **ancora** *deciso dove andare a scuola l'anno prossimo* – Chiara has not yet decided where to go to school next year

- **Non... da nessuna parte** – nowhere or not... anywhere

*Non riuscivo a trovare il mio telefono **da nessuna parte*** – I couldn't find my phone anywhere

- **Non... più** – no longer, no more, not anymore

*Che io sappia, Paolo e Lucrezia **non** escono **più** insieme* – As far as I know, Paolo and Lucrezia are not going out together anymore

- **Non... affatto / non... mica** – not at all

*Non è **affatto** vero!* – It's not true at all!

*Non l'ho **mica** detto!* – I didn't say it at all!

*Non è **mica** male!* – It's not bad at all!

Listen to track 230

A Tuscan regionalism, **non... punto** has exactly the same meaning as *non... affatto/ mica*. Remember that *punto* always goes between the auxiliary verb and the past participle. For example:

*Benedetta **non è punto** arrivata* – Benedetta hasn't arrived at all

Note that, when using the expressions **non...ancora** (not yet), **non...più** (no more, no longer, not anymore) and **non...affatto** (not at all), the words *affatto, ancora* or *più* can be placed either after the past participle or between the auxiliary verb and the past participle. Here are some examples:

*I problemi **non** sono **affatto** finiti / I problemi **non** sono finiti **affatto*** – The problems are not over at all

*Rossella **non è ancora** arrivata / Rossella **non è** arrivata **ancora*** – Rossella hasn't arrived yet

*Non ci ho **più** visto e ho reagito / Non ci ho visto **più** e ho reagito* – (Literally: I haven't seen it anymore and I reacted) I lost my temper and reacted badly

As mentioned previously, it is not unusual to use three or even four negatives in the same sentence. For example:

*Filippo **non** ha **mai** voglia di fare **niente*** – Filippo never feels like doing anything

*Emanuele **non** dice mai **niente** a **nessuno*** – Emanuele never says anything to anyone

Note: both *niente* (nothing, anything) and *nessuno* (nobody, no one, anybody, anyone) can be either subjects or direct objects.

Word order in negative sentences

Negative interrogative sentences

Listen to track 231

Negative interrogative sentences have the same word order as statements. You only need to use a rising intonation of your voice or add a question mark to the end of the sentence. For example:

Non dovevamo vederci oggi alle ore 11:00? – Weren't we supposed to meet today at 11am?

If you need to use a question word, place it before the negation *non* (not). Look at the following example:

*Perchè **non** ne parli con loro?* – Why don't you talk to them instead?

Negative imperative

Listen to track 232

The imperative (*imperativo*) is used to order or exhort others to do or not to do something. The negative form of the Italian *imperativo* is formed quite easily.

The **imperativo informale** is formed by the verb in the infinitive form preceded by *non* (not). For example:

***Non** entrare!* – Do not enter!

***Non** fare il guastafeste!* – Don't be such a party pooper!

The **imperativo formale** is formed by placing the negation *non* (not) in front of the verb that has been conjugated in the imperative mood. For example:

***Non** mi **interrompa** quando parlo* – Don't interrupt me when I'm talking

***Non** se ne **vada**, signor Beretta* – Please don't go, Mr. Beretta

To express negative commands using the **voi** (y'all) form, just add *non* (not) in front of the affirmative form. Have a look at these examples to get an idea of how it works:

*Ragazzi, **non** fate rumore!* – Don't make a noise, guys!

***Non** dite sciocchezze!* – Don't talk nonsense!

Direct and indirect object pronouns

Listen to track 233

If there are **direct and indirect object pronouns,** such as *mi* (to me, me), *ti* (to you, you), *lo* (him), *la* (her), *ci* (us, to us), *vi* (to you, you), *li* (them) or *le* (them), *non* goes immediately in front of them.

Non mi piacciono le persone false e ipocrite – I don't like false and two-faced people

Non l'ho fatto apposta – I didn't do it on purpose

Non me lo ricordo – I can't remember

Nobody, nothing, not even

Listen to track 234

If you begin a sentence with a negative word, like *nessuno* (nobody, no one), *niente/nulla* (nothing) and *neanche/nemmeno/neppure* (not even), don't use the negation *non* (not) with the verb that comes after it. For example:

Niente succede per caso – Nothing happens by chance

Neanche Danilo ha passato l'esame – Not even Danilo passed the exam

Nessuno si è degnato di avvertirmi – No one has bothered to inform me

But:

Non succede niente per caso – Nothing happens by chance

Non ha passato l'esame neanche Danilo – Not even Danilo passed the exam

Non si è degnato di avvertirmi nessuno – No one has bothered to inform me

As in English, **negative words** can be used on their own to answer questions. For example:

Ti piace il rugby? No (make sure you say "no" with an Italian accent) – *Do you like rugby? No*

Cosa ti hanno regalato a Natale? Niente – What did you get for Christmas? Nothing

Chi te l'ha detto? Nessuno – Who told you that? Nobody

Adverbs of time and frequency

Listen to track 235

In compound verbs, **mai** (never), **più** (anymore, any longer), **ancora** (yet, again, still) and **già** (already) have to be placed between the auxiliary verb and the past participle. For example:

*Miriam **non è mai stata** a New York* – Miriam has never been to New York

*La mia amica di penna **non ha più risposto** alle mie lettere* – My pen pal no longer replies to my letters

Non ho ancora trovato ciò che cerco – I still haven't found what I'm looking for

Non abbiamo ancora visto alcun cambiamento – We haven't seen any changes yet

Watch out for Italian false negatives

Listen to track 236

Finché non means "until the moment in which" and is usually translated as simply *until*. In this case, the particle ***non*** (not) is a false negative and is not to be translated. ***Fino a quando non*** has exactly the same meaning as *finché non*, and they are interchangeable. Let's look at the following examples:

Finché non *avrai finito i compiti non potrai andare a giocare con Andrea e Mattia* – You can't go out to play with Andrea and Mattia until you will have finished your homework

Vittoria sostituirà Stella ***fino a quando non*** *tornerà dalla maternità* – Vittoria is going to replace Stella until she returns from maternity leave

To sum up...

- To convert an affirmative sentence to a negative one, just place *non* (not) in front of the main verb.
- Double negatives in Italian are okay.
- Unlike in English, in Italian it is good grammar to use three or even four negative words in the same sentence.

Well done for making it to the end of this lesson! Practice a little every day until you get the hang of it!

Workbook Lesson 14. Negation

Exercise 14.1: Make these affirmative sentences negative:

Affirmative	Negative
1. Mi piace ballare. (I like dancing.)	
2. Luca suona la chitarra. (Luca plays the guitar.)	
3. Il divano è rosso. (The sofa is red.)	
4. I bambini stanno giocando. (The children are playing.)	
5. Avete ragione. (You are right.)	

Exercise 14.2: Choose the right translation for each sentence:

1. Lunch is not ready.

    1) Il pranzo è non pronto

    2) Il pranzo non è pronto.

    3) Il pranzo non sarà pronto.

2. Don't be late!

   1) Non siate tardi!

   2) Non essere tardi!

   3) Non arrivare tardi!

3. He never does what he says.

   1) Non fare mai quello che dice.

   2) Non fa quello che dice.

   3) Non fa mai quello che dice.

4. I don't want to see him anymore.

   1) Non voglio più vederlo.

   2) Non voglio mai vederlo.

   3) Non voglio vederlo.

5. Don't you want some cake?

   1) Non volete la torta?

   2) Non volete un po' di torta?

   3) Non volete mai un po' di torta?

Exercise 14.3: Make these negative sentences affirmative:

Negative	Affirmative
Non mangiare la pizza! (Don't eat pizza!)	
Dario non vuole andare all'università. (Dario doesn't want to go to university.)	
Non abbiamo bisogno del tuo aiuto. (We don't need your help.)	
La televisione non è rotta. (The television is not broken.)	
I fiori non sono gialli. (The flowers are not yellow.)	

Exercise 14.4: Complete the following sentences:

1. Non ci hanno ____ salutati! (They didn't even greet us!)

2. Non importa a ____ quello che state dicendo! (No one cares what you are saying!)

3. Non mangia ____ carne ____ pesce. (He eats neither meat nor fish.)

4. Il nuovo tecnico non sa fare ____. (The new technician can't do anything.)

5. Non andrò ____ a chiederle scusa! (I will never go and apologize!)

Exercise 14.5: Tick the right answer:

1. Non posso crederci. ____ io! (I can't believe it. Me neither/Nor me!)
   1) Neanche   2) Nulla   3) Mai

2. Non dirlo a ____ ! (Don't tell anyone!)
   1) niente   2) tutti   3) nessuno

3. Non fate ____ senza il mio permesso! (Don't do anything without my permission!)
   1) niente   2) mai   3) nessuno

4. Non sono ____ arrivati. (They haven't arrived yet.)
   1) mai   2) ancora   3) già

5. Non mi hai ____ disturbato. (You didn't bother me at all.)
   1) nulla   2) mai   3) affatto

Answers:

Exercise 14.1:

1. Non mi piace ballare.
2. Luca non suona la chitarra.
3. Il divano non è rosso.
4. I bambini non stanno giocando.
5. Non avete ragione.

Exercise 14.2:

1) Il pranzo non è pronto.
2) Non arrivare tardi!
3) Non fa mai quello che dice.
4) Non voglio più vederlo.
5) Non volete un po' di torta?

Exercise 14.3:

1. Mangia la pizza!
2. Dario vuole andare all'università.
3. Abbiamo bisogno del tuo aiuto.
4. La televisione è rotta.
5. I fiori sono gialli.

Exercise 14.4:

1. Non ci hanno neanche/neppure salutati!

2. Non importa a nessuno quello che state dicendo!

3. Non mangia né carne né pesce.

4. Il nuovo tecnico non sa fare nulla/niente.

5. Non andrò mai a chiederle scusa!

Exercise 14.5:

1) Neanche; 2) nessuno; 3) niente; 4) ancora; 5) affatto

LESSON 15. PASSATO PROSSIMO

Passato prossimo, imperfetto, passato remoto... Unlike in English, there are many different past tenses in Italian and the difference between them can be tricky. The **passato prossimo** is the main tense used in Italian to describe an action which has been completed in the near past.

In this lesson, we will show you how to use it and give you some tips to help you with how to use these three past tenses.

Using the passato prossimo

Listen to track 237

As mentioned previously, the *passato prossimo* refers to something that happened in the past. It is used in the following situations:

- an action which occurred in the recent past

Sono andata dal parrucchiere ieri pomeriggio – I went to the hairdresser yesterday afternoon (the action took place a short time ago)

- an action which is clearly defined in time

Ho lavorato dalle 8:00 alle 19:00, sono esausto – I worked from 8am to 7pm, I'm exhausted

- an action which occurred some time ago and the results of the action can still be felt in the present day

Nel 2002 è entrato in vigore l'Euro – The euro was introduced in 2002 (the effects of the action are still felt in the present)

- an experience in your life

Ho frequentato un corso di italiano all'università - I attended an Italian course at university

- an action which was concluded but the time period (for example, today, this week) hasn't finished yet

Quest'anno siamo andati in vacanza insieme – This year we went on holiday together (this year hasn't finished yet)

- an unusual action that happened in the past

Due anni fa siamo andati a Torino – We went to Turin two years ago

The closeness of a past action to the present can be based either on time or on feelings.

How to form the passato prossimo

As you might have noticed, the *passato prossimo* is a compound tense, which means that it has more than one word in its construction.

The *passato prossimo* is formed by using two verbs:

- the **present form** of the auxiliary verbs *essere* or *avere*
- the **past participle** (*participio passato*) of the verb expressing the meaning.

To make the **past participle** of regular verbs you just have to take off the infinitive ending *-are, -ere* or *-ire,* and add the correct ending. Just follow this simple rule:

- the past participle of verbs ending in *-are* is **-ato**: *lavorare>lavorato, mangiare>mangiato, preparare>preparato*
- the past participle of verbs ending in *-ere* is **–uto**: *conoscere>conosciuto, temere>temuto, piovere>piovuto*
- the past participle of verbs ending in *-ire* is **–ito**: *partire>partito, gestire>gestito, stupire>stupito.*

Listen to track 238

Parlare

*Ho parl**ato*** - I spoke or have spoken

*Hai parl**ato*** - You spoke or have spoken

*Ha parl**ato*** - He/She/It spoke or has spoken

*Abbiamo parl**ato*** - We spoke or have spoken

*Avete parl**ato*** - Y'all spoke or have spoken

*Hanno parl**ato*** - They spoke or have spoken

Credere

Listen to track 239

*Ho cred**uto*** - I believed or have believed

*Hai cred**uto*** - You believed or have believed

*Ha cred**uto*** - He/She/It believed or has believed

*Abbiamo cred**uto*** - We believed or have believed

*Avete cred**uto*** - Y'all believed or have believed

*Hanno cred**uto*** - They believed or have believed

Listen to track 240

Sentire

Ho sentito - I heard or have heard

Hai sentito - You heard or have heard

Ha sentito - He/She/It heard or has heard

Abbiamo sentito - We heard or have heard

Avete sentito - Y'all heard or have heard

Hanno sentito - They heard or have heard

There are many irregular verbs in the past participle, so check them out. **Some of the common irregular past participle are:**

Listen to track 241

fare (to do/make) – fatto

dire (to say/tell) - detto

prendere (to take) - preso

aprire (to open) - aperto

bere (to drink) - bevuto

chiedere (to ask) - chiesto

chiudere (to close) - chiuso

scrivere (to write) - scritto

tradurre (to translate) - tradotto

vivere (to live) - vissuto

vedere (to see) - visto

How do you choose the auxiliary verb?

Listen to track 242

Does the verb you want to use need the auxiliary verb 'to be' or 'to have'? The majority of verbs take "avere" (to have) as their auxiliary verb.

Transitive verbs always use the auxiliary "avere". What is a **transitive verb**? A transitive verb only makes sense if it exerts its action on an object. Without an object to affect, a transitive verb cannot function and the sentence that it inhabits will seem incomplete. A transitive verb typically answers the question "Who/What".

Ho scritto una lettera di reclamo – I wrote a letter of complaint

Ieri ho mangiato i ravioli con ricotta e spinaci – Yesterday I had ravioli stuffed with ricotta and spinach

You have to use "essere" with:

- all **reflexive verbs**;

Mi sono svegliato presto - I woke up early

A che ora ti sei alzato? – What time did you get up?

Ci siamo innamorati cinque anni fa – We fell in love five years ago

- most **intransitive verbs**: verbs that do not require an object to act upon;
- verbs that express movement, like *andare* (to go), *venire* (to come), *uscire* (to go out), *partire* (to leave), *tornare* (to come back), *arrivare* (to arrive);

Sono andato in Italia l'anno scorso – I went to Italy last year

- verbs that express lack of movement, like *stare* (to stay) and *rimanere* (to remain);
- verbs that express a state of being, a physical or mental state, or processes of change, like *essere* (to be), *nascere* (to be born), *morire* (to die);
- verbs which do not have a subject as such *succedere (happen), accadere (occur/ happen)*.

Here are some things to remember:

- though intransitive, *dormire* (to sleep), *rispondere* (to answer), *viaggiare* (to travel) and *vivere* (to live) require the auxiliary "avere";
- the verb *piacere* (to like) requires the auxiliary "essere";
- when you use a verb in the *passato prossimo* with the auxiliary verb *essere* (to be), the past participle must agree with the subject in gender (masculine or feminine) and number (singular or plural).

Listen to track 243

Hai visto Lorenzo? Sì, l'ho visto – Have you seen Lorenzo? Yes, I've seen him

Hai visto Gabriella? Non l'ho vista – Have you seen Gabriella? No, I haven't seen her

I ragazzi sono andati a sciare – The guys went skiing

Le tue amiche sono arrivate – Your friends have arrived

Here is a list of **verbs that take "essere" as their auxiliary verb:**

Listen to track 244

Andare: *Dove sei andato stamattina? Sono andato in banca* – Where did you go this morning? I went to the bank

Venire: *Paola e Simone sono venuti a trovarci domenica scorsa* – Paola and Simone came to see us last Sunday

Partire: *Patrizia è partita ieri* – Patrizia left yesterday

Uscire: *Questa mattina sono uscito presto* – This morning I left early

Tornare: *Nadia è tornata a Edimburgo la scorsa settimana* – Nadia went back to Edinburgh last week

Arrivare: *Monica e Antonella sono arrivate* - Monica and Antonella have arrived

Stare: *Sei mai stata a Palermo, Elena?* – Have you ever been to Palermo, Elena?

Rimanere: *Giulia è rimasta a casa tutto il giorno* – Giulia stayed at home all day

Nascere: *Tommaso è nato a luglio* – Tommaso was born in July

Morire: *È morto il famoso scrittore Andrea Camilleri* – The renowned writer Andrea Camilleri died

Diventare: *Federica è diventata mamma* – Federica has become a mom

Piacere: *Le foto sono piaciute a tutti* – Everyone liked the photos

When do you use the imperfect tense instead of the passato prossimo?

It may be difficult to correctly choose between the *passato prossimo* and the **imperfect tense** (*imperfetto*) when you try and talk about the past in Italian. Here are some tips which we hope will help you with the use of these two tenses.

In Italian the ***passato prossimo*** refers to one-off actions that happened in the past – maybe just one time – and are not repeated through time. If the action is seen as a completed/finished event in the recent past, then you use the *passato prossimo* in Italian.

Listen to track 245

Tre anni fa sono andata a Treviso – I went to Treviso three years ago

Sono andata in Toscana l'anno scorso – I went to Tuscany last year

In other words, I didn't keep on going to Treviso or Tuscany. I went and the event was concluded. If you are describing events that happened regularly in the past, then you have to use the ***imperfetto***, which corresponds to "used to...".

Ogni anno andavamo in Toscana – Every year we used to go to Tuscany

If you want to talk about events that happened repeatedly in the past or describe something that happened over a period of time, like, for instance, going to your Italian lesson every Wednesday, you will need to use the **imperfetto**.

When describing how a place, person or thing was, you use the **imperfetto** in Italian.

Da piccola avevo i capelli biondi – When I was little, I used to have blonde hair

Faceva troppo caldo – It was too hot

If you are describing something in the past that happened at the same time as something else, then you use both. The **imperfetto** is used to describe the action that was taking place when something else happened.

Mentre andavo al supermercato ho visto Davide – While I was going to the supermarket, I saw Davide

Mentre guardavo la televisione è suonato il telefono – While I was watching TV, the phone rang

Which phrases are typically used with the **passato prossimo**? Here is a list of expressions that are usually used with the present perfect tense in Italian:

Listen to track 246

Stamattina – this morning

Ieri – yesterday

Ieri pomeriggio – yesterday afternoon

Ieri sera – last night

L'altro giorno – the other day

Tre giorni fa – three days ago

Il mese scorso – last month

What's the difference between passato remoto and passato prossimo?

The remote past tense (*passato remoto*) refers to events further in the past, and the *passato prossimo* refers to recent ones. We use the **passato remoto** to describe actions that are concluded and that we consider distant in time.

Listen to track 247

Cristoforo Colombo scoprì l'America nel 1492 – Columbus discovered America in 1492

Michelangelo nacque nel 1475 - Michelangelo was born in 1475

We use the ***passato prossimo*** to talk about something that still has an impact on the present.

Siamo sposati da 11 anni – We have been married for 11 years (we are still married)

We know that *passato prossimo* is not so easy to understand. In English, you do not distinguish at all between a remote or recent past event, because there is no separate past tense for this distinction.

Used to translate both the English perfect and the simple past, the *passato prossimo* is used much more frequently than the remote past tense in Italy. Northern Italians tend to use almost exclusively the *passato prossimo*, whereas further south, especially in Sicily, Campania, Basilicata, Apulia and Calabria, the remote past tense is often used to describe fairly recent events.

To sum up...

Listen to track 248

- The *passato prossimo* is used to say what you have done at some time in the recent past.

Ieri sera ho cucinato per i miei amici – Last night I cooked for my friends

Mi sono iscritto all'università due anni fa – I entered University two years ago

- You need to use the present tense of either the **auxiliary verb** "essere" or "avere" and the **past participle** of the verb expressing the action.
- Unlike in English, the Italian *passato prossimo* is used to say exactly when something happened and what you did at a particular time in the recent past.

Ho visto quel film giovedì scorso – I saw that film last Thursday

Roberta gli ha parlato ieri sera – Roberta spoke to him last night

Remember that **English** and Italian have different tense forms and most of the time you can't make an exact correlation between Italian and English tenses. The choice of an English tense when translating from Italian depends more on conveying the right meaning than trying to use a corresponding tense form.

BEWARE: the Italian *passato prossimo* is used to translate both the English present perfect and the **simple past**, and many students find it hard to understand when to use it. The best way for English speakers to understand this tense is to be found in the action described by the main verb: it is an action that has been completed/ finished/concluded in the recent past.

Workbook Lesson 15. Past Tenses

Exercise 15.1: Conjugate the verb "essere" in the "passato prossimo"

1. Io_____ _____
2. Tu_____ _____
3. Lui/Lei _____ _____
4. Noi _____ _____
5. Voi _____ _____
6. Loro _____ _____

Exercise 15.2: Conjugate the verb "avere" in the "passato prossimo"

1. Io_____ _____
2. Tu_____ _____
3. Lui/Lei _____ _____
4. Noi _____ _____
5. Voi _____ _____
6. Loro _____ _____

Exercise 15.3: Choose the right option

1. Ho _____ una torta buonissima ieri.
   a. Ascoltato   b. Camminato   c. Mangiato
2. Emma mi ha _____ due giorni fa, ma non ieri.
   a. Salutato   b. Seduto   c. Creduto
3. I miei amici mi hanno _____ a una festa.
   a. Consigliato   b. Invitato   c. Gustato
4. Maria e Luca _____ visto Alice ieri.
   a. Ha   b. Hanno   c. Ho
5. Tu _____ mai mangiato la pizza con le acciughe?
   a. Ho   b. Hanno   c. Hai
6. Noi non _____ mai andati a Roma.
   a. Abbiamo   b. Siamo   c. Sono

Exercise 15.4: Translate the following sentences into Italian

English	Italian
1. I saw that movie last week.	
2. We went there together.	

3. She ate the whole pizza on her own!	
4. They didn't invite us to the party.	
5. Have you talked to Giulia recently?	
6. He ran 4 kms in two hours!	

Exercise 15.5: "Essere" or "avere"? Choose the right "ausiliare"

1. ____ mangiato

2. _____ andato

3. _____ pianto

4. _____ arrivato

5. _____ apparso

6. _____ visto

7. _____ scomparso

8. _____ sperato

Answers:

Exercise 15.1:

1. Io sono stat; 2. tu sei stato; 3. lui/lei è stato/stata; 4. noi siamo stati; 5. voi siete stati; 6. loro sono stati

Exercise 15.2:

1. Io ho avuto; 2. tu hai avuto; 3. lui/lei ha avuto; 4. noi abbiamo avuto; 5. voi avete avuto; 6. loro hanno avuto.

Exercise 15.3:

1) c; 2) a; 3) b; 4) b; 5) c; 6) b

Exercise 15.4:

1. Ho visto quel film la settimana scorsa.

2. Siamo andati là insieme.

3. Ha mangiato tutta la pizza da sola!

4. Non ci hanno invitati alla festa.

5. Hai parlato con Giulia di recente?

6. Ha corso 4 km in due ore!

Exercise 15.5:

1. avere; 2. essere; 3. avere; 4. essere; 5. essere; 6. avere; 7. essere; 8. avere

LESSON 16. RELATIVE PRONOUNS

Welcome to this lesson on Italian relative pronouns (*pronomi relativi*). In the following paragraphs, we will teach you what a relative pronoun is, what the most common ones in Italian are and how to use each of them. Ready? Let's begin!

What's a relative pronoun?

Simply put, **relative pronouns** (*pronomi relativi*) serve as links and introduce the relative clause that provides more information on a previous proposition, establishing a relationship between the two clauses.

In other words, Italian relative pronouns connect clauses that have one element in common, and replace it in the second clause. The clause introduced by the pronoun is subordinate and is dependent on the main one. The **relative pronoun** refers back to a noun, pronoun or phrase called the antecedent, and is used to avoid repetitions.

Listen to track 249

The most common relative pronouns in Italian are:

- **che** (which, that, who, whom);
- **cui** (who, whom, which, whose, that, to which, of which);
- **chi** (those who, the person who, everyone who);
- **il quale** (who, which, that).

We will take you through each of them one by one. Let's start from the top.

The main relative pronouns in Italian

Listen to track 250

Che (which, that, who, whom)

As you know, in English *which* and *that* are used to talk about things, while *who, whom* and *that* are used to talk about people. In Italian, you use *che* for all of these without distinction. Pronounced /ke/, the relative pronoun *che* can refer to people, animals and objects, both in the singular and in the plural.

Have a look at some examples:

*Quello è il treno **che** va a Savona* – That is the train that goes to Savona

Ho letto il saggio sulla Rivoluzione Francese **che** *hai scritto ieri* – I read the paper on the French Revolution you wrote yesterday

L'uomo **che** *è appena entrato è il marito di Cristina* – The man who has just come in is Cristina's husband

La torta **che** *hai preparato è deliziosa* – The cake you made is delicious

Gli occhiali da sole **che** *mi ha regalato Gianni hanno le lenti polarizzate* – The sunglasses Gianni gave me as a present have polarized lenses

The hero of Italian relative pronouns, *che* is invariable in gender and number and doesn't change according to the subject or direct object complement it replaces in the relative clause. For example:

Questo è il vestito **che** *ho comprato online* (*che* is the object of *ho comprato*) – This is the dress that I bought online

Questo è il vestito **che** *costa un occhio della testa* (*che* is the subject for the verb *costa*) – This is the dress that costs an arm and a leg

As you may have noticed from some of the above examples, there is one main difference between Italian and English relative pronouns: while in English you can omit the relative pronoun, you can never miss out *che* in Italian.

Listen to track 251

Le lasagne vegetariane **che** *ho mangiato a pranzo erano buonissime* – The vegetarian lasagna (that) I had for lunch was delicious

In Italian you cannot say "*le lasagne vegetariane ho mangiato a pranzo erano buonissime*".

Note: the relative pronoun *che* preceded by the definite article *il* replaces a whole sentence. Here are some examples:

Sento un continuo sparlare nei miei confronti, **il che** *mi rattrista* – I hear people saying bad things about me all the time, which makes me sad

Si tratta di un ente finanziato dal sistema di tassazione collettiva, **il che** *significa che le spese sono coperte dai contribuenti* – It is an organization funded by the collective taxation system, which means that the expenses are covered by the tax payers

Remember that the relative pronoun *che* is never preceded by a preposition.

BEWARE: in Italian there are other uses of *che*. It can actually be a conjunction, a comparative, an interrogative adjective or pronoun, or an exclamatory adjective or pronoun. To know if it is a relative pronoun, try and substitute *che* with *il quale*.

Cui (who, whom, which, to which, whose, of which)

Listen to track 252

Pronounced /*kui*/, **cui** is an invariable pronoun, replaces the indirect complement, and is always preceded by a preposition (*di, a, da, in, con, su, per, tra/fra*).

Let's look at the following examples:

*L'ufficio **a cui** ci siamo rivolti non ha saputo risolvere la nostra pratica* – The office which we were bound to did not know how to handle our paperwork

*Riccardo è una persona **di cui** è meglio non fidarsi* – Riccardo is a person you should not trust

*Si può sapere il motivo **per cui** state bisticciando?* – May I know the reason why you are arguing?

You can also use *cui* preceded by a definite article to connect two clauses that have an element in common expressing a form of possession. Have a look at these examples to get an idea of how it works:

*Quante persone conosci **i cui** genitori sono divorziati?* – How many people do you know whose parents are divorced?

Chi (those who, the person who, everyone who)

Listen to track 253

Pronounced /*kee*/, *chi* is invariable, refers only to people and functions as subject and object. The relative pronoun *chi* in Italian literally means *those who, the person who* and *everyone who*. For example:

*Non mi piace **chi** si lamenta sempre* – I don't like those who always complain

***Chi** rompe, paga* – Who breaks, pays / You break it, you own it

***Chi** trova un amico, trova un tesoro* – He/she who finds a friend, finds a treasure

***Chi** dorme non piglia pesci* – (Literally: Those who sleep don't catch any fish) You snooze, you lose

***Chi** fa da sé, fa per tre* – (Literally: Those who make themselves do it for three) If you want a thing done well, do it yourself

***Chi** cerca trova* – He/she who seeks will find

***Chi** non risica non rosica* – (Literally: Those who don't risk can't win) No pain, no gain

Chi *la fa, l'aspetti* – (Literally: Those who do it, should wait for it) What goes around comes around

Chi *disprezza compra* – (Literally: He/she who despises, buys) The more you despise, the more you like / The more you hate, the more you love

Chi *tace acconsente* – (Literally: Who keeps silent, consents) Silence means consent

Chi *la dura la vince* – It will be worth it in the end

As you can see, *chi* is widely used in Italian proverbs

- Sometimes *chi* functions as an indirect complement if it is preceded by a preposition. Here you have some examples:

Listen to track 254

*Dovresti dare una mano **a chi** ha bisogno* – You should help those in need

*Non fidarti **di chi** non conosci abbastanza* – Don't trust those you don't know well-enough

*Diffida **da chi** non ama gli animali* – Beware of those who do not like animals

*Sii sempre gentile con tutti, anche **con chi** non se lo merita* – Always be kind to everyone, even those who don't deserve it

Il quale (who, which, that)

Listen to track 255

Next up is *il quale*, which has exactly the same meaning as *che* and *cui*, but is a little bit more formal and you will mostly come across it in written Italian. For example:

*Gli inquirenti hanno parlato con i colleghi di Davide, **i quali** sostengono di non averlo visto* – Investigators talked to Davide's colleagues, who say they haven't seen him

As you may have already guessed, the relative pronoun *il quale* changes according to the gender and number of the noun it refers to. Depending on whether you have a masculine, feminine, singular or plural antecedent, you will have to choose a different form:

- *il quale* for masculine singular;
- *la quale* for feminine singular;
- *i quali* for masculine plural;
- *le quali* for feminine plural.

Here are some examples:

*Non puoi dimenticarti delle persone con **le quali** hai passato i momenti più belli della tua vita* – You can't forget about the people with whom you spent the best moments of your life

*Questo è l'indirizzo dell'agenzia con **la quale** collaboro da anni* – This is the address of the agency I have been working with for years

*Quali sono gli interventi edilizi per **i quali** è possibile usufruire della detrazione fiscale?* – Which are the building works whose cost can be deducted from taxes?

*Quel film vanta un cast di prim'ordine, tra **il quale** spicca il nome di Pierfrancesco Favino* – That film boasts a first-rate cast, including Pierfrancesco Favino

As you can see, *il quale, la quale, i quali* and *le quali* are often used with prepositions.

If you use *il quale* to express possession, remember that it agrees in gender and number with the person who possesses. Here is an example:

*Mio figlio Mattia, la moglie **del quale** è svedese, vive in Svezia da quindici anni / Alternative: Mi figlio Mattia, **(la) cui** moglie è svedese, vive in Svezia da quindici anni* – My son Mattia, whose wife is Swedish, has lived in Sweden for fifteen years

How to use prepositions with relative pronouns

Listen to track 256

If you need to use a preposition with a relative pronoun, use **cui** instead of *che*, and place the preposition in front of it. Easy, right? Let's look at a few examples:

*Questo è il libro **di cui** ti ho parlato* – This is the book I told you about

*Alghero è un'antica città sul mare **a cui** deve il suo nome* – Alghero is an ancient town on the sea which gives it its name

*L'album **da cui** è tratto il brano è del 1972* – The album from which the song is taken was released in 1972

*Il paese **in cui** vivono i miei zii ha meno di mille abitanti* – The town where my uncles live has less than a thousand inhabitants

*Il ragazzo **con cui** sono uscita è di origini bosniache* – The guy with whom I went out is of Bosnian descent

*Sono stati traditi i princìpi **su cui** si fonda la Federazione* – The principles upon which the Federation was founded were betrayed

*L'azienda **per cui** lavoro è quotata in borsa* – The company I work for is listed on the stock exchange

*Il parco ospita numerose specie animali, **tra cui** spicca il rinoceronte, a rischio di estinzione* – The park is home to many animal species, most notably the endangered rhino

As you can see, in Italian you cannot split the relatives like in English, and prepositions never go at the end of the phrase. It doesn't matter how awkward it sounds to you, you simply cannot do it.

To sum up...

- Relative pronouns connect phrases and sentences replacing one or more elements.
- Italian relative pronouns can never be omitted.
- *Che* (which, that, who, whom) is the most used relative pronoun in Italian.
- *Che* can't be used after a preposition.
- *Cui* is to be used after a preposition.
- *Il quale, la quale, i quali* and *le quali* may replace both *che* and *cui*, especially in writing.

Don't worry if you don't get it all at first. There is a lot to take in here, we know. Lots of practice usually helps. The more you practice using Italian **relative pronouns** and hear them being used in conversation, the less weird it will feel.

Workbook Lesson 16. Relative Pronouns

Exercise 16.1: Translate the following sentences into Italian

English	Italian
1. The flowers you bought me are very pretty.	
2. The person I met yesterday is my cousin.	
3. I don't like someone who complains about everything.	
4. The school I went to as a kid is closed now.	
5. The real winner is the one who does his best.	

Exercise 16.2: Complete with the right relative pronoun

1. Dario, con _____ sono uscito, è molto simpatico.

2. Il libro di _____ ti ho parlato, è interessante.

3. Il film _____ abbiamo visto, ci è piaciuto.

4. L'automobile _____ mi piacerebbe possedere è una Ferrari.

5. Sei entusiasta del viaggio _____ hai partecipato?

6. Il negozio _____ abitualmente faccio spese è chiuso.

Exercise 16.3: Choose the right option

1. Sul prato c'è una pecora chi/che ha avuto un agnellino.

2. La bambina chi/che ho incontrato ha nove anni.

3. Ho visto le amiche che/chi tu mi avevi presentato.

4. Hai ascoltato i CD che/chi ti ho regalato?

5. Giovanni, che/chi mi ha detto una bugia, ora si è pentito.

Exercise 16.4: Complete with the right preposition + cui

1. L' atleta _____ tutti chiedono l'autografo è un campione olimpionico.

2. La vacanza _____ ti ho parlato è stata entusiasmante.

3. La ragione _____ ti ho lasciata è seria.

4. Le aiuole _____ piantai i tulipani sono bellissime.

5. I ragazzi _____ sono uscito abitano nel mio palazzo.

6. Il romanzo, _____ è stato tratto il film è avvincente.

Exercise 16.5: Underline the relative pronouns

Eccoli questi grandi uccelli bianchi dalle ali nere, i lunghi colli protesi, che volteggiano al di sopra dei tetti con le lunghe zampe rosa. Scendendo sopra i tetti alla ricerca di un comignolo su cui costruirsi il nido al quale, la primavera successiva, talvolta qualcuno di loro fa ritorno. Le altre, le più sfortunate, quelle a cui il vento e il gelo dell'inverno hanno distrutto il nido, si rimettono subito a lavoro. C'è qualche nido, invece, che ha bisogno solo di essere riparato per diventare nuovamente abitabile. Le cicogne amano il nido che costruiscono.

Answers:

Exercise 16.1:

1. I fiori che mi hai regalato sono bellissimi.
2. La persona che ho incontrato ieri è mio cugino.
3. Non mi piace chi si lamenta di tutto.
4. La scuola che ho frequentato da bambino adesso è chiusa.
5. Il vero vincitore è chi fa del proprio meglio.

Exercise 16.2:

1. con il quale/ con cui; 2. di cui / del quale; 3. che; 4. Che; 5. al quale/ a cui; 6. nel quale/ in cui

Exercise 16.3:

1. che; 2. Che; 3. Che; 4. Che; 5. che

Exercise 16.4:

1. L' atleta a cui tutti chiedono l'autografo è un campione olimpionico.

2. La vacanza di cui ti ho parlato è stata entusiasmante.

3. La ragione per cui ti ho lasciata è seria.

4. Le aiuole in cui piantai i tulipani sono bellissime.

5. I ragazzi con cui sono uscito abitano nel mio palazzo.

6. Il romanzo, da cui è stato tratto un film, è avvincente.

Exercise 16.5:

Eccoli questi grandi uccelli bianchi dalle ali nere, i lunghi colli protesi, che volteggiano al di sopra dei tetti con le lunghe zampe rosa. Scendendo sopra i tetti alla ricerca di un comignolo su cui costruirsi il nido al quale, la primavera successiva, talvolta qualcuno di loro fa ritorno. Le altre, le più sfortunate, quelle a cui il vento e il gelo dell'inverno hanno distrutto il nido, si rimettono subito a lavoro. C'è qualche nido, invece, che ha bisogno solo di essere riparato per diventare nuovamente abitabile. Le cicogne amano il nido che costruiscono.

LESSON 17: MI PIACE! HOW TO EXPRESS LIKES & DISLIKES IN ITALIAN

Mi piace is one of the most useful expressions in Italian, as it is very important to be able to say what you like and what you don't like. But the Italian verb *piacere* can be tricky and a bit mind-boggling, as it works differently from *to like* in English.

Fear not, by the end of this lesson you will get it. Let's get started!

How to use the Italian verb piacere

Listen to track 257

Piacere (to like, to appreciate, to be pleasing) is a common yet irregular and quite insidious verb, which literally twists the Anglo-Saxon mindset. That is because the Italian verb *piacere* doesn't actually mean that someone likes something, but rather that something is pleasing to someone.

In English there is an active subject who likes something, and you simply say that A likes B. Sentences constructed with the verb *piacere* don't function the same as in English, as *piacere* is intransitive. In Italian, the same meaning is expressed in different terms: B is pleasing to A.

Have a look at the following examples:

Mi **piace** *viaggiare* – (Literally: traveling is pleasing to me) I like traveling

Agli italiani **piace** *il calcio* – (Literally: Football is pleasing to Italians) Italians like football

As you can see, the subject of the sentence is the thing that is being liked, while in English it is the object. The person who likes something is the **indirect object**.

The sentence structure is:

Indirect object + verb + subject

Piacere is a reverse-construction verb and, as you can see, the word order of sentences involving it gets all twisted up. That's the reason why the verb *piacere* makes most English-speaking Italian learners crazy.

As mentioned previously, in Italian when we say that we like something, we are actually saying that something is pleasing to us. The best thing for you to do when learning **how to use the Italian verb *piacere*** is to think of it as *to be pleasing* instead of *to like*.

Listen to track 258

*Ci **piace** la musica grunge* – We like grunge music / Grunge music is pleasing to us

*Mi **piacciono** le fragole* – I like strawberries / Strawberries are pleasing to me

As you can see, the Italian verb *piacere* is conjugated to match the subject of the sentence. **Piace** is to be used if the thing you like is a singular item or an infinitive, which counts as masculine singular for the purpose of agreement. It doesn't matter if the number of people liking it changes from singular to plural. As long as it is a single item or an individual person, you use *piace*.

If what you like is plural, you say *mi **piacciono*** plus the things you like. *Piacciono* is always used when the items or people being liked are plural. Again, it doesn't matter if the number of people liking them changes. For example:

Listen to track 259

*Mi **piace** la pizza / Ci **piace** la pizza* – (Literally: Pizza is pleasing to me/us) I/we like pizza

*Mi **piacciono** gli animali / Ci **piacciono** gli animali* – (Literally: Animals are pleasing to me/us) I/we like animals

*Ti **piace** disegnare? / Vi **piace** disegnare?* – (Literally: Is drawing pleasing to you/y'all?) Do you/y'all like drawing?

*Ti **piacciono** i ravioli? / Vi **piacciono** i ravioli?* – (Literally: Are ravioli pleasing to you/y'all?) Do you/y'all like ravioli?

To say how much you like something you can add *molto* (a lot), *tanto/tantissimo* (a lot, very much) or *da impazzire* (madly) immediately after the verb. For instance:

Listen to track 260

*Mi **piace molto** suonare il basso* – I really like playing the bass guitar

*Ti piace l'arte contemporanea? Sì, **mi piace tantissimo*** – Do you like contemporary art? Yes, I like it a lot

*Mi **piaci da impazzire*** – I like you madly

Saying *mi piaci* to someone you are dating means that you find them nice and attractive. It is much less serious than *ti amo*, which means "I'm in love with you". *Ti amo* is very strong and it is better to use it only when things get really serious.

How to conjugate the verb piacere

Piacere is an irregular verb mostly used in the third person singular *piace*, pronounced /*pee-yah-chay*/, and plural *piacciono*, pronounced /*pee-yah-cho-no*/.

Here are the other forms, just in case you ever need to use them:

Listen to track 261

(io) **piaccio**

(tu) **piaci**

(lui / lei) **piace**

(noi) **piacciamo**

(voi) **piacete**

(loro) **piacciono**

Here are some examples:

Listen to track 262

***Piaci** molto a mio cugino* – My cousin likes you a lot

*Purtroppo, mi innamoro sempre di ragazze a cui non **piaccio*** – Unfortunately, I always fall in love with girls who don't like me

*Sono sicuro che **piacete** molto alla vostra maestra* – I am sure that your teacher likes you a lot

*Gli uomini saccenti e arroganti non **piacciono** alle donne* – Women don't like arrogant men

Piacere and indirect object pronouns

As was mentioned earlier, the little word you put in front of the conjugated verb to express who is doing the liking is not a subject, it is actually an **indirect object pronoun**.

Here is a quick review of the Italian **unstressed indirect object pronouns**:

Listen to track 263

mi – to me (first person singular)

ti – to you (second person singular)

gli – to him (third person masculine singular)

le, Le – to her (third person feminine singular); to you (polite singular)

ci – to us (first person plural)

vi – to you (second person plural)

gli – to them (third person plural)

Take a look at the following examples:

Listen to track 264

Mi piace il gelato (I am the person to whom ice-cream is pleasing) – I like ice-cream

Gli piace studiare – He likes studying

To emphasize who likes something or someone, you can use the **stressed indirect object pronouns**:

Listen to track 265

a me – (to) me (first person singular)

a te – (to) you (second person singular)

a lui – (to) him (third person masculine singular)

a lei, a Lei – (to) her (third person feminine singular), (to) you (polite singular)

a noi – (to) us (first person plural)

a voi– (to) you (second person plural)

a loro – (to) them (third person plural)

Let's look at a few examples:

Listen to track 266

A me piace il teatro classico, eccome se mi piace – I like classical theatre, I like it a lot

A me piace il mare, mentre **a lei piace** la montagna – I like the sea whereas she likes the mountains

You may hear people say *a me mi piace*. Ugh, it's incorrect and sounds very strange because it is a repetition.

Different tenses and moods

Like any verb, *piacere* can be conjugated in any tense. For example:

Listen to track 267

Ti piacerà l'Italia (*futuro semplice*) – You will like Italy

Quando ero più giovane, **mi piaceva** *andare a ballare* (*imperfetto*) – When I was younger, I used to like going clubbing

Mi piacerebbe *rivedere Apocalypse Now* (*condizionale presente*) – I would like to see Apocalypse Now again

Ti piacerebbe! (*condizionale presente*) – In your dreams! / You wish!

Ci sarebbe piaciuto *andare a vedere la partita* (*condizionale passato*) – We would have liked to go and see the match

In compound tenses, like the present perfect (*passato prossimo*), past perfect (*trapassato prossimo*), future perfect tense (*futuro anteriore*) and so on, use the auxiliary verb *essere* (to be). Remember that the past participle agrees with the subject of the sentence in gender and number. Use *piaciuto/piaciuta* with singular objects and *piaciuti/piaciute* with plural ones, depending on the gender of what you are talking about.

For example:

Listen to track 268

Mi è piaciuto *molto lo spezzatino, era buonissimo* – I really liked the stew, it was delicious

Il mio articolo **è piaciuto** *al caporedattore* – The editor liked my article

Enrico voleva sapere se la commedia **ci era piaciuta** – Enrico wanted to know if we liked the play

Gli sono piaciute *le nostre fotografie* – He liked our photographs

Non potevamo immaginare che i cannelloni **non vi fossero piaciuti** – We couldn't imagine that you didn't like our stuffed cannelloni

How to say you dislike something in Italian

To turn an affirmative sentence with *piacere* into a negative one, all you have to do is place the negation **non** (not) in front of the verb or in front of the indirect object pronoun. It couldn't be easier. Here are some examples:

Listen to track 269

Non *mi piace stirare* – I don't like ironing

Ai miei figli **non** *piace la pallacanestro* – My kids don't like basketball

Ti piace l'opera? **No, non mi piace**, *preferisco il balletto* – Do you like lyrical opera? No, I don't like it, I prefer ballet

Listen to track 270

To say how much you dislike something you can add *per niente* (not at all, at all, in no way), *affatto* (absolutely not, not at all, by no means) or *neanche un po'* (not even a bit) immediately after the verb. For example:

Ti piacciono i reality show? No, **non mi piacciono per niente** – Do you like reality television series? No, I don't like them at all

Italian verbs that behave like piacere

Piacere is not the only verb that follows this unusual sentence structure. Here is a list of Italian verbs that behave similarly to *piacere*:

Listen to track 271

- **bastare** (to suffice, to be enough, to be sufficient):

Pensi che **ti basteranno** *200 euro?* – Do you think that 200 euros will suffice?

Ti bastano *due giorni per scrivere questo articolo?* – Are two days sufficient for you to write this article?

- **dispiacere** (to be sorry, to displease):

Mi dispiace *che non possiate venire con noi* – I'm sorry that you can't come with us

- **mancare** (to miss, to be lacking)

Mi manca *molto la mia famiglia* – I miss my family a lot

Ti sono mancata? – Did you miss me?

- **occorrere** (to need, to require):

Devo preparare una torta per la quale **mi occorrono** *300 grammi di zucchero* – I have to make a cake for which I need 300 grams of sugar

- **servire** (to be needed, to serve, to be necessary, to need, to be of use):

Le serviranno *dei chiodi per appendere i nuovi quadri* – She will need a couple of nails to hang up her new paintings

Mi servono *20 euro, me li puoi prestare?* – I need 20 euros, can you lend them to me?

- **interessare** (to interest):

Ti interessa *questo documentario?* – Are you interested in this documentary?

Other meanings of piacere

Listen to track 272

Aside from a verb, *piacere* is also a noun spelled the same way. It means *delight, pleasure* or *joy*. Here are some examples:

*Per noi vederti è sempre un **piacere*** – It's always a delight to see you

*Il **piacere** è mio* – The pleasure is mine / It's my pleasure

*Con chi ho il **piacere** di parlare?* (on the phone) – To whom do I have the pleasure of speaking?

Piacere! (when you greet someone for the first time) – Pleased to meet you, lovely to meet you

*Con **piacere*** – With pleasure

*A cosa devo il **piacere**?* – To what do I owe the pleasure?

Listen to track 273

Piacere can also mean *favor* or *courtesy*.

*Mi fai un **piacere**?* – Would you do me a favor?

*Ma fammi il **piacere**!* (in an exasperated or sarcastic tone) – Oh please! / Oh, come on! / Do me a favor!

You can express a request in a more polite way by adding **per piacere**, which means *please,* just like *per cortesia* and *per favore*. For example:

*Spegni la luce, **per piacere*** – Turn off the light, please

To sum up...

- The Italian verb *piacere* works a little differently from *to like* in English.
- *Piacere* is an intransitive verb.
- In Italian, the thing you like or dislike is the subject of the verb *piacere*. The subject of the verb *piacere* is what in English would be the object.
- The indirect object is the person to whom something is pleasing.
- *Piacere* needs either an indirect object pronoun (*mi, ti, gli, le, ci, vi, gli*) or the preposition "a" followed by the person to whom something is pleasing.
- When talking about an activity, use the infinitive with *piace*.
- Italian verbs *dispiacere* (to be sorry), *mancare* (to miss), *occorrere* (to require), *servire* (to need), *interessare* (to interest) and *bastare* (to suffice, to be enough) follow the same construction as *piacere*.

As I have said before, once you get *to like* out of your head and start to think of the verb *piacere* as *to be pleasing*, it is actually not too difficult to use. Read and listen to Italian as much as you can and practice in real-life situations until you get the hang of it. Happy language learning!

Workbook Lesson 17. How to Express Likes & Dislikes in Italian

Exercise 17.1: Reply with "yes" and "no"

1. – Ti piace il cioccolato? – Sì, _____. / – No, non _____.

2. – Ti piace la Formula 1? – Sì, _____. / – No, non _____.

3. – Ti piacciono gli spaghetti? – Sì, _____. / – No, _____.

4. – Ti piacciono i biscotti? – Sì, _____. / No, _____.

5. – Ti piace il cibo cinese? – Sì, _____. / – No, _____.

Exercise 17.2: Complete the following sentences

a. (she likes) _____ le lingue straniere.

b. (we don't like) Non _____ i locali rumorosi

c. (I don't like) Non _____ la violenza nello sport.

d. (they like) _____ le opere di Verdi.

e. (do you like?) _____ i gelati e i dolci?

f. (he doesn't like) Non _____ la pizza.

Exercise 17.3: Translate the following sentences into Italian

English	Italian
1. I didn't know you liked horror movies.	
2. I'm sure she will like your present.	
3. They'd like going to China next year.	
4. She won't like this mess.	
5. He would like to join our team.	

Exercise 17.4: Complete the dialogues, as in the example

Es.: A. – Mi piace il colore arancione. B. – [Anche a me]. C. – [A me invece] piace il colore blu.

1. A. – Mi piace ascoltare la musica jazz.

   B. - Anche a me.

   C. –_____ la musica classica.

2. A. – Mi piacciono i libri gialli.

   B. – Anche a me.

   C. – _____ i libri di avventure.

3. A. – Mi piace stare in compagnia.

   B. – Anche a me.

   C. –_____ stare solo.

4. A. – Mi piacciono le feste in campagna.

   B. - Anche a me.

   C. –_____le feste in casa.

5. A. – Mi piace la cucina italiana.

   B. – Anche a me.

   C. – _____ la cucina francese.

Exercise 17.5: Choose the correct option

1. Mi chiedevo se ti piacesse/piacerebbe andare a Venezia con me.

2. Se mi piacesse/piacerebbe la pizza, la mangerei tutti i giorni.

3. Non mi piace/non mi è piaciuto il film di ieri.

4. Chissà se a Marta piacciono/piacerebbero i pomodori.

5. Ti piace/piacciono le rose?

Answers:

Exercise 17.1:

1. – Ti piace il cioccolato?

   – Sì, mi piace. / – No, non mi piace.

2. – Ti piace la Formula 1?

   – Sì, mi piace. / – No, non mi piace.

3. – Ti piacciono gli spaghetti?

   – Sì, mi piacciono. / – No, non mi piacciono.

4. – Ti piacciono i biscotti?

   – Sì, mi piacciono. / – No, non mi piacciono.

5. – Ti piace il cibo cinese?

   – Sì, mi piace. / – No, non mi piace.

Exercise 17.2:

a. Le piacciono le lingue straniere.

b. Non ci piacciono i locali rumorosi.

c. Non mi piace la violenza nello sport.

d. A loro piacciono le opere di Verdi.

e. Ti piacciono i gelati e i dolci?

f. Non gli piace la pizza.

Exercise 17.3:

1. Non sapevo che ti piacessero i film horror.

2. Sono sicuro che le piacerà il tuo regalo.

3. Gli piacerebbe andare in Cina l'anno prossimo.

4. Non le piacerà questo disordine.

5. Gli piacerebbe unirsi al nostro gruppo.

Exercise 17.4:

1) A. – Mi piace ascoltare la musica jazz.

   B. - Anche a me.

   C. - A me invece piace la musica classica.

2) A. – Mi piacciono i libri gialli.

   B. – Anche a me

   C. – A me invece piacciono i libri di avventure.

3) A. – Mi piace stare in compagnia.

   B. – Anche a me.

   C. – A me invece piace stare solo.

4) A. – Mi piacciono le feste in campagna.

   B. - Anche a me.

   C. – A me invece piacciono le feste in casa.

5) A. – Mi piace la cucina italiana.

   B. – Anche a me.

   C. – A me invece piace la cucina francese.

Exercise 17.5:

1. piacerebbe

2. piacesse

3. non mi è piaciuto

4. piacciono

5. piacciono

LESSON 18: THE IMPERATIVE

The Italian **imperative** (*imperativo*) is used to order, exhort or suggest someone to do something. It comes up quite a lot, especially in spoken Italian.

The ***imperativo*** is simpler than other moods and just needs some attention. Would you like to master this essential aspect of Italian grammar? Here is a guide to help you avoid some common pitfalls.

Using the imperative

Listen to track 274

The Italian imperative is used to:

- give orders or commands:

Siediti! – Sit down! (I am telling someone to do something)

Non entrare! – Do not enter! (I am telling someone not to do something)

- give advice:

Prendi *un'aspirina e* ***riposati*** – Take an aspirin and rest

- give directions:

Prosegua *dritto poi* ***giri*** *a sinistra* – Go straight on and then turn left

- express exhortations:

Siate *affamati.* ***Siate*** *folli.* (cit. Steve Jobs) – Stay hungry. Stay foolish.

Tieni *duro!* – Hang in there!

Batti *il cinque!* – Gimme a high five!

Sbrigati! – Hurry up!

- scold, reprimand someone harshly:

Vergognati! – Shame on you!

- make direct suggestions:

Vai *a casa, sei ubriaco!* – Go home, you're drunk!

- make requests:

Fammi *sapere, per favore* – Let me know, please

- give instructions (especially in recipes):

Portate *il composto a ebollizione, mescolando costantemente* – *Bring the mixture to the boil, stirring frequently*

- implore someone:

Abbi *pietà di me* – Have mercy on me

Sia *clemente* – Be merciful to me

The Italian imperative is also used in exclamations. Here are some examples:

Listen to track 275

*Ma **dai**!* – Come on!

*Ma **va'**!* – No way!

*Non **dirmelo**!* – You don't say!

As you can see, when we use the *imperativo* in Italian, we don't include the subject pronouns in our sentences.

Listen to track 276

Abbi *fede!* – Have faith!

"Tu abbi fede" is incorrect and sounds very strange.

How to form the imperativo

The *imperativo* is the only mood in Italian that has only one tense: the present. It changes depending on the verb's subject and can be used with:

tu – second person singular "you"

Lei – the formal way of saying "you" in Italian

voi – second person plural "y'all"

Loro – formal plural form

To make suggestions, you can also use **noi** (the first person plural "we") in the imperative, which corresponds to the English phrase "let's (do something)".

Listen to track 277

Sbrighiamoci, *è tardi!* – Let's hurry up, it's late!

Andiamo! – Let's go!

*Bene, allora **cominciamo***! – OK, let's get started then!

In Italian, we use a different form of the *imperativo* depending on whether we are speaking formally or informally.

1. Imperativo informale

The ***imperativo informale*** is used with a peer your age, close friends, family members, children and people you know well. Use **tu** (informal singular "you") to address a single person informally.

Listen to track 278

Finiscila, *Gemma!* – Stop it, Gemma!

Se ci sei ***batti*** *un colpo!* – If you can hear me, knock once for yes!

Sparecchia *la tavola e* ***porta*** *fuori la spazzatura, per favore* – Clear the table and take out the trash, please

Sappi *che non ho assolutamente nulla contro di te* – Know that I have absolutely nothing against you

Use **voi** (y'all) to tell two or more people what to do.

Dite *la verità!* – Tell the truth!

Accorrete *numerosi!* – Come one, come all!

Venite *a trovarmi!* – Come and see me!

Per ulteriori informazioni non ***esitate*** *a contattarci* – If you require more information, don't hesitate to contact us

2. Imperativo formale

Listen to track 279

The ***imperativo formale*** is to be used in formal contexts, when you are addressing:

* someone in a polite and respectful way;
* someone you don't know well;
* someone with whom you have a professional relationship;
* someone to whom you want to show your deference by using polite language.

Use **Lei** (formal singular "you") to address a single person.

Si accomodi, *signora* – Take a seat, madam!

Compili *il modulo e* ***attenda*** *il suo turno, signor Rossi* – Please fill in the form and wait your turn, Mr. Rossi

Salga *in macchina* – Get in the car

In some parts of Italy, especially in the South among older people, "voi" is still used as the formal singular "you" for telling a single person what to do. This polite form has almost completely become extinct, though.

Loro (formal plural form) is used in extremely formal situations when addressing more than one person.

Prego signore e signori, **si accomodino** – Please have a seat, ladies and gentlemen

The use of the formal plural form "Loro" is declining with each passing generation and is gradually being replaced by the "voi" form.

Constructing the imperativo

The **imperativo** of regular verbs is formed by adding the appropriate endings to the stem of the verb. There are different endings for -**are**, -**ere** and -**ire** verbs.

To make the *imperativo* of regular verbs ending in -**are**, take off the infinitive ending to find the stem of the verb and add the following endings:

- -**a** for "tu"
- -**i** for "Lei"
- -**iamo** for "we" (let's)
- -**ate** for "voi"
- -**ino** for "Loro" polite plural.

Not too bad, right? With regular -**are** verbs, like *guardare* (to look at, to watch), the conjugation looks like this:

Listen to track 280
Guardare

(tu) guard**a**

(Lei) guard**i**

(noi) guard**iamo**

(voi) guard**ate**

(Loro) guard**ino**

To make the *imperativo* of regular verbs ending in -**ere**, take off the infinitive ending to find the stem of the verb and add the following endings:

- -**i** for "tu"
- -**a** for "Lei"
- -**iamo** for "we" (let's)

- **-ete** for "voi"
- **-ano** for "Loro" (polite plural)

With regular **-ere** verbs, like *scendere* (to get off, to get out), the conjugation looks like this:

Listen to track 281

Scendere

(tu) scend**i**

(Lei) scend**a**

(noi) scend**iamo**

(voi) scend**ete**

(Loro) scend**ano**

To make the *imperativo* of most regular verbs ending in **-ire**, take away the infinitive ending and add the following endings:

- **-i** for "you"
- **-a** for "Lei"
- **-iamo** for "we" (let's)
- **-ite** for "voi"
- **-ano** for "Loro" (polite plural)

With **-ire** verbs like *partire* (to leave), the conjugation looks like this:

Listen to track 282

Partire

(tu) part**i**

(Lei) part**a**

(noi) part**iamo**

(voi) part**ite**

(Loro) part**ano**

Some verbs ending in **-ire**, like *finire* (to finish), *pulire* (to clean), *fornire* (to provide) and *dimagrire* (to lose weight), take the following endings:

- **-isci** for "tu"
- **-isca** for "Lei"
- **-iamo** for "we" (let's)

- **-ite** for "voi"
- **-iscano** for "Loro" (polite plural)

Note: in Italian "sca" and "sci" are pronounced /*ska*/ and /*she*/ respectively.

Listen to track 283

Finire (to finish)

(tu) fin**isci**

(Lei) fin**isca**

(noi) fin**iamo**

(voi) fin**ite**

(Loro) fin**iscano**

Listen to track 284

To construct the "noi" form of the Italian *imperativo*, just use the present tense conjugation for whichever verb you are dealing with.

Scappiamo! – Let's run away!

Vediamoci *una di queste sere!* – Let's hang out one day soon!

Irregular verbs in the imperativo

There are some **irregular verbs** in the *imperativo*. First, we will look at the imperfect conjugations of *essere* (to be) and *avere* (to have):

Listen to track 285

Essere (to be)

(tu) sii

(Lei) sia

(noi) siamo

(voi) siate

(Loro) siano

Listen to track 286

Avere (to have)

(tu) abbi

(Lei) abbia

(noi) abbiamo

(voi) abbiate

(Loro) abbiano

Some of the commonest verbs in Italian form the *imperativo* irregularly and just have to be committed to memory because they do not follow any grammatical rules. Here is a list:

Listen to track 287

Andare (to go)

(tu) vai / va'

(Lei) vada

(noi) andiamo

(voi) andate

(Loro) vadano

Listen to track 288

Fare (to do, to make)

(tu) fai / fa'

(Lei) faccia

(noi) facciamo

(voi) fate

(Loro) facciano

Listen to track 289

Dare (to give)

(tu) dai / da'

(Lei) dia

(noi) diamo

(voi) date

(Loro) diano

Listen to track 290

Sapere (to know)

(tu) sappi

(Lei) sappia

(noi) sappiamo

(voi) sapete

(Loro) sappiano

Listen to track

Dire (to say)

(tu) di'

(Lei) dica

(noi) diciamo

(voi) dite

(Loro) dicano

Listen to track 292

Stare (to stay)

(tu) stai / sta'

(Lei) stia

(noi) stiamo

(voi) state

(Loro) stiano

Listen to track 293

Venire (to come)

(tu) vieni

(Lei) venga

(noi) veniamo

(voi) venite

(Loro) vengano

Listen to track 294

Tenere (to hold)

(tu) tieni

(Lei) tenga

(noi) teniamo

(voi) tenete

(Loro) tengano

Imperative of reflexive verbs

To form the imperative of reflexive verbs, like *alzarsi* (to get up), *preoccuparsi* (to worry) and *svegliarsi* (to wake up), you have to add the same imperative endings listed above. The only difference is the reflexive pronoun.

Look at this example:

Listen to track 295

Reflexive verb **svegliarsi** (to wake up)

(tu) sveglia**ti**

(Lei) **si** svegli

(noi) svegliamo**ci**

(voi) svegliate**vi**

(Loro) **si** sveglino

As you can see, the reflexive pronoun is joined to the verb in the "tu", "noi" and "voi" forms and the result is written as a single word. When addressing someone with "Lei" and "Loro", the reflexive pronouns always come before the verb.

Let's see another example:

Listen to track 296

Reflexive verb **fermarsi** (to stop)

(tu) ferma**ti** – non fermar**ti** – non **ti** fermare

(Lei) **si** fermi – non **si** fermi

(noi) fermiamo**ci** – non fermiamo**ci** – non **ci** fermiamo

(voi) fermate**vi** – non fermate**vi** – non **vi** fermate

(Loro) **si** fermino – non **si** fermino

In the negative form the reflexive pronoun can either be added to the verb or placed before it. The pronoun always precedes the verb in the formal "Lei" and "Loro" forms.

Listen to track 297

Non fermarti adesso, Massimo! – ***Non ti fermare*** adesso, Massimo! – Don't stop now, Massimo!

*Non **si fermi**, signor Verdi* – Don't stop, Mr. Verdi

Negative form of the imperativo

Lucky for you, the negative form of the Italian imperative is formed quite easily. If you are talking to one person informally, just put the negation **non** (not) in front of the verb in the infinitive form.

Here are some examples:

Listen to track 298

Non piangere – Don't cry

***Non** mi **interrompere** quando parlo* – Don't interrupt me when I'm talking

***Non** ti **azzardare** a toccarmi* – Don't touch me

For all the other persons, just add the negation **non** (not) in front of the "Lei", "noi, "voi" and "Loro" conjugation of the verb in the *imperativo*.

***Non** lo **dica** neanche per scherzo, signor Bianchi!* – Don't even say it as a joke, Mr. Bianchi!

*Ragazzi, **non abbassiamoci** al loro livello* – Let's not lower ourselves to their level, guys

***Non dite** sciocchezze!* – Don't talk nonsense!

***Non se ne vadano**, signori* – Don't leave, gentlemen

Where do direct and indirect object pronouns go?

In Italian, direct and indirect object pronouns come after the ***imperativo informale*** in the "tu" and "voi" forms, and join with the verb to make a single word.

Listen to track 299

*Ha telefonato il commercialista, **richiamalo**!* – The accountant called, call him back!

Ascoltatemi! – Listen to me, guys!

BEWARE: with monosyllabic verbs in the *imperativo*, the pronoun doubles the last consonant. "Mi" becomes **-mmi**, "ti" becomes **-tti** and so on.

Here are some examples:

***Dimmi** l'ora, per piacere* – Tell me the time, please

***Fatti** sentire* – Get in touch!

*Vai dalla mamma e **dalle** un bacio!* – Go to mom and give her a kiss!

***Fallo** subito!* – Do it now!

Listen to track 300

When the pronouns "mi", "ti", "ci" and "vi" are followed by an additional pronoun, they become:

- **me-**
- **te-**
- **ce-**
- **ve-**

"Gli" and "le" become **glie-**.

Dammeli! – Give them to me

Diglielo – Say it to her / Tell her

As you may have noticed from previous examples, direct and indirect object pronouns come after the "noi" form of the Italian *imperativo*, joining onto it to make a single word.

***Scopriamolo** insieme!* – Let's find out together!

*Al nonno piacerebbe molto questo dipinto, **regaliamoglielo**!* – Grandpa would love this artwork, let's give it to him

Unlike with the other command forms, direct and indirect object pronouns always come before the "Lei" form and the polite plural form, and don't join onto the verbs.

*Buongiorno, signora. Mi **dica*** – Good morning, Ma'am. Tell me

*Mi **dia** sei melograni, per favore* – Give me six pomegranates, please

*Non lo **faccia**, signore* – Don't do it, sir

*Ne **prendano** una fetta, signori!* – Take a slice, gentlemen!

Courtesy words to use with the imperativo

Using the *imperativo* is a very direct way to give orders and puts you at risk of sounding rude. In order to express a request in a less strong and more polite way, we suggest using courtesy words, such as:

Listen to track 301

Per favore – Please

Per piacere – Please

Per cortesia – Please

Cortesemente – Please

Se non ti / Le / vi dispiace – If you don't mind

Ti / Le / vi dispiace…? – Do you mind …?

Ti / La / vi prego… – I beg you to…

Let's see some examples:

Listen to track 302

Abbassa la voce! – Lower your voice!

Abbassa la voce, per favore – Lower your voice, please

Ti dispiace abbassare la voce? – Do you mind lowering your voice?

Spenga la luce! – Turn off the light!

Spenga la luce, per piacere – Turn off the light, please

Spenga la luce, se non Le dispiace – Turn off the light, if you don't mind

To sum up…

Listen to track 303

- The Italian imperative is used to give orders, express exhortations, make direct suggestions and give advice, indications and instructions.

Scarica l'app gratuitamente – Download the app for free

- There are formal and informal forms of the Italian *imperativo*.

Fai in fretta, Damiano – Hurry up, Damiano

Faccia attenzione, signora – Be careful, Ma'am

- The -iamo form corresponds pretty neatly to "let's" in English.

Aspettiamo qui! – Let's wait here!

Workbook Lesson 18. The Imperative

Exercise 18.1: Translate the following sentences from Italian into English:

Italian	English
1. Spegni la luce!	
2. Non lasciare la porta aperta!	
3. Non parlare mentre mangi!	
4. Chiama tua mamma!	
5. Metti in ordine la tua stanza!	

Exercise 18.2: Complete the following sentences with the verbs in the imperative mood:

1. (voi) (lasciare) ____in pace quel gatto! (Leave that cat alone!)

2. (voi) (stare) ____zitti! (Shut up!)

3. (tu) Non (correre) ____! (Don't run!)

4. (voi) Non (toccare) ____ le mie cose! (Don't touch my things!)

5. (tu) (mettere) ____ la giacca! (Put on your jacket!)

Exercise 18.3: Tick the right answer:

1. ____ in pace! (Leave me alone!)

   1) Lasciare   2) Lasciami   3) Lascia

2. Non ____ la carne! (Don't burn the meat!)

   1) brucia   2) bruciato   3) bruciare

3. Non ____ troppo! (Don't think about it too much!)

   1) pensarci   2) pensare   3) pensiamo

4. ____ la medicina! (Take the medicine!)

   1) prendere   2) prendiamo   3) prendi

5. Non ____! (Do not shout!)

   1) urla   2) urlate   3) urlo

Exercise 18.4: Translate these sentences from English into Italian:

English	Italian
1. Do me a favor!	
2. Don't sit down!	
3. Water the plants!	
4. Add more sugar!	
5. Tell me the truth!	

Exercise 18.5: Change these sentences into their singular form:

Plural	Singular
1. Non mangiate troppi dolci! (Don't eat too many sweets!)	
2. Non guidate ubriachi! (Don't drive drunk!)	
3. Non credeteci! (Don't believe it!)	
4. Riflettete prima di parlare! (Think before you speak!)	
5. Mettetevi a dieta! (Go on a diet!)	

Answers:

Exercise 18.1:

1. Turn off the light!
2. Don't leave the door open!
3. Don't talk while you're eating!
4. Call your mom!
5. Put your room in order!

Exercise 18.2:

1. Lasciate in pace quel gatto!
2. State zitti!
3. Non correre!
4. Non toccate le mie cose!
5. Metti la giacca!

Exercise 18.3:

1) lasciami
2) bruciare
3) pensarci
4) prendi
5) urlate

Exercise 18.4:

1. Fammi/fatemi un favore!
2. Non sederti/sedetevi!
3. Annaffiate/annaffia le piante!

4. Metti/mettete più zucchero!

5. Ditemi/dimmi la verità!

Exercise 18.5:

1. Non mangiare troppi dolci!

2. Non guidare ubriaco!

3. Non crederci!

4. Rifletti prima di parlare!

5. Mettiti a dieta!

LESSON 19: IMPERFETTO

Most Italian language learners are a little intimidated by the **_imperfetto_**, one of the main past tenses in Italian. The **imperfect tense** (_imperfetto_) refers to both distant and recent past occurrences that happened on a regular basis.

In this lesson, we will show you how to use the _imperfetto_ tense and will give you some tips to help you avoid some common pitfalls. Its rules are pretty straightforward and once you learn them, it will begin to come naturally.

Using the imperfetto

Listen to track 304

The **imperfect tense** in Italian can be a little tricky at first, because it doesn't have an exact equivalent in English.

The **_imperfetto_** is a past tense used to:

- talk about repeated or habitual actions in the past:

Ogni giovedì ci incontravamo al bar – We used to meet at the bar every Thursday (the action happened continually in the past)

Quando Virginia era piccola, si svegliava alle 7:30 per andare a scuola – When Virginia was a kid, she used to wake up at 7:30 a.m. to go to school (a habitual action in the past)

- describe a situation in the past:

La strada non era asfaltata – The road wasn't paved

La città era deserta – The city was empty

Quando andavo a scuola odiavo la matematica – When I was at school, I used to hate maths

- talk about one's age at a point in the past:

Nel 2000, Alessia aveva 16 anni – In 2000, Alessia was 16 years old

- describe time or weather in the past:

C'era il sole ma faceva freddo – It was sunny but cold

Erano le sette – It was seven o'clock

- describe the ongoing state of objects, places and people in the past:

Listen to track 305

Da piccola, Sabrina aveva i capelli ricci – When she was little, Sabrina used to have curly hair (you are talking about how she looked in the past)

Caterina era una donna coraggiosa – Caterina was a brave woman

- express an emotional or physical state that occurred in the past, and is now over:

Ieri avevo mal di testa – I had a headache yesterday

Eravamo così felici – We were so happy

- talk about two or more events that happened simultaneously in the past:

Mentre studiavo in camera mia, Tommaso guardava la televisione (parallel activities) – While I was studying in my room, Tommaso was watching TV

- describe an action that was taking place when something else happened:

Mentre passeggiavo nel parco, ho visto uno scoiattolo – While I was having a stroll in the park, I saw a squirrel (you are talking about what you were doing when something else occurred)

As you can see, that's a lot of uses!

How to Construct the Italian imperfetto

Lucky for you, the ***imperfetto*** is one of the most stable Italian tenses and is formed by adding the same endings to all three verb types.

The *imperfetto* is formed by taking the *-re* off the end of the infinitive and replacing it with:

- *-vo* for "I"
- *-vi* for "you"
- *-va* for "he" / "she" / "it"
- *-vamo* for "we"
- *-vate* for "y'all"
- *-vano* for "they"

That's it! This works with all regular verbs. As you might have noticed, the characteristic letter of the *imperfetto* tense is the letter "v":

- Parla**vo** (I spoke or used to speak)
- Legge**vo** (I read or used to read)
- Dormi**vo** (I slept or used to sleep)

Once you've learnt one set of endings, it's easy to learn the subsequent two because they all follow a similar pattern.

Listen to track 306

Parlare

Io parlavo - I spoke or used to speak

Tu parlavi - You spoke or used to speak

Lui/lei parlava - He/She/It spoke or used to speak

Noi parlavamo - We spoke or used to speak

Voi parlavate - Y'all spoke or used to speak

Loro parlavano - They spoke or used to speak

Listen to track 307

Leggere

Io leggevo - I read or used to read

Tu leggevi - You read or used to read

Lui/lei leggeva - He/She/It read or used to read

Noi leggevamo - We read or used to read

Voi leggevate - Y'all read or used to read

Loro leggevano - They read or used to read

Listen to track 308

Dormire

Io dormivo - I slept or used to sleep

Tu dormivi - You slept or used to sleep

Lui/lei dormiva - He/She/It slept or used to sleep

Noi dormivamo - We slept or used to sleep

Voi dormivate - Y'all slept or used to sleep

Loro dormivano - They slept or used to sleep

There are some **irregular verbs** in the imperfect form. First, we'll look at the imperfect conjugations of ***essere*** (to be):

Listen to track 309

Io ero

Tu eri

Lui/lei era

Noi eravamo

Voi eravate

Loro erano

Aside from the Italian verb "essere", the other irregular verbs to beware of in the imperfect form are those that end in *-orre, -urre* and *-arre*, such as:

Listen to track 310

- porre (to put, to place);
- tradurre (to translate);
- trarre (to pull, to draw);

and also:

- fare (to make, to do);
- dire (to say, to tell);
- bere (to drink).

While the endings are similar, the stem used is not as easy to form. Fortunately, they tend to be the same troublesome verbs that are also irregular in other tenses in Italian, so they are easy to spot. Let's go over some of the most common **irregular verbs in the imperfect form**:

Listen to track 311

Fare

Io facevo

Tu facevi

Lui/lei faceva

Noi facevamo

Voi facevate

Loro facevano

Listen to track 312
Dire

Io dicevo

Tu dicevi

Lui/lei diceva

Noi dicevamo

Voi dicevate

Loro dicevano

Listen to track 313
Bere

Io bevevo

Tu bevevi

Lui/lei beveva

Noi bevevamo

Voi bevevate

Loro bevevano

Listen to track 314
Porre

Io ponevo

Tu ponevi

Lui/lei poneva

Noi ponevamo

Voi ponevate

Loro ponevano

Listen to track 315
Tradurre

Io traducevo

Tu traducevi

Lui/lei traduceva

Noi traducevamo

Voi traducevate

Loro traducevano

Listen to track 316

Trarre

Io traevo

Tu traevi

Lui/lei traeva

Noi traevamo

Voi traevate

Loro traevano

We recommend committing those to memory.

Fortunately, the Italian verb "**avere**" is regular in the imperfect tense:

Listen to track 317

Avere

Io avevo

Tu avevi

Lui/lei aveva

Noi avevamo

Voi avevate

Loro avevano

Which phrases are typically used with the Italian imperfect tense?

Here is a list of adverbial expressions that are usually used with the *imperfetto* in Italian:

Listen to track 318

A volte – at times

Continuamente – continuously / continually

Giorno dopo giorno – day in, day out

Mentre – while / as

Ogni tanto – every so often

Sempre – always

Spesso – often

Tutti i giorni – every day

Imperfetto or passato prossimo?

Confused by the past tenses in Italian? Understanding when to use the *imperfetto* over the *passato prossimo* can be tough at first, and most English speakers who decide to learn Italian struggle with this. Here are some tips to help you with the use of these two past tenses.

As mentioned previously, the *imperfetto* describes repeated or habitual actions in the past as well as the characteristics and frequency of past situations.

Listen to track 319

L'estate scorsa andavo in piscina ogni domenica – Last summer, I used to go to the pool every Sunday

A 11 anni Cinzia aveva i capelli lunghissimi – When Cinzia was 11, she had very long hair

On the other hand, the *passato prossimo* refers to events which are clearly defined in time and describes things that happened only once in the recent past.

Due anni fa siamo andati a Firenze – We went to Florence two years ago (we didn't keep on going to Florence)

Events that happened long ago may be expressed using the *passato prossimo* when they still have an active relationship to the present.

If you are talking about an action in the past that happened at the same time as something else, then you use both.

Mentre andavo a scuola ho incontrato Francesca – While I was going to school, I met Francesca

Colloquial uses of the imperfetto

There are colloquial uses of the *imperfetto* which are well worth learning. It is quite common in colloquial speech to skip complicated grammar structures and use the imperfect tense instead.

In spoken everyday language, the *imperfetto* is commonly used instead of the conditional and past subjunctive, which take longer to say. So, the *imperfetto* has become an acceptable alternative in **casual, informal conversation**. It is crucial for foreigners to learn its colloquial uses to understand what people are talking about.

The following example is a classic **use of the *imperfetto* in place of a subjunctive tense**, which would have been grammatically correct.

Listen to track 320

Se sapevo che eri vegetariana, non preparavo l'arrosto (only acceptable in spoken Italian) – Had I known you were a vegetarian, I wouldn't have made the roast.

The above is considered incorrect but it is what most native Italian speakers would actually say when speaking at a **colloquial and informal level**. The technically correct but rather complex version is appropriate in formal communication and written Italian:

Se avessi saputo che eri vegetariana, non avrei preparato l'arrosto.

Here are other examples:

Potevate avvisarmi che arrivavate in ritardo (informal communication)

Avreste potuto avvisarmi che sareste arrivati in ritardo (formal communication)

You guys could have told me that you were late.

Se Fabio mi mandava una mail, rispondevo subito (informal communication)

Se Fabio mi avesse inviato una mail, avrei risposto subito (formal communication)

If Fabio had sent me an email, I would have replied right away.

The imperfect tense is also used **in place of the conditional** to make a request sound less imperative.

Listen to track 321

Buongiorno, volevo un caffè per favore (*volevo* instead of *vorrei*) – Good morning, I'd like a coffee please.

Volevo prenotare una camera per due notti (*volevo* instead of *vorrei*) – I'd like to book a room for two nights.

How to translate the *imperfetto* into English

English and Italian have different past tenses and there is no exact one-to-one correspondence between how they are used. The ***imperfetto*** corresponds roughly to "used to" or the past continuous tense. The most similar phrasing you have in English is perhaps the expression "used to," but it is not a direct translation.

Widely used both in the spoken and written language, the *imperfetto* in Italian may need to be translated with:

- the past continuous tense:

Listen to track 322

Pioveva forte – It was raining heavily

- "used to":

Andavo a trovare Emanuele ogni giorno – I used to visit Emanuele every single day

- the simple past tense:

Marta faceva la babysitter dopo la scuola – Marta worked as a babysitter after school (this was a regular happening)

- "would":

Silvia lo seguiva dovunque andasse – Silvia would follow him everywhere

How to pronounce verbs in the imperfect form

Lots of students get tripped up on which syllable to stress in Italian imperfect verbs.

You should stress the penultimate syllable on *imperfetto* verb conjugations, except in the **third person plural** (*loro*), when, as in the present, the stress falls on the third to last syllable (antepenultimate).

Listen to track 323

*Andrea e Adele and**a**vano al cinema ogni mercoledì sera* – Andrea and Adele used to go to the cinema every Wednesday evening

This might sound a bit weird to you at first but this rhythm will come to feel natural with a bit of practice.

To sum up...

- The imperfect tense is used for situations and events that continued for some time in the past.
- It is used to describe things that happened continuously in the past on a regular basis, kind of like the expression "used to" in English:

Listen to track 324

Quando ero in Sicilia parlavo italiano ogni giorno – When I was in Sicily, I used to speak Italian every day

Quando ero piccolo, mangiavo la pasta tutti i giorni – When I was a kid, I used to eat pasta every day

- The verb forms are made by removing the letters -re of the infinitive and simply adding the endings -vo, -vi, -va, -vamo, -vate and -vano. There are a few irregular forms.

- The Italian *imperfetto* has various ways of being translated into English.

Developing an understanding for which tense to use in a sentence is not something you can learn by simply studying grammar rules. It will take time and requires you to spend a lot of time with the language until you develop a natural feel for the correct tense form to use.

Read and listen to Italian as much as you can to speed up this process. The more you expose yourself to Italian, the more natural this and other grammatical structures will become for you.

Workbook Lesson 19. Imperfect Tenses

Exercise 19.1: Conjugate the verbs in their imperfetto form

	Mangiare	Credere	Dormire
Io	Mangiavo		
Tu		Credevi	
Lui/Lei			
Noi			
Voi			
Loro			Dormivano

Exercise 19.2: Complete the sentences with the verb "essere" in its imperfetto form

1. Ieri non ___ in casa, studiavo in biblioteca.
2. Da bambino Matteo ___ una vera peste!
3. Noi _____ affamati, ma la mamma voleva continuare lo shopping.
4. Ieri né Luca né Andrea ____ alla partita.
5. ____ davvero tu l'altro giorno al lago?

Exercise 19.3: Choose the right option

1. Non vedevo/vedevi l'ora di incontrarti!
2. Emma volevi/voleva parlarti.
3. Anna e Rita vivevamo/vivevano insieme all'università.
4. Voi da bambini giocavate/giocavamo insieme?
5. Lei eri/era stanca ma noi eravate/eravamo ancora pieni di energie.
6. Mattia da bambino odiavi/odiava le verdure.

Exercise 19.4: Translate the following sentences containing irregular verbs into Italian

English	Italian
When I was in high school I used to translate Latin.	
They used to drink a lot of beer in their teenage years.	
My grandma always used to say: beware of strangers!	
We made a big effort back in middle school.	
While coming here, I saw a person saying weird things.	

Exercise 19.5: Change the following present tense sentences into the imperfetto

Present Tense	Imperfetto
Marco è famoso anche in America.	
Oggi è davvero una bella giornata.	
Ecco il programma che guardo sempre.	
I miei gatti sanno sempre dove nascondo il loro cibo.	
Ma voi non avete qualcosa da fare?	

Answers:

Exercise 19.1:

	Mangiare	Credere	Dormire
Io	Mangiavo	Credevo	Dormivo
Tu	Mangiavi	Credevi	Dormivi
Lui/Lei	Mangiava	Credeva	Dormiva
Noi	Mangiavamo	Credevamo	Dormivamo
Voi	Mangiavate	Credevate	Dormivate
Loro	Mangiavano	Credevano	Dormivano

Exercise 19.2:

1. ero; 2. era; 3. eravamo; 4. erano; 5. eri

Exercise 19.3:

1. vedevo; 2. voleva; 3. vivevano; 4. giocavate; 5. era; eravamo; 6. odiava

Exercise 19.4:

1. Quando ero al liceo traducevo il Latino.
2. Bevevano un sacco di birra quand'erano adolescenti.
3. Mia nonna diceva sempre: stai attento agli sconosciuti!

4. Facevamo un sacco di sforzi ai tempi delle medie.
5. Mentre venivo qui, ho visto una persona che diceva cose strane.

Exercise 19.5:

1. Marco era famoso anche in America.
2. Ieri era davvero una bella giornata.
3. Ecco il programma che guardavo sempre.
4. I miei gatti sapevano sempre dove nascondevo il loro cibo.
5. Ma voi non avevate qualcosa da fare?

LESSON 20: HOW TO USE THE ITALIAN VERB *STARE* IN THE PRESENT PROGRESSIVE

Ciao! In this lesson, we will be looking at what the Italian **present progressive** (*presente progressivo*) is and how to use it. We will give you the essential grammar know-how you need to form this useful tense and use it in real-world speech and writing. Luckily, it isn't a terribly tricky element of Italian grammar.

Let's get right into it!

Using the Italian present progressive

The Italian **presente progressivo**, also known as the present continuous, is used to:

- talk about actions that are happening right as you speak:

Listen to track 325

Fai silenzio, per favore! **Sto ascoltando** *un podcast* – Be silent, please! I'm listening to a podcast (I am listening to a podcast right now as I am speaking)

Guarda! Il treno **sta partendo***!* – Look! The train is leaving! (the train is leaving right now as I am speaking)

Un attimo, **mi sto allacciando** *le scarpe* – Wait a minute, I'm tying my shoe laces

Abbassa la voce! I bambini **stanno dormendo** – Please be quiet, the children **are sleeping**

- express what someone is in the process of doing at this moment:

Listen to track 326

Cosa **stai facendo? Sto guardando** *il telegiornale* – What are you doing? I'm watching the news on TV

A cosa **stai pensando***?* – What are you thinking about?

Dove **state andando***, ragazzi? Stiamo andando in discoteca* – Where are you going, guys? We are going to the club

Viviana **sta passando** *un brutto periodo* – Viviana is going through a hard time

- indicate that something is changing, growing or developing:

Listen to track 327

Il clima **sta cambiando** *rapidamente* – The climate is changing rapidly

I tempi **stanno cambiando**, *e non per il meglio* – Times are changing and not for the better

Sento che **sta nascendo** *qualcosa di bello tra di noi* – I feel that something beautiful is developing between us

Questo ematoma **sta crescendo** *a vista d'occhio* – This lump on my head is getting bigger by the second

• express gradual processes of change:

Listen to track 328

Mi congratulo con te, Ivana, il tuo italiano **sta migliorando** *giorno per giorno* – Congratulations, Ivana, your Italian is improving day by day

What's the difference between Italian and English present continuous?

Listen to track 329

The **Italian** *presente progressivo* corresponds to the **English present continuous**, made from the present tense of the verb to be (*essere*) and the present participle of the verb describing the action, with an -ing ending. In Italian, the present progressive is used less frequently than in English, but it is still really common.

There are some important differences between the Italian and English present continuous tenses, though. First of all, you cannot use the Italian *presente progressivo* to talk about **future plans** or arrangements in the way you use the present continuous in English. For example:

I'm leaving tomorrow → **Partirò** *domani /* **Parto** *domani*

Lisa is going to a new school next term → *Lisa* **andrà** *in un'altra scuola l'anno prossimo / Lisa* **va** *in un'altra scuola l'anno prossimo*

I'm holidaying in Greece next summer → *Quest'estate* **andrò** *in vacanza in Grecia / Quest'estate* **vado** *in vacanza in Grecia*

In Italian you need to use the simple future tense (*futuro semplice*) or the present tense to talk about the future. It doesn't matter how awkward it sounds to you, you cannot say "*sto partendo domani*", "*Lisa sta andando in un'altra scuola l'anno prossimo*" or "*sto andando in vacanza in Grecia quest'estate*". Ugh, it is ungrammatical and sounds so strange.

As mentioned previously, in Italian the present progressive tense only refers to present-time actions in progress. In other words, it is a way to convey any action, event or condition that is happening right now, at this very minute. In Italian this tense is known as the "progressive" because it is used to **emphasize that an action is in progress as you speak**. For example:

Listen to track 330

*Cesare **sta facendo** la doccia* – Cesare is taking a shower

***Sto cercando** il mio passaporto* – I'm looking for my passport

***Stai cercando** lavoro?* – Are you looking for a job?

*Luana **sta facendo** una foto* – Luana is taking a photo

In many situations in which English uses the present continuous, we simply use the present tense in Italian. To talk about fixed habits and ongoing actions, always use the present simple tense. For example:

Listen to track 331

*Vittorio **studia** medicina all'università di Bologna* – Vittorio is studying medicine at the University of Bologna

***Lavori** ancora da McDonald's?* – Are you still working at McDonald's?

The present progressive is to be used only to refer to actions that are taking place at the time of speaking:

Sto uscendo – I'm leaving, I'm on my way out

Stanno arrivando! – They're coming!

Stai scherzando? – Are you joking?

*Sbrigati! Ti **stiamo aspettando*** – Hurry up! We are all waiting for you

*Sabrina **sta ridendo** a crepapelle* – Sabrina is laughing out loud

As you can see, the Italian *presente progressivo* is much more limited in its uses than the English present continuous tense.

Constructing the Italian present progressive

As you may have noticed from the above examples, the **Italian present progressive** is a compound tense, which means that it is made up of two separate parts.

The *presente progressivo* in Italian is formed by the present tense of the verb **stare** (to stay) and the gerund of the verb expressing the action. In this verbal construction, the verb *stare* loses its original meaning and works something like the English auxiliary verb *to be* (essere) in the present continuous.

Listen to track 332

Stare is an intransitive and irregular verb, which means that it doesn't follow the typical **-are** verb ending pattern. Its conjugation is irregular:

(io) **sto** – I am

(tu) **stai** – you are

(lui/lei) **sta** – he/she is

(noi) **stiamo** – we are

(voi) **state** – y'all are

(loro) **stanno** – they are

The present progressive is one of the simplest tenses to form and use. To make a full phrase, all you have to do is combine the conjugated form of *stare* with the gerund of the main verb. For example:

Listen to track 333

(io) sto aspettando – I am waiting

(lui) sta scrivendo – He is writing

(loro) stanno parlando – They are talking

You don't necessarily need to state the subject pronoun if it is obvious from the ending of the conjugated verb.

Listen to track 334

Reflexive verbs, like divertirsi (to have fun), vestirsi (to get dressed), prepararsi (to get ready), addormentarsi (to fall asleep), svegliarsi (to wake up), alzarsi (to get up), annoiarsi (to get bored), perdersi (to get lost) e ricordarsi (to remember), can have a progressive form.

When using the present progressive with a personal pronoun, it can either come before **stare** or be joined onto the gerund. Let's look at a few examples:

Listen to track 335

Marisa e Chiara **si stanno divertendo** / *Marisa e Chiara* **stanno divertendosi** – Marisa and Chiara are having fun

Stefania **si sta annoiando** / *Stafania* **sta annoiandosi** – Stefania is getting bored

Danilo **si sta vestendo** / *Danilo* **sta vestendosi** – Danilo is getting dressed

Which one is more common? The first one.

How to form the Italian gerund

The **gerund** (*gerundio*) corresponds to the -ing form of the verb in English. Lucky for you, it is formed quite easily.

To form the gerund of regular verbs ending in -**are**, all you have to do is remove the infinitive ending to find the stem of the verb and add -**ando**. For example:

Listen to track 336

Andare (to go) → **andando** (going)

Guardare (to watch, to look at) → **guardando** (watching, looking at)

Tornare (to return, to go back) → **tornando** (returning, going back)

Lavorare (to work) → **lavorando** (working)

Camminare (to walk, to stroll) → **camminando** (walking, strolling)

Listen to track 337

Let's take a look at the verb *aspettare* (to wait) in the present progressive.

Aspettare

(io) sto aspettando – I am waiting

(tu) stai aspettando – You are waiting

(lui/lei) sta aspettando – He/she is waiting

(noi) stiamo aspettando – We are waiting

(voi) state aspettando – Y'all are waiting

(loro) stanno aspettando – They are waiting

To form the gerund of regular verbs ending in -**ere**, remove the infinitive ending to find the stem of the verb and add -**endo**. For example:

Listen to track 338

Prendere (to take, to catch) → **prendendo** (taking, catching)

Vendere (to sell) → **vendendo** (selling)

Chiedere (to ask) → **chiedendo** (asking)

Scendere (to get off, to get out) → **scendendo** (getting off, getting out)

Fortunately, the Italian verbs essere (to be) and avere (to have) are regular in the gerund.

Essere (to be) → **essendo** (being)

Avere (to have) → **avendo** (having)

Let's take a look at the verb *chiedere* (to ask) in the present progressive:

Listen to track 339
Chiedere

(io) sto chiedendo – I am asking

(tu) stai chiedendo – You are asking

(lui/lei) sta chiedendo – He/she is asking

(noi) stiamo chiedendo – We are asking

(voi) state chiedendo – Y'all are asking

(loro) stanno chiedendo – They are asking

To form the gerund of regular verbs ending in **-ire**, remove the infinitive ending to find the stem of the verb and add **-endo**. For example:

Listen to track 340

Partire (to leave) → **partendo** (leaving)

Dormire (to sleep) → **dormendo** (sleeping)

Sentire (to hear, to feel) → **sentendo** (hearing, feeling)

Finire (to finish) → **finendo** (finishing)

Let's take a look at the verb *pulire* (to clean) in the present progressive:

Listen to track 341
Pulire

(io) sto pulendo – I am cleaning

(tu) stai pulendo – You are cleaning

(lui/lei) sta pulendo – He/she is cleaning

(noi) stiamo pulendo – We are cleaning

(voi) state pulendo – Y'all are cleaning

(loro) stanno pulendo – They are cleaning

Easy, huh? As you can see, all you have to remember is:

- *-are* → **-ando**
- *-ere* and *-ire* → **-endo**

And there's good news. These forms are invariable and never change to agree with the subject of the sentence. The Italian gerund is always the same.

Irregular verbs in the gerund

There are some irregular forms, which have to be committed to memory. Here is a list:

Listen to track 342

Fare (to do, to make) → **facendo** (doing, making)

Dire (to say) → **dicendo** (saying)

Bere (to drink) → **bevendo** (drinking)

Nuocere (to harm, to damage) → **nocendo/ nuocendo** (harming, damaging)

Trarre (to pull) → **traendo** (pulling)

Porre (to put, to place) → **ponendo** (putting, placing)

Addurre (to advance) → **adducendo** (advancing)

Attrarre (to attract) → **attraendo** (attracting)

Comporre (to compose) → **componendo** (composing)

Condurre (to lead) → **conducendo** (leading)

Contrarre (to contract) → **contraendo** (contracting)

Distrarre (to distract) → **distraendo** (distracting)

Estrarre (to extract) → **estraendo** (extracting)

Indurre (to induce) → **inducendo** (inducing)

Produrre (to produce) → **producendo** (producing)

Proporre (to propose) → **proponendo** (proposing)

Ridurre (to reduce) → **riducendo** (reducing)

Supporre (to suppose) → **supponendo** (supposing)

Sottrarre (to subtract) → **sottraendo** (subtracting)

Tradurre (to translate) → **traducendo** (translating)

Which phrases are typically used with the present progressive?

Here is a list of marker words that are usually used with the **present progressive** to talk about actions taking place at the moment of speaking:

Listen to track 343

- **Ora** – now, just now

Elena sta parlando ora al telefono con il nuovo direttore del personale – Elena is talking on the phone with the new personnel manager now

- **Adesso** – right now

Sto rileggendo l'articolo proprio adesso – I'm reading the article again right now

- **In questo momento** – at the (present) moment

Aurora sta facendo i compiti in questo momento – Aurora is doing her homework right now

- **Guarda!** – Look!

Guarda! Sta nevicando – Look! It's snowing

Here are marker words that are usually used with the ***presente progressivo*** to describe something changing or developing:

Listen to track 344

- **Gradualmente, progressivamente** – gradually, progressively

Le condizioni di salute della signora Bernabini **stanno** *gradualmente* **migliorando** – Mrs Bernabini's health is gradually improving

- **Costantemente** – steadily

L'universo **si sta** *costantemente* **espandendo** – The universe is steadily expanding

- **Giorno per giorno** – day by day

La clientela **sta crescendo** *giorno per giorno* – The clientele is growing day by day

To sum up...

- To make the present progressive, use the present tense of the verb *stare* and the gerund of the verb describing the action.
- Instead of the auxiliary verb *essere* (to be), Italian uses the verb *stare* (to stay) followed by the gerund of the main verb.
- To form the gerund, add **-ando** to the stem of verbs whose infinitive ends in **-are,** and **-endo** to the stem of verbs whose infinitive ends in **-ere** and **-ire**. There are only two forms of gerund in Italian.
- Only use the present progressive in Italian to explain what's going on in the here-and-now.
- You can't use the *presente progressivo* to talk about the future in Italian.

There you have it! Ready to roll out the Italian **present progressive** on your own? Practice this tense by role-playing situations and it will start coming naturally to you. *A presto!*

Workbook Lesson 20. How to Use the Italian Verb Stare in the Present Progressive

Exercise 20.1: Translate the following sentences into Italian

English	Italian
1. Shhh! The baby is sleeping!	
2. The book I'm reading is very interesting.	
3. What's the brand of the sweater you're wearing?	
4. Where are you? I've been waiting for hours!	
5. Emma is eating a lot today.	

Exercise 20.2: Choose the right option

1. Marco non risponde al telefono perché ha/sta facendo la doccia.

2. A scuola noi sto/stiamo studiando il passato prossimo in italiano.

3. Non parlare con me perché stai/sto leggendo!

4. Oggi non esco perché è/sta nevicando.

5. Tu e Rita state/siete facendo tardi!

Exercise 20.3: Complete with the present progressive

1. In questo momento *(io, vedere)* _____un film.

2. Marica e Antonio *(loro, andare)* _____al cinema.

3. Luca, tu *(tu, sprecare)* _____il tuo tempo!

4. Io e Francesca *(noi, pulire)* _____il garage.

5. Caro Marco, tu e Michele *(voi, studiare)* _____ molto bene.

6. Marta *(lei, scrivere)* _____una lunga lettera.

Exercise 20.4: Choose the right option

1. Marina ha/sta mettendo la torta nel forno.

2. La dottoressa arriva subito: sta/è facendo una telefonata ed è subito da voi.

3. - Sei arrivato? - Arrivo tra 5 minuti: sto/sono scendendo dal treno.

4. Io ho/sto navigando in Internet.

5. Noi abbiamo/stiamo prenotando l'hotel su "Booking.com".

Exercise 20.5: Correct the mistakes

1. Non ho ancora finito il lavoro: ho scrivendo la fine della storia.
2. Il dottor Rossi non può rispondere: è parlando con un cliente.
3. Che fai? – Sono leggendo un libro molto difficile ma interessante.
4. Mio figlio è studiando molto perché la settimana prossima ha un esame.
5. Siamo uscendo. Puoi chiamare ancora una volta più tardi?

Answers:

Exercise 20.1:

1. Shhh! Il bambino sta dormendo!
2. Il libro che sto leggendo è davvero interessante.
3. Di che marca è la felpa che stai indossando?
4. Dove sei? Ti sto aspettando da ore!
5. Emma sta mangiando un sacco oggi.

Exercise 20.2:

1. sta; 2. stiamo; 3. sto; 4. sta; 5. state

Exercise 20.3:

1. sto vedendo
2. stanno andando
3. stai sprecando
4. stiamo pulendo
5. state studiando
6. sta scrivendo

Exercise 20.4:

1. sta; 2. sta; 3. sto; 4. sto; 5. stiamo

Exercise 20.5:

1. Non ho ancora finito il lavoro: **sto** scrivendo la fine della storia.
2. Il dottor Rossi non può rispondere: **sta** parlando con un cliente.
3. Che fai? – **Sto** leggendo un libro molto difficile ma interessante.
4. Mio figlio **sta** studiando molto perché la settimana prossima ha un esame.
5. **Stiamo** uscendo. Puoi chiamare ancora una volta più tardi?

LESSON 21: THE ITALIAN PRONOUNS NE AND CI

The tiny words **ne** and **ci** are two useful yet extremely confusing pronouns in Italian. They sneak in here and there and vex even the most diligent English-speaking Italian learners. And, to make matters worse, in English there are no single word equivalents to *ne* and *ci*.

Fear not: here is a guide to help you understand and use these useful pronominal particles. Sound good? Ok, let's get started!

Round 1: *Ne*

Listen to track 345

Technically called a pronominal particle, **ne** is used in lots of different scenarios in Italian and has several meanings. Like all pronouns, it is there to make it possible for you to have a conversation without constantly repeating what you are talking about.

Ne can mean:

- **of it, of which, of them**

*Che **ne** pensi?* – What do you think **of it**?

***Ne** siamo consci* – We are aware **of it**

- **of this, of that, of these, of those**

*Sono sazio, non **ne** voglio più* – I'm full, I don't want any more **of this**

*Quanti **ne** vuole, signora?* – How many (of these) do you want?

*Basta, **ne** ho abbastanza* – Stop! I've had enough

- **about it, about him, about her, about them**

*Cosa **ne** dici?* – What do you say **about it**?

*Parliamo**ne**!* – Let's talk **about it**!

***Ne** sono molto contenta* – I'm very happy **about it**

***Ne** sei veramente sicuro?* – Are you really sure **of it**?

*L'amministratore **ne** ha parlato ampiamente durante l'assemblea* – The condominium manager talked extensively **about it** at the meeting

Listen to track 346

- **some, any**

Vuoi altri spaghetti, Elisabetta? **Ne** *ho, grazie* – Elisabetta, would you like some more spaghetti? I've got **some**, thanks

- **for it, for them**

Agnese si è offesa e non **ne** *capisco il motivo* – Agnese got offended and I don't understand the reason **for it**

- **from it, from them**

Abbiamo raccolto molte olive e **ne** *abbiamo estratto un ottimo olio* – We picked a lot of olives, and we extracted a really good oil from them

As you can see, **ne** can replace a noun introduced by an expression of quantity, such as a number or *molto/i/e, tanti/e, un po'* and so on.

With verbs and adjectives followed by the preposition **di** (of, about), *ne* can be used to refer to nouns that have already been mentioned. Let's look at some examples:

Listen to track 347

Alberto è partito, **ne** *sento molto la mancanza* – Alberto has gone, I really miss him

Chi parla di semiotica? **Ne** *parla Umberto Eco* – Who talks about semiotics? Umberto Eco talks about it

Hai ancora bisogno del cacciavite? No, grazie, non **ne** *ho più bisogno* – Do you need the screwdriver? No, thanks, I don't need it anymore

Where to put *ne* in a sentence

Listen to track 348

Widely used in Italian, **ne** usually comes **before the conjugated verb**.

Chiedi a Lorella, io non **ne** *so nulla* – Ask Lorella, I know nothing about it

Ne is **joined onto the verb** with the imperative and gerund. For example:

*Parla***ne** *con il medico* – Talk to your doctor about it

*Non staremmo nemmeno parlando***ne** *se avessi avuto il coraggio di dire a Sara la verità* – We wouldn't even be talking about it if you had the courage to tell Sara the truth

When **ne** comes after the infinitive, the final -e of the verb is dropped.

*Volevo parlar***ne** *con il commercialista* – I wanted to talk about it with my accountant

*Non c'è più pane, andiamo a prender***ne** *altro* – We've run out of bread, let's go buy some

Ne with compound tenses

If you need to use *ne* with a compound tense, like the present perfect (*passato prossimo*), past perfect (*trapassato prossimo*), future perfect tense (*futuro anteriore*), remember that the verb needs to agree in gender and number with the direct object. Have a look at these examples to get an idea of how it works:

Listen to track 349

Quanti paesi hai visitato in Asia? **Ne ho visitati** *tre, Vietnam, Giappone e Cina* – How many countries have you visited in Asia? I've visited three, Vietnam, Japan and China

Ne *ho prese due* – I took two (oranges)

Non me **ne** *ero accorta* - I didn't realize it

Idiomatic verbs with *ne*

Listen to track 350

You can find *ne* in a number of idiomatic verbs, such as:

- **Andarsene** – to leave

Mi mancheresti se **te ne andassi** – I will miss you if you go away

- **Farne a meno** – to do without

Non è facile **farne a meno** – It is not easy to do without it

- **Averne abbastanza** – to have enough of something

Considerami fuori, **ne ho abbastanza** – Count me out, I've had enough

- **Fregarsene** – to care nothing for, to not care at all

Il direttore **se ne frega** *dei dipendenti* – The director really doesn't care about his employees

- **Non poterne più** – to be sick of

Sarà un sollievo, **non ne posso più** – It will be a relief, I'm sick of this

- **Valerne la pena** – to be worth it

Ne è valsa la pena – It was worth it

- **Combinarne di tutti i colori** – to get up to all sorts of mischief

Greta è una bambina molto vivace e ne combina di tutti i colori ogni giorno – Greta is a lively child who gets up to all sorts of mischief every single day

Round 2: Ci

Most likely you have already seen the tricky little word **ci** in the expressions *c'è* (there is) and *ci sono* (there are). In full, *c'è* would look like *ci è*. In this case, *ci* means **there** or **here**. For example:

Listen to track 351

*Non **c'è** fretta* – There is no hurry

*Non **c'è** nessuno* – Nobody is here

*Non **ci sono** più le mezze stagioni* – There are no more middle seasons

***Ci sono** sedici alunni in quella classe* – There are sixteen students in that class

Especially when used with certain verbs followed by *a*, like *pensare a* (to think of, to think about), *credere a* (to believe in), *riuscire a* (to succeed at) and *tenere a* (to care about, to consider important), *ci* can mean:

- **it, them**

Listen to track 352

*Non **ci** credo* – I don't believe **it**

*Credi agli alieni? No, non **ci** credo* – Do you believe in aliens? No, I don't believe in **them**

*Riesci a farmi avere l'indirizzo entro le ore 18:00? Sì, **ci** riesco* – Can you send me the address by 6pm? Yes, I can do **it**

*Non **ci** capisco un bel niente* – I can't understand **it** at all

- **about it**

Listen to track 353

***Ci** penserò* – I'll think **about it**

*Non perdere quel bracciale, **ci** tengo molto* – Don't lose that bracelet, I care a lot **about it**

*Non so che far**ci*** – I don't know what to do **about it**

With verbs followed by the preposition ***in*** (in), ***da*** (to), ***a*** (to) and ***su*** (on), *ci* can be used to refer to nouns or places that have already been mentioned. For example:

Listen to track 354

Sei andato in banca? Sì, **ci** *sono andato stamattina* – Did you go to the bank? Yes, I went there this morning

Vieni alla festa domani? **Ci** *vengo eccome!* – Are you coming to the party tomorrow? Of course I'm coming!

Reflexive, direct and indirect object pronoun

Listen to track 355

Ci is also used as a reflexive, direct or indirect pronoun meaning *us* or *to us*.

Domani **ci** *dobbiamo alzare presto* – We have to get up early tomorrow

Ci *conosciamo?* – Have we met before?

Ci *vediamo domani!* – (Literally: we see each other tomorrow) See you tomorrow!

Ci *sentiamo* – We'll be in touch

Where to put *ci* in a sentence

Listen to track 356

Ci usually comes before the conjugated verb.

Sei mai stato in Italia? Sì, **ci** *vado ogni anno* – Have you ever been to Italy? Yes, I go there every year

Ci is joined onto the verb with the imperative and gerund. For example:

*Aiuta***ci** *invece di startene lì impalato!* – Help us instead of just standing there!

*Non vedendo***ci** *arrivare, la nonna si è preoccupata* – Grandma got worried when she didn't see us arrive

When **ci** comes after the infinitive, the final -e of the verb is dropped.

*Vorremmo andar***ci** – We would like to go there

*Puoi venire a prender***ci** *alla stazione?* – Can you pick us up at the station?

In a negative sentence the pronoun *ci* remains right in front of the verb.

Non **ci** *vado* – I don't go there

Non **ci** *posso credere* – I can't believe it

Using *ci* with the verb *entrare*

Listen to track 357

The pronoun *ci* is used with the verb **entrare** (to enter, to go in) to form a very common and useful expression in Italian, which literally means *to go in there*, but whose idiomatic meaning is actually *having to do with, being involved* or *being related to*.

Let's look at some examples:

*Cosa **c'entra**?* – What's that got to do with it?

*Io non **c'entro*** – It has nothing to do with me

*Il conflitto per l'eredità non **c'entra** con questo delitto* – The fight over inheritance has nothing to do with this crime

Using *ci* with the verb *volere*

Ci can be used with the verb **volere** (to want, to desire) to mean *"it takes"*. Use *ci vuole* when the following word is singular.

Listen to track 358

*Ci **vuole** coraggio* – It takes courage

*Per andare a Firenze **ci vuole** un'ora in macchina* – It takes an hour to get to Florence by car

Use *ci vogliono* when the following word is plural.

*Da Monza a Ferrara **ci vogliono** tre ore di treno* – It takes three hours to go from Monza to Ferrara by train

*Ci **vogliono** solo cinque minuti per andare da casa mia allo stadio* – It takes only five minutes to go from my house to the stadium

Using *ci* with the verb *avere*

Listen to track 359

When speaking at a colloquial and informal level, *ci* can be used with the verb **avere** (to have) to express possession. Note: when using different pronouns in the same sentence, *ci* changes its form. The spelling of *ci* will change to *ce* when followed by a direct object pronoun (*lo, la, li* and *le*).

Here are some examples:

*Hai una sigaretta? Sì, **ce** l'ho* – Do you have you a cigarette? Yes, I have (one)

Edoardo, ce l'hai la ragazza? No, non ce l'ho – Edoardo, do you have a girlfriend? No, I don't

So, when you see a direct object pronoun next to *ci*, remember that it will change its spelling.

Ci will also change when combined with **ne**. For example:

Ci *sono delle mandorle? Si, ce ne dovrebbero essere in cucina* – Are there any almonds? Yes, there should be some in the kitchen

Idiomatic verbs with *ci*

Listen to track 360

Finally, there are quite a few idiomatic verbs which have *ci/ce* built into them. Here is a list:

- **Avercela** – to be mad at someone

Perché ce l'hai con me, Luca? – Why are you mad at me, Luca?

- **Farcela** – to manage, to cope

Non ce la faccio più – I can't take it any more

- **Metterci** – to take time

Quanto **ci metti** *per andare a Torino in macchina?* **Ci metto** *due ore* – How long does it take to go to Turin by car? It takes two hours

- **Entrarci** – to have to do with, to be involved

Non ti arrabbiare con me. Io non c'entro, è tutta colpa di Gianluca – Don't get mad at me. It has nothing to do with me, it's Gianluca's fault

- **Mettercela tutta** – to try one's hardest

Ce l'ho messa tutta – I put my heart and soul into it!

- **Passarci sopra** – to get over something

Sono passati anni ma non riesco a passarci sopra – It's been years but I can't get over it

- **Provarci** – to try

Sarebbe inutile provarci? – Would it be pointless to try?

To sum up...

- *Ne* is used to mean *some*.
- *Ne* is used to mean *of it/them* when talking about amounts and quantities.
- *Ne* can be used to mean *about it/them* with adjectives and verbs followed by *di* (of).
- *Ci* can be used to mean *it* or *about it*.
- *Ci* is used with verbs that can be followed by the preposition *a* (to).
- *Ne* and *ci* usually come before the verb.

All this *ne* and *ci* stuff can get super confusing, I know. Don't worry if you don't fully get it at first. That's okay. Once you start giving *ne* and *ci* more attention and practicing a little every day, you should start to notice the kinds of sentences where these tricky words are used and they will start to make more sense to you. I promise!

Workbook Lesson 21. The Italian Pronouns Ne and Ci

Exercise 21.1: Translate the following sentences into Italian using the pronoun "ne"

English	Italian
1. Do you like this pizza? Do you want more of it?	
2. Yesterday's homework? Ask Marco, I don't know anything about that.	
3. I don't want to hear about that.	
4. Lucia's home? I didn't realize that.	
5. Please, don't go away!	

Exercise 21.2: Translate the following sentences into Italian using the pronoun "ci"

English	Italian
1. Emma's pregnant? I can't believe it!	
2. Saturday's party? I'll be there for sure.	
3. Let's meet at 7.	
4. Do you think you can talk with that Italian customer? Yes, I think I can.	
5. Even if they are way too old to believe in Santa Claus, they do still believe in him.	

Exercise 21.3: Complete with "ci" or "ne"

1. Sono stata a Parigi e _____ voglio ritornare il prossimo anno.

2. Come vai in stazione? _____ vado a piedi.

3. Quanti libri hai letto quest'anno? _____ ho letti tanti.

4. Vieni al cinema con noi? No, non _____ posso venire.

5. Quanti fratelli hai? _____ ho uno.

6. Hai incontrato i miei amici dell'università? Sì, _____ ho incontrato uno.

Exercise 21.4: Choose the right option

1. Andiamo in campeggio e ci/ne restiamo una settimana.

2. Studiate tutti i giorni in biblioteca? No, ci/ne studiamo solo il martedì.

3. Questo treno è molto scomodo, ma io ci/ne viaggio lo stesso.

4. Cosa metti nel caffè? Ci/Ne metto un po' di latte.

5. Voglio organizzare una bella festa. Che ci/ne dici?

6. Fumare fa male, ma io non ci/ne posso fare a meno.

Exercise 21.5: Complete with "ci", "ce" or "ne"

1. Quanto _____ metti per arrivare a casa di Marco?

2. Che sonno! Non _____ la faccio più a stare sveglio.

3. Vuoi un po' di caffè? – Sì, grazie, _____ voglio una tazzina.

4. Rimani in biblioteca? – No, me _____ vado a casa.

5. Da quanto tempo abiti in Catalogna? – _____ abito da dieci anni.

6. Ti penti di non avere studiato? – Sì, me _____ pento.

Answers:

Exercise 21.1:

1. Ti piace questa pizza? Ne vuoi ancora?

2. I compiti di ieri? Chiedi a Marco, io non ne so nulla.

3. Non ne voglio sentir parlare.

4. Lucia è a casa? Non me ne ero accorta.

5. Per favore, non andartene!

Exercise 21.2:

1. Emma è incinta? Non posso crederci!

2. La festa di sabato? Ci sarò di sicuro.

3. Incontriamoci alle 7.

4. Pensi di riuscire a parlare con quel cliente italiano? Sì, credo di riuscirci.

5. Anche se sono decisamente troppo grandi per credere a Babbo Natale, ci credono ancora.

Exercise 21.3:

1. ci; 2. Ci; 3. Ne; 4. ci; 5. Ne; 6. ne

Exercise 21.4:

1. ci; 2. ci; 3. ci; 4. Ci; 5. ne; 6. ne

Exercise 21.5:

1. ci; 2. ce; 3. ne; 4. ne; 5. Ci; 6. ne

LESSON 22: TRAPASSATO PROSSIMO

The **Italian past perfect** (*trapassato prossimo*) may sound incredibly scary at first – but there's good news. We use it in a similar way to how you use the past perfect in English.

In this lesson, we will show you how to use the ***trapassato prossimo*** in Italian. Once you've got the hang of it, you will easily master this tense.

Using the *trapassato prossimo*

Listen to track 361

In Italian, the past perfect (*trapassato prossimo***)**, or more properly said **pluperfect** or **plusquamperfect**, is a past tense used to talk about what had happened at a point in the past.

It is used to:

- talk about past occurrences that took place before something else happened.

*Quando siamo arrivati in aeroporto, l'aereo **era** già **decollato*** – When we arrived at the airport, the airplane had already taken off (i.e. the plane took off before we arrived)

*Sara non è andata a teatro perchè **aveva** già **visto** lo spettacolo* – Sara didn't go to the theater because she had already seen the show

*Riccardo mi ha restituito i soldi che gli **avevo prestato** due mesi fa* – Riccardo gave me back the money I had lent him two months ago

- refer to something that had already begun at a past time:

***Aveva** già **piovuto** per due settimane quando è arrivata l'alluvione* – It had already been raining for two weeks when the flood came

- create suspense in narrative/storytelling:

*Sofia quel giorno **si era alzata** come tutte le mattine* – That day, Sofia got up/had got up just like every other morning (i.e. this looks just like a regular day in Sofia's life, but you would expect something unusual to happen on that specific day)

Constructing the *trapassato prossimo*

As you might have noticed, the *trapassato prossimo* is a compound tense, which means that it is formed by more than one word.

In Italian, the ***trapassato prossimo***, also called *piuccheperfetto*, is formed with:

- the imperfect indicative form of the appropriate auxiliary verb (*avere* or *essere*);
- the past participle of the main verb.

We will be using *avere* (to have) and *essere* (to be) as auxiliary verbs like with the *passato prossimo*. The only difference is that we will be conjugating them in the imperfect tense. Their conjugations are as follows:

Listen to track 362

Avere

Io avevo - I had

Tu avevi - You had

Lui/lei aveva - He/She/It had

Noi avevamo - We had

Voi avevate - Y'all had

Loro avevano - They had

Listen to track 363

Essere

Io ero - I was

Tu eri - You were

Lui/lei era - He/She/It was

Noi eravamo - We were

Voi eravate - Y'all were

Loro erano - They were

To make the **past participle of regular verbs**, you just have to remove the infinitive ending *-are, -ere* or *-ire* and replace it with the past participle ending as shown below:

- verbs ending in -are use **-ato**: parlare>parlato, realizzare>realizzato, sognare>sognato;
- verbs ending in -ere use **-uto**: credere>creduto, ricevere>ricevuto, possedere>posseduto;
- verbs ending in -ire use **-ito**: dormire>dormito, agire>agito, diminuire>diminuito.

There are some **irregular verbs in the past participle**. We recommend committing them to memory:

Listen to track 364

Aprire (to open) - aperto

Bere (to drink) - bevuto

Chiedere (to ask) - chiesto

Chiudere (to close) - chiuso

Dire (to say, to tell) - detto

Fare (to do, to make) - fatto

Prendere (to take) - preso

Scrivere (to write) - scritto

Tradurre (to translate) - tradotto

Vedere (to see) - visto

Vivere (to live) - vissuto

How do you choose the right auxiliary verb?

That's a complex question. The answer depends on the verb which is expressing the meaning of the sentence. In order to choose which helping/auxiliary verb is used, the same rules used in *passato prossimo* apply.

Using the auxiliary verb *avere*

Listen to track 365

The Italian verb "avere" is used as the auxiliary for most **transitive verbs**. What is a **transitive verb**, you ask? A transitive verb expresses an action that carries over from the subject to an object. Without a direct object to affect, transitive verbs like *dire* (to say), *portare* (to bring), *leggere* (to read), *dimenticare* (to forget) and *comprare* (to buy) cannot function.

*Solo il 42% degli intervistati **aveva letto** un libro negli ultimi 6 mesi* – Only 42 per cent of the adults surveyed had read a book in the past 6 months

As you might have noticed, the past participle is invariable when the *trapassato prossimo* is constructed with "avere".

Listen to track 366

BEWARE: though intransitive, *viaggiare* (to travel), *rispondere* (to answer), *vivere* (to live) and *dormire* (to sleep) take "avere" as their auxiliary verb.

Using the auxiliary verb *essere*

While "to have" acts as an auxiliary for a myriad of Italian verbs, there is a group of verbs that conjugate with "to be". You often have to learn whether to use the auxiliary verb "essere" on a case-by-case basis, but there are some general guidelines that are well worth following.

You have to use the auxiliary verb "essere" with:

- all **reflexive verbs**:

*Mi **ero** già **svegliato** quando è suonata la sveglia* – I had already woken up when the alarm clock sounded

- most **intransitive verbs**, especially those expressing motion, like *andare* (to go), *arrivare* (to arrive), *partire* (to leave), *tornare* (to come back, to return) and *uscire* (to go out);
- verbs that express lack of movement, like *restare* (to stay, to remain) and *stare* (to stay, to be);
- verbs that express state of being, like *essere* (to be), or processes of change, like *nascere* (to be born) and *morire* (to die);
- verbs like *succedere* (to happen) and *accadere* (to occur), which do not have a subject as such.

When you use a verb in the *trapassato prossimo* with "essere", the past participle must agree with the subject of the sentence in number (singular or plural) and gender (masculine or feminine). Therefore, it can have four endings:

- -o for masculine singular;
- -a for feminine singular;
- -i for masculine plural;
- -e for feminine plural.

In Italian, the verb "essere" can be conjugated with itself as the auxiliary verb.

Gianluca **era stato** a casa da solo tutto il fine settimana – Gianluca had been home alone the whole weekend

Here is a list of the **most common verbs that form compound tenses with "essere"**:

Listen to track 367

***Andare** (to go): Pietro ed Elisa **erano andati** al museo* – Pietro and Elisa had gone to the museum

Arrivare *(to arrive): Marina è andata via quanto Barbara **era** già **arrivata*** – Marina left when Barbara arrived

Cadere *(to fall, to drop): Un albero gigantesco **era caduto** durante la notte* – A giant tree had fallen over during the night

Costare *(to cost): Il suo nuovo abito **era costato** una fortuna* – Her new outfit had cost an arm and a leg

Crescere *(to grow): I capelli di Elisabetta **erano** talmente **cresciuti** da arrivarle quasi alla vita* – Elisabetta's hair had grown so long it nearly reached her waist

Diventare *(to become): I Nirvana **erano** rapidamente **diventati** una delle rock band <u>più influenti del mondo.</u>*– Nirvana had quickly become one of the most influential rock bands in the world

Durare *(to last, to continue): Anche dopo la riconciliazione, i litigi **erano continuati*** – Even after their reconciliation, the arguments had continued

Entrare *(to enter): Linda è arrivata dopo che tutte le sue amiche **erano** già **entrate** nel locale* – Linda arrived after all of her friends had already gone into the club

Morire *(to die): **Era** già **morto** quando è arrivata l'ambulanza* – He had already died by the time the ambulance arrived

Nascere *(to be born): Nel 2005 mia figlia **era** già **nata*** – My daughter was already born in 2005

Partire *(to leave, to depart): La moto che **era partita** per prima è arrivata ultima* – The motorbike that started first arrived last

Restare *(to stay, to remain): Mentre i prezzi **erano rimasti** stabili, le tasse continuavano ad aumentare* – While prices had remained stable, the taxes continued to increase

Stare *(to stay, to be): **Eravate** già **stati** a Napoli prima dell'estate scorsa?* – Had you already been to Naples before last summer?

Tornare *(to come back, to return): Non appena **eravamo tornati** a casa, ha iniziato a piovere* – Right after we had returned home, it started raining

Uscire *(to go out, to exit): Il professore ci ha informato che Dario **era uscito** da scuola senza permesso* – The teacher informed us that Dario had gone out of school without permission

Venire *(to come): Era mezzanotte quando gli agenti **erano venuti** a bussare alla nostra porta* – It was midnight when the officers had come to knock at our door

How do *passato prossimo* and *trapassato prossimo* work together?

Listen to track 368

As we mentioned earlier, we use the *trapassato prossimo* whenever we want to talk about something that happened before something else in the past.

The **trapassato prossimo** and the **passato prossimo** are often used together in the same sentence. In this type of construction, the action expressed by the *trapassato prossimo* happened before the event you are referring to with the *passato prossimo*.

*Chiara è partita in ritardo perché **aveva dimenticato** il passaporto a casa* – Chiara left late because she had left her passport at home

*Alessandro non ha salutato subito Serena perché non l'**aveva riconosciuta** –* Alessandro didn't greet Serena right away because he **had not recognized** her

The **trapassato prossimo** makes it clear that the event it describes is placed earlier in the past than the action expressed by the *passato prossimo*.

Grammatically, the difference between them is like this:

Passato prossimo

Listen to track 369

Io ho parlato - I spoke or have spoken

Tu hai parlato - You spoke or have spoken

Lui/lei ha parlato - He/She/It spoke or has spoken

Noi abbiamo parlato - We spoke or have spoken

Voi avete parlato - Y'all spoke or have spoken

Loro hanno parlato - They spoke or have spoken

Listen to track 370

Trapassato prossimo

Io avevo parlato - I had spoken

Tu avevi parlato - You had spoken

Lui/lei aveva parlato - He/She/It had spoken

Noi avevamo parlato - We had spoken

Voi avevate parlato - Y'all had spoken

Loro avevano parlato - They had spoken

How to translate the *trapassato prossimo* into English

Listen to track 371

The *trapassato prossimo* is the natural equivalent of the past perfect in English and is mostly used for the same purposes. Somewhat unusually, the similarity in the way the two tenses are used in Italian and English is striking.

*Quando ho sentito il telefono squillare **ero** già **uscita** di casa* – When I heard the phone ringing, I had already gone out of the house

*Avevo fame perché non **avevo mangiato** nulla tutto il giorno* – I was hungry because I **had not eaten** anything all day

The actions expressed by the *trapassato prossimo* and past perfect had finished before another event took place in the past.

*Prima di trasferirti a Milano **avevi** già **studiato** l'italiano?* – Had you already studied Italian before you moved to Milan?

*Giuliano **aveva prenotato** il volo cinque giorni prima di partire* – Giuliano had booked the flight three days before leaving

*La mia vita **era stata** infelice fino a quando ho conosciuto Samuele* – My life had been unhappy until I met Samuele

In the last example you might well say "was" instead of "had been" in English, but note that Italian is more steadfast in its use of the *trapassato prossimo* in past-before-the-past situations.

To sum up...

Listen to track 372

- In Italian, the *trapassato prossimo* is used to talk about what had already happened in the past.

*Dopo solo due ore, **avevamo** già **finito** gli argomenti di conversazione* – After just a couple of hours, we had already run out of things to say

- It is used to talk about something that happened in the past before another event you are usually refer to with the *passato prossimo* or *imperfetto* tense

*Quando Vincenzo iniziò a parlare, **avevo** già **capito** cosa aveva in mente* – When Vincenzo started talking, I had already understood what he had in mind

- In English, the **past perfect tense** acts in the same way.

***Avevamo deciso** di andare a fare una passeggiata al parco, ma poi ha cominciato a piovere* – We had decided to go for a walk in the park, but then it started raining

- It is made with the imperfect of the auxiliary verb "avere" or "essere" and the past participle.

Practice as much as you can until you get the hang of it. *A presto*!

Workbook Lesson 22. Past perfect

Exercise 22.1: Complete the following sentences with the trapassato prossimo

1. Avevate mal di pancia perché _____ _____(mangiare) troppe ciliegie.
2. Daniele era nervoso perché _____ _____(avere) una discussione con il capo.
3. Ho rotto il vaso che _____ _____(comprare) a Volterra.
4. Sofia _____ _____(arrivare) in ritardo.
5. Pietro _____ _____(uscire) per andare al cinema.
6. La colf _____ appena _____(lavare) il pavimento quando i bambini sono entrati con le scarpe sporche.

Exercise 22.2: Choose the right ausiliare

1. Non hai passato l'esame perché non avevi/eri studiato abbastanza.
2. Quando sono arrivata all'appuntamento la mia fidanzata aveva/era già andata via.
3. Siccome avevo/ero rimasto senza benzina, sono andato a piedi fino al distributore.
4. Sono andata dai carabinieri perché mi avevano/erano rubato la borsa.
5. Siccome mi avevo/ero dimenticato il portafoglio, non ho potuto pagare il conto.

Exercise 22.3: Translate the following sentences into Italian

English	Italian
They had already arrived home.	
I didn't consider that option.	
We didn't eat anything weird, but we felt sick.	
She had never been to Italy.	
Marta and Michela didn't go to school last February.	

Exercise 22.4: Complete the sentences with the appropriate given verb

Litigare/Mangiare/Aprire/Venire/Riunirsi/Assegnare/Ricordarsi

1. Luigi non aveva fame perché _____ _____ troppo.
2. Non volle parlare con l'amico con cui _____ _____ .
3. _____ _____da voi fiducioso, perché sapevo che mi avreste aiutato.
4. L'insegnante_____ _____ una relazione ma gli alunni non si_____ _____ di consegnarla.

5. I vecchi compagni di classe _____ _____ per festeggiare, ma non si divertirono.

6. Non _____ _____ le sbarre del passaggio a livello, perciò il traffico rimase bloccato.

Exercise 22.5: Choose the correct verb

1. (Aveva dimenticato / dimenticava) l'appuntamento, per questo venne rimproverato.

2. Quella notte non (dormì / aveva dormito), poiché aveva visto un film pauroso.

3. Non (ha voluto / ebbe voluto) parlare con l'amico con cui aveva litigato.

4. (Avevano bevuto / Bevono) troppo quella sera perciò fecero molta confusione.

5. Non (siamo partiti / eravamo partiti) anche se eravamo riusciti a liberarci dagli impegni familiari.

6. Le strade erano allagate perché (pioverà / aveva piovuto) tanto.

Answers:

Exercise 22.1:

1. Avevate mal di pancia perché avevate mangiato troppe ciliegie.

2. Daniele era nervoso perché aveva avuto una discussione con il capo.

3. Ho rotto il vaso che avevo comprato a Volterra.

4. Sofia era arrivata in ritardo.

5. Pietro era uscito per andare al cinema.

6. La colf aveva appena lavato il pavimento quando i bambini sono entrati con le scarpe sporche.

Exercise 22.2:

1. avevi; 2. era; 3. ero; 4. avevano; 5. ero

Exercise 22.3:

1. Erano già arrivati a casa.

2. Non avevo considerato quell'opzione.

3. Non avevamo mangiato nulla di strano, ma stavamo male.

4. Non era mai stata in Italia.

5. Marta e Michela non erano andate a scuola lo scorso febbraio.

Exercise 22.4:

1. Luigi non aveva fame perché aveva mangiato troppo.
2. Non volle parlare con l'amico con cui aveva litigato.
3. Ero venuto da voi fiducioso, perché sapevo che mi avreste aiutato.
4. L'insegnante aveva assegnato una relazione ma gli alunni non si erano ricordati di consegnarla.
5. I vecchi compagni di classe si erano riuniti per festeggiare, ma non si divertirono.
6. Non avevano aperto le sbarre del passaggio a livello, perciò il traffico rimase bloccato.

Exercise 22.5:

1. Aveva dimenticato
2. aveva dormito
3. ha voluto
4. Avevano bevuto
5. siamo partiti
6. aveva piovuto

LESSON 23: THE FUTURO SEMPLICE

In Italian, the **simple future tense** (*futuro semplice*) refers to actions which have yet to happen. Fortunately, it is much simpler than the present and the past, and both its use and conjugations are pretty straightforward.

In this lesson we will show you how to conjugate and use the *futuro semplice*. It is not a hard tense to master.

Using the *futuro semplice*

Listen to track 373

In Italian, the *futuro semplice* is used to:

- talk about events that will take place in the future. Unlike in English, it doesn't matter if the action is far or close in the future:

*La finale di Champions League **si terrà** sabato prossimo* – The Champions League final is going to take place next Saturday

*Tra un centinaio di anni la Terra **sarà** invivibile* – The earth will be uninhabitable within a hundred years

- plan an action that will happen:

*La prossima estate io e Filippo **andremo** in Brasile* – Filippo and I are going to Brazil next summer

*Diego **inizierà** la dieta domani* – Diego will start the diet tomorrow

- express a polite order:

***Farai** tutto quello che ti dico, va bene?* – You will do what I say, alright?

- make a statement sound less strong and authoritative:

***Ammetterai** che non hai avuto un comportamento adeguato* – You have to admit that you didn't behave properly

- express hypothesis, a guess or doubt:

*Dove **sarà** Camilla?* – Where could Camilla be? (I am wondering where Camilla is right now, not asking where she will be at some point in the future)

*Da qui al parco **saranno** tre chilometri* – It must be two miles from here to the park

In the spoken language, the *futuro semplice* is often replaced with the **present tense** to:

- refer to the future:

Il corso intensivo di italiano comincia domani – The intensive Italian course starts tomorrow

Mi sposo tra due settimane – I am getting married in two weeks

- say what you are about to do:

Pago io! – I'll pay!

- ask for suggestions:

Cosa facciamo? – What shall we do?

Note: unlike in English, both parts of a future sentence can be in the future tense in Italian.

Ci **crederò** *quando lo* **vedrò** – I'll believe it when I see it

Chi **vivrà**, **vedrà** – Only time will tell

We suggest studying the *futuro semplice* and its uses within the context of speaking Italian. Try and think in Italian when you speak, and don't look for a correspondence with any particular tense in English. Italian and English have different tense forms and most of the time you cannot make an exact correspondence between their tenses.

Constructing the *futuro semplice*

Lucky for you, the *futuro semplice* is easy to form in Italian. You start by removing the verb's ending, and then add the appropriate simple future ending.

There is one form for first-conjugation and second-conjugation regular verbs, and a second form for third-conjugation regular verbs.

- For regular verbs ending in **-are** and **-ere**, the simple future endings are:
- -erò for "I"
- -erai for "you"
- -erà for "he"/ "she" / "it"
- -eremo for "we"
- -erete for "y'all"
- -eranno for "they"

So, for instance, to form the future tense of *cantare* (to sing) and *vendere* (to sell), you have:

Listen to track 374

Cantare (to sing)

Io cant**erò** - I will sing

Tu cant**erai** - You will sing

Lui/lei cant**erà** - He/She/It will sing

Noi cant**eremo** – We will sing

Voi cant**erete** - Y'all will sing

Loro cant**eranno** - They will sing

Vendere (to sell)

Io vend**erò** - I will sell

Tu vend**erai** - You will sell

Lui/lei vend**erà** - He/She/It will sell

Noi vend**eremo** - We will sell

Voi vend**erete** - Y'all will sell

Loro vend**eranno** – They will sell

As you can see, the future endings for both **-are** and **-ere** verbs begin with an "e".

For regular verbs ending in **-ire**, the simple future endings are:

- -irò for "I"
- -irai for "you"
- -irà for "he"/ "she" / "it"
- -iremo for "we"
- -irete for "y'all"
- -iranno for "they"

Note: they are the same as above except for the first letter. So, for instance, to form the future tense of *sentire* (to hear), you have:

Listen to track 375

Sentire (to hear)

Io sent**irò** - I will hear

Tu sent**irai** - You will hear

Lui/lei sent**irà** - He/She/It will hear

Noi sent**iremo** - We will hear

Voi sent**irete** - Y'all will hear

Loro sent**iranno** - They will hear

Listen to track 376

For verbs ending in **-are**, there are some spelling changes to learn. Verbs ending in **-care** and **-gare**, such as cercare (to look for, to try), pubblicare (to publish), seccare (to annoy/ to dry), pagare (to pay), delegare (to delegate) and spiegare (to explain), add an "h" to the future tense stem after the "c" or "g", in order to preserve the hard sound of the infinitive.

Pubblicare (to publish)

Io pubblic**herò** - I will publish

Tu pubblic**herai** - You will publish

Lui/lei pubblic**herà** - He/She/It will publish

Noi pubblic**heremo** - We will publish

Voi pubblic**herete** - Y'all will publish

Loro pubblic**heranno** - They will publish

Delegare (to delegate)

Io deleg**herò** - I will delegate

Tu deleg**herai** - You will delegate

Lui/lei deleg**herà** - He/She/It will delegate

Noi deleg**heremo** - We will delegate

Voi deleg**herete** - Y'all will delegate

Loro deleg**heranno** - They will delegate

Listen to track 377

Verbs ending in **-giare** and **-ciare**, such as mangiare (to eat), parcheggiare (to park), cominciare (to start) and viaggiare (to travel), remove the "i" before adding the future-tense endings.

Mangiare (to eat)

Io mang**erò** - I will eat

Tu mang**erai** - You will eat

Lui/lei mang**erà** - He/She/It will eat

Noi mang**eremo** - We will eat

Voi mang**erete** - Y'all will eat

Loro mang**eranno** - They will eat

Viaggiare (to travel)

Io viagg**erò** - I will travel

Tu viagg**erai** - You will travel

Lui/lei viagg**erà** - He/She/It will travel

Noi viagg**eremo** - We will travel

Voi viagg**erete** - Y'all will travel

Loro viagg**eranno** - They will travel

That's all there is to forming the simple future verb conjugations in Italian.

Irregular verbs in the Italian simple future tense

Listen to track 378

In the future tense, some verbs are irregular, which means they do not follow the regular conjugation patterns.

The auxiliary verbs *essere* (to be) and *avere* (to have) have **irregular future forms**. The stem of the verb "essere" is *sar-*.

Essere (to be)

Io sar**ò**

Tu sar**ai**

Lui/lei sar**à**

Noi sar**emo**

Voi sar**ete**

Loro sar**anno**

Avere (to have)

Io av**rò**

Tu av**rai**

Lui/lei av**rà**

Noi av**remo**

Voi av**rete**

Loro av**ranno**

Irregular verbs have to be committed to memory, but here are two main categories for classifying them.

Listen to track 379

1. Verbs that lose the ending except for the letter "r."

Dovere (to must, to have to)

Io dovrò

Tu dovrai

Lui/lei dovrà

Noi dovremo

Voi dovrete

Loro dovranno

Sapere (to know)

Io saprò

Tu saprai

Lui/lei saprà

Noi sapremo

Voi saprete

Loro sapranno

Potere (to be able to)

Io potrò

Tu potrai

Lui/lei potrà

Noi potremo

Voi potrete

Loro potranno

Vedere (to see)

Io vedrò

Tu vedrai

Lui/lei vedrà

Noi vedremo

Voi vedrete

Loro vedranno

Vivere (to live)

Io vivrò

Tu vivrai

Lui/lei vivrà

Noi vivremo

Voi vivrete

Loro vivranno

Cadere (to fall)

Io cadrò

Tu cadrai

Lui/lei cadrà

Noi cadremo

Voi cadrete

Loro cadranno

2. Verbs that lose both the ending and part of the root, and add "rr" instead.

Listen to track 380

Venire (to come)

Io verrò

Tu verrai

Lui/lei verrà

Noi verremo

Voi verrete

Loro verranno

Tenere (to keep)

Io terrò

Tu terrai

Lui/lei terrà

Noi terremo

Voi terrete

Loro terranno

Volere (to want)

Io vorrò

Tu vorrai

Lui/lei vorrà

Noi vorremo

Voi vorrete

Loro vorranno

Bere (to drink)

Io berrò

Tu berrai

Lui/lei berrà

Noi berremo

Voi berrete

Loro berranno

Condurre (to drive)

Io condurrò

Tu condurrai

Lui/lei condurrà

Noi condurremo

Voi condurrete

Loro condurranno

Tradurre (to translate)

Io tradurrò

Tu tradurrai

Lui/lei tradurrà

Noi tradurremo

Voi tradurrete

Loro tradurranno

The verbs **fare** (to do, to make), **dare** (to give) and **stare** (to stay, to be) simply drop the final -e of their infinitives and form the stems *far-*, *dar-* and *star-* respectively. These stems are then combined with the regular simple future endings listed above.

Listen to track 381

Fare (to do, to make)

Io farò

Tu farai

Lui/lei farà

Noi faremo

Voi farete

Loro faranno

Dare (to give)

Io darò

Tu darai

Lui/lei darà

Noi daremo

Voi darete

Loro daranno

Stare (to stay, to be)

Io starò

Tu starai

Lui/lei starà

Noi staremo

Voi starete

Loro staranno

As you might have noticed, the tail end of the future-tense endings is always the same for each subject even with these irregular conjugations.

Which phrases are typically used with the *futuro semplice*?

Listen to track 382

Here is a list of marker words that are usually used with the *futuro semplice* in Italian:

- Domani – Tomorrow

Domani Matilde e Giulia **canteranno** *nel coro* – Tomorrow Matilde and Giulia will sing in the chorus

- *Un giorno* – One day

Un giorno ci **rideremo** *su* – One day we will laugh about this

- *Stasera* – Tonight, this evening

Letizia **riceverà** *il premio stasera* – This evening, Letizia will receive the award

- Domani mattina/pomeriggio/sera – Tomorrow morning/afternoon/evening

Domani mattina non **sarò** *a casa* – Tomorrow morning I will not be home

- *La prossima settimana/mese/anno* – Next week/month/year

Mia cugina Mara **avrà** *un bambino il mese prossimo* – My cousin Mara will have a baby next month

- *Tra ... giorni/settimane/mesi/anni* – In ... days/weeks/months/years

Tra due settimane **sarà** *il nostro terzo anniversario di matrimonio* – In two weeks, it will be our third wedding anniversary

- *Mai più* – Never again

Non **tornerò** *mai più in quel ristorante* – I will never go back to that restaurant again

Non mi **vedrai** *mai più* – You will never see me again

What's the difference between *futuro semplice* and *futuro anteriore*?

Listen to track 383

In Italian, the future tense is made up of two tenses: the *futuro semplice* (future tense) and the ***futuro anteriore*** (future perfect), both belonging to the indicative mood.

As mentioned previously, the *futuro semplice* is used to talk about something that will happen in the close or distant future.

Un giorno **canterò** *in un coro* – One day I will sing in a choir

*A metà settembre i bambini **dovranno** tornare a scuola* – The children will have to go back to school in mid-September

Typically, you will use the ***futuro anteriore*** when you are unsure about something that is happening in the future or that has happened in the past.

*Emanuele non è venuto a lezione, **sarà stato** molto impegnato* – Emanuele didn't come to the class, he must have been very busy

*Non ho più visto Pamela a scuola, probabilmente si **sarà trasferita*** – I haven't seen Pamela at school for a while, she must have moved

You can also use the ***futuro anteriore*** when you are talking about an action in the future before something else happens.

*Entro i 30 anni, **avrai messo** da parte abbastanza soldi per comprare una casa* – By the age of 30, you will have saved enough money to buy a house

*Alle nove **avremo** già **cenato*** – By 9 p.m. we will already have had dinner

The Italian future perfect is also used to talk about what will have happened by a point in time in the future.

*Domani a quest'ora **sarò** già **arrivato** a New York* – By this time tomorrow I will already have arrived in New York

*Entro la fine dell'anno Viviana **avrà lavorato** qui per 10 anni* – By the end of the year, Viviana will have worked here for 10 years

To sum up...

Listen to track 384

- The *futuro semplice* is to be used to talk about something that will happen in the future.

*Alberto **venderà** la sua moto per pagare i debiti* – Alberto will sell his motorcycle to pay his debts

- Native Italian speakers use the present tense a lot to talk about their future plans.
- The simple future endings of regular **-are** and **-ere** verbs are **-erò, -erai, -erà, -eremo, -erete** and **-eranno.**
- The simple future endings of regular **-ire** verbs are **-irò, -irai, -irà, -iremo, -irete** and **-iranno.**
- In Italian, both speculative and definite future are expressed with the *futuro semplice*, which is commonly used to express suppositions and doubts:

*Qualcuno sta bussando alla porta, chi **sarà** mai?* – Someone is knocking at the door, who could it be?

Workbook Lesson 23. Simple Future Tense

Exercise 23.1: Translate the following sentences into Italian

English	Italian
1. We will eat sushi tomorrow.	
2. If he keeps playing like that he'll trip up, for sure.	
3. If you keep shouting, the teacher will hear you.	
4. I feel like something weird will happen soon.	
5. I don't believe you'll read that book.	

Exercise 23.2: Choose the right verb

1. Domani comprorò/comprerò un nuovo rossetto.

2. Verrai/verrei alla festa di sabato?

3. Non so se Marco verrò/verrà, ma io ci sarà/sarò.

4. Luna e Asia mangeranno/mangeremo a casa loro martedì.

5. Credi che il professore ci interrogherà/interrogheremo domani?

Exercise 23.3: Complete these sentences with the right verb

1. Mi _____ (complain) con la segreteria.

2. Credo che io e Marco_____ (study) domani.

3. Sono sicura che mio figlio _____ (play) tutto il pomeriggio.

4. Loro _____ (listen) i loro genitori di sicuro.

5. _____ (you, live) con i tuoi genitori fino ai 40 anni?

6. Marzia _____ (write) una lettera al ragazzo che le piace.

Exercise 23.4: Conjugate the verbs correctly

1. _____(venire) anche i bambini al museo con voi?

2. Credo che Sara _____(dovere) risparmiare di più per poter andare in vacanza!

3. Quest'anno _____(iniziare-voi) un nuovo corso di danza?

4. Da oggi _____(ricordare-noi) sempre di pagare le bollette prima della scadenza.

5. Giulia, _____(rimanere) sempre nel mio cuore.

Exercise 23.5: Erase the verb that's not in the future tense

a. andrebbero – andrà – andremo

b. verrò – verremo – veniranno

c. daremmo – daremo – darai

d. faranno – farai – faremmo

e. berresti – berrai – berranno

f. diranno – direbbe - direte

g. saremo – sarai – sarei

h. avessi – avrete – avrà

Answers:

Exercise 23.1:

1. Domani mangeremo sushi.
2. Se continua a giocare così inciamperà di sicuro.
3. Se continui a urlare, l'insegnante ti sentirà.
4. Sento che succederà presto qualcosa di strano.
5. Non credo che leggerai quel libro.

Exercise 23.2:

1. omprerò
2. Verrai
3. verrà, sarò
4. mangeranno
5. interrogherà

Exercise 23.3:

1. lamenterò
2. studieremo
3. giocherà
4. ascolteranno
5. Vivrai
6. scriverà

Exercise 23.4:

1. Verranno
2. dovrà
3. inizierete
4. ricorderemo
5. rimarrai

Exercise 23.5:

a. **andrebbero** – andrà – andremo
b. verrò – verremo – **veniranno**
c. **daremmo** – daremo – darai
d. faranno – farai – **faremmo**
e. **berresti** – berrai – berranno
f. diranno – **direbbe** - direte
g. saremo – sarai – **sarei**
h. **avessi** – avrete – avrà

LESSON 24: GETTING TO KNOW THE ITALIAN REFLEXIVE PRONOUNS

Welcome to this guide to the **Italian reflexive pronouns** (*pronomi riflessivi*). With this lesson we aim to show you how to use them in real-world speech and writing, and not to confuse them with direct and indirect object pronouns. Let's get started!

Italian reflexive pronouns

Listen to track 385

Even someone who knows very basic Italian is already familiar with the *pronomi riflessivi*. How come? The very first sentence most language learners ever learn is:

Mi chiamo... – (Literally: I call myself...) My name is...

The above is an example of a **reflexive verb** (*verbo reflessivo*). Simply put, a reflexive verb is a verb where the subject is carrying out the action on itself. Reflexive verbs can't function on their own, and require a **reflexive pronoun**.

You can easily recognize **Italian reflexive verbs** because in the infinitive form they all end in **-si**. *Si* means *to oneself* and it lets us know that the action expressed by the verb is being done to the subject. In other words, the subject and the object of a reflexive verb are the same person. Let's look at some examples:

*Come **ti** chiami?* – (Literally: how are you called?) What's your name?

***Mi** guardo allo specchio* – I look at myself in the mirror

*Con il calore, il ghiaccio **si** scioglie* – Ice melts with heat

*Luana e Patrizia **si** stanno preparando* – Luana and Patrizia are getting ready

We use **reflexive pronouns** when the subject and object of the sentence coincide. In a reflexive sentence, the action of the verb refers back to the subject.

Here are the Italian reflexive pronouns:

mi (myself)

ti (yourself)

si (himself)

si (herself)

ci (ourselves)

vi (yourselves)

si (themselves)

As you can see, Italian reflexive pronouns (*pronomi riflessivi*) look similar to direct and indirect object pronouns, except for the third-person form *si*, which is the same in the singular and in the plural. How to distinguish between reflexive and object pronouns? The best thing for you to do is to keep in mind that reflexive pronouns reflect back upon a sentence's subject. For example:

Listen to track 386

*Elsa **si** guarda allo specchio* – Elsa looks at herself in the mirror

As you can see, the *pronome riflessivo* is used when the subject and the object of a sentence are the same.

Reflexive pronouns tell us that a verb is reflexive. Let's see some reflexive verbs in action.

Vestirsi (to get dressed)

(io) **mi** vesto – I get dressed

(tu) **ti** vesti – you get dressed

(lui/lei) **si** veste – he/she/it gets dressed

(noi) **ci** vestiamo – we get dressed

(voi) **vi** vestite – y'all get dressed

(loro) **si** vestono – they get dressed

Preoccuparsi (to worry)

(io) **mi** preoccupo – I worry

(tu) **ti** preoccupi – you worry

(lui/lei) **si** preoccupa – he/she/it worries

(noi) **ci** preoccupiamo – we worry

(voi) **vi** preoccupate – y'all worry

(loro) **si** preoccupano – they worry

Lavarsi (to wash oneself)

(io) **mi** lavo – I wash myself

(tu) **ti** lavi – you wash yourself

(lui/lei) **si** lava – he/she/it washes himself/herself/itself

(noi) **ci** laviamo – we wash ourselves

(voi) **vi** lavate – y'all wash yourselves

(loro) **si** lavano – they wash themselves

Not so bad, right?

Where to put the Italian reflexive pronouns in a sentence

Listen to track 387

In the **present tense**, Italian reflexive pronouns are usually placed before the conjugated verb but after the subject, if you are using one. For example:

*Benedetta **si** alza ogni giorno alle 6:00* – Benedetta gets up at six o'clock every day

*(Io) **mi** chiedo perché non si riesca a trovare un accordo* – I wonder why we can't reach an agreement

*(Io) **mi** arrendo, hai vinto* – I surrender, you win

This is the same as for any of the other simple tenses, like the imperfect tense (*imperfetto*), remote past tense (*passato remoto*), simple future tense (*futuro semplice*) and present conditional (*condizionale presente*), just to mention a few. Check out these examples:

***Mi** sentii in colpa per molti anni* – I felt guilty for many years

*Da piccole, le gemelle **si** vestivano sempre uguali* – As kids, the twins always dressed the same

*Vorrei che **ti** dedicassi di più a nostra figlia* – I would like you to dedicate more of your time to our daughter

*Nicola **si** scuserebbe se non fosse così orgoglioso* – Nicola would apologize if he wasn't so proud

In **compound tenses**, like the present perfect (*passato prossimo*), past perfect (*trapassato prossimo*), future perfect tense (*futuro anteriore*) and pluperfect subjunctive (*congiuntivo trapassato*), the reflexive pronoun goes right at the start, before both the auxiliary and main verb. For example:

Listen to track 388

*Questa mattina **mi** sono svegliata prima dell'alba* – This morning I woke up before sunrise

***Mi** sono laureata nel 2009* – I graduated in 2009

***Ci** siamo divertiti molto stasera* – We had a great time tonight

*Speravo che Flavio **si** fosse ricordato di comprare i francobolli* – I hoped that Flavio had remembered to buy stamps

If the verb is in the **infinitive** form (non-conjugated form), the reflexive pronoun is attached to the end of the verb, which drops its final -e. Sometimes it is also possible to put it before the verb. For example:

*Voglio vestir**mi** da Harley Quinn ad Halloween / **Mi** voglio vestire da Harley Quinn ad Halloween* – I want to dress up as Harley Quinn for Hallowe'en

The same goes with the **gerund** (*gerundio*). For example:

*Un attimo, **mi** sto pettinando / Un attimo, sto pettinando**mi*** – Wait a minute, I'm combing my hair

With the **positive imperative** and past participle, the reflexive pronoun gets tacked onto the end of the verb. See some examples below:

Listen to track 389

*Sbriga**ti**!* – Hurry up!

*Copri**ti** bene perchè fuori fa molto freddo!* – Put something warm on because it's very cold outside!

*Sveglia**ti**!* – Wake up!

*Divertite**vi**!* – Have fun!

*Appena svegliato**si** dal coma, il paziente riconobbe subito i genitori* – As soon as he woke from the coma, the patient immediately recognized his parents

If you need to use the **positive imperative** with the formal Lei or Loro form, the reflexive pronoun always goes before the verb. For example:

***Si** accomodi, signora!* – Take a seat, Madam!

***Si** accomodino, signore e signori!* – Please have a seat, ladies and gentlemen!

In the **negative imperative**, the reflexive pronoun can either be joined onto the verb or go between the *non* (not) and the verb. For example:

Listen to track 390

*Non **ti** preoccupare! / Non preoccupar**ti**!* – Don't worry!

*Non **vi** preoccupate! / Non preoccupate**vi**!* – Don't worry!

*Non **ti** lamentare sempre! / Non lamentar**ti** sempre!* – Don't complain all the time!

*Non **vi** lamentate sempre! / Non lamentate**vi** sempre!* – Don't complain all the time!

If the verbs **dovere** (to must, to have to), **potere** (to can, to be able to) and **volere** (to want, to desire) precede the infinitive of the reflexive verb, the reflexive pronoun can either be placed before the conjugated verb or be attached to the infinitive, which loses the final -e. Let's look at some examples:

*Mara **si** poteva fare male tuffandosi da quella scogliera / Mara poteva far**si** male tuffandosi da quella scogliera* – Mara could get hurt by diving off that cliff

***Mi** volevo mettere la gonna, ma poi ho scelto i jeans / Volevo metter**mi** la gonna, ma poi ho scelto i jeans* – I wanted to wear a skirt, but then I chose a pair of jeans

***Ti** dovevi riposare invece di stare alzato fino a tardi / Dovevi riposar**ti** invece di stare alzato fino a tardi* – You should have been getting some rest instead of staying up late

Listen to track 391

In a **negative sentence**, the reflexive pronoun remains in front of the verb.

***Non** mi sento a mio agio qui* – I don't feel comfortable here

***Non** ci siamo accorti di nulla* – We didn't notice anything wrong

***Non** fermandoti allo stop hai infranto il codice della strada* – By not stopping at a stop sign, you haven't followed the traffic rules

Reflexive pronouns and *ne* in the same sentence

Some reflexive verbs in Italian, like *andarsene* (to leave, to go away), add the pronominal particle **ne** after the reflexive pronoun.

Listen to track 392

Me ne vado – I'm leaving

Vattene! – Go away!

Ilaria e Federico se ne sono andati – Ilaria and Federico have left

When followed by another pronoun, such as *ne*, the reflexive pronouns *mi, ti, si, ci* and *vi* change their spelling as follows:

- *mi* becomes **me**
- *ti* becomes **te**
- *si* becomes **se**
- *ci* becomes **ce**
- *vi* becomes **ve**

See some examples below:

*Non me **ne** ero accorta* – I didn't realize it

*Le mancheresti se **te** ne andassi* – She will miss you if you go away

*Giorgio ha conosciuto una ragazza finlandese e **se** ne è innamorato perdutamente* – Giorgio met a Finnish girl and fell in love with her

Ce ne infischiamo di quello che dici! – We don't care about what you say!

Ve ne siete accorti? – Have you noticed?

Listen to track 393

Other uses of the Italian reflexive pronouns

The plural forms *ci, vi* and *si* can be used to mean **each other** and **one another**.

Let's look at some examples:

Vi conoscete? – Do you know each other?

Andrea e Chiara si vogliono molto bene – Andrea and Chiara love each other a lot

*Si vede lontano un miglio che **si** detestano* – You can see they hate one another

Ci siamo abbracciati – We hugged

Ci siamo baciati – We kissed each other

*Marzia e Roberto **si** sono conosciuti a Verona* – Marzia and Roberto met in Verona

In Italian, we often talk about actions that have to do with our body and clothing using a reflexive verb. For example:

Listen to track 394

Mi lavo i denti dopo ogni pasto – I brush my teeth after every meal

Lavati le mani prima di pranzo! – Wash your hands before lunch!

Mettiti il cappotto! – Put your coat on!

Common reflexive verbs

Reflexive pronouns are mostly used with reflexive verbs. There are many more reflexive verbs in Italian than in English. Here is a list of the most common ones:

Listen to track 395

Abbronzarsi – to tan

Accorgersi di – to notice

Accomodarsi – to make oneself comfortable

Addormentarsi – to fall asleep

Alzarsi – to get up

Arrabbiarsi – to get angry

Arrangiarsi – to manage, to get by

Arrendersi – to surrender

Avviarsi – to start out

Avvicinarsi – to come near, to approach

Cambiarsi – to change one's clothes

Chiamarsi – to be called

Chiedersi – to wonder

Coprirsi – to cover oneself

Dedicarsi a – to dedicate oneself, to devote oneself

Depilarsi – to shave

Divertirsi – to enjoy oneself, to have a good time, to have fun

Farsi male – to get hurt, hurt oneself

Fermarsi – to stop

Imbattersi in – to bump into

Incontrarsi con – to meet with

Infilarsi – to put on, to wear

Infischiarsene – to not care about

Innamorarsi – to fall in love

Lamentarsi – to complain

Laurearsi – to graduate

Lavarsi – to wash oneself

Mettersi – to put on, to wear

Organizzarsi – to prepare for, to get ready

Perdersi – to get lost

Pettinarsi – to comb one's hair

Pentirsi – to regret, to be sorry

Portarsi dietro – to carry around

Preoccuparsi – to worry

Prepararsi – to get ready

Raccomandarsi – to beg, to implore

Radersi – to shave

Ricordarsi – to remember

Riposarsi – to rest

Sbrigarsi – to hurry

Sciogliersi – to melt

Sedersi – to sit down

Scusarsi – to excuse oneself, to apologize

Sdraiarsi – to lie down, to stretch out

Sentirsi – to feel

Spogliarsi – to undress

Sposarsi con – to get married

Struccarsi – to remove one's make-up

Svegliarsi – to wake up

Tenersi – to hold, to take place

Trattarsi di – to be a matter of

Trovarsi – to be located

Truccarsi – to put on make-up

Tuffarsi – to dive

Vergognarsi – to be ashamed, to be embarrassed

Vestirsi – to dress oneself, to get dressed

As you can see, there are quite a few of them and a lot of the most common ones refer to daily routine, like *svegliarsi* (to wake up), *alzarsi* (to get up), *lavarsi* (to wash oneself), *pettinarsi* (to comb one's hair) and so on.

To sum up...

- Reflexive pronouns *mi, ti, si, ci* and *vi* are used when the subject and the object of a sentence are the same.
- Reflexive verbs are used exclusively with reflexive pronouns.
- With reflexive verbs, the subject and the object always coincide.
- Don't confuse reflexive pronouns with direct and indirect object pronouns, which look similar but aren't quite the same.

All done for now! I hope this guide has given you a solid foundation for using Italian reflexive pronouns in conversation and writing. Have fun practicing them a little each day! *Alla prossima!*

Workbook Lesson 24. Getting to Know the Italian Reflexive Pronouns

Exercise 24.1: Conjugate the following verbs

I dress up: _____

You worry: _____

He/she falls asleep: _____

We put on make-up: _____

You feel good: _____

They stop: _____

Exercise 24.2: Complete with reflexive pronouns

1. io _____ alzo

2. tu _____ alzi

3. lui/lei _____ alza

4. noi _____ alziamo

5. voi _____ alzate

6. loro _____ alzano

Exercise 24.3: Choose the right option

1. Se una persona beve troppo vino, può ubriacarmi/ubriacarsi.

2. Qual è il segreto per non arrabbiarti/arrabbiarsi più e non perdere la pazienza?

3. Prima di una gara gli atleti devono allenarci/allenarsi per molte ore.

4. A Carnevale tutti i bambini vogliono mascherarsi/mascherarmi.

5. Una persona vanitosa ama guardarsi/guardare allo specchio per ore.

Exercise 24.4: Complete with reflexive verbs in their passato prossimo tense

1. Marco, che cosa è successo ai tuoi capelli? Non _____ (*pettinarsi*) questa mattina?

2. Per la gara del mese scorso, io e mio fratello _____ (*allenarsi*) due volte al giorno.

3. Sono molto stanca. Ieri sera _____ (*addormentarsi*) molto tardi.

4. L'anno scorso a Carnevale gli studenti _____ (*mascherarsi*) per la festa.

5. Anna, Rita, come _____ (*vestirsi*) per il colloquio di lavoro?

Exercise 24.5: Complete with the given verbs in their passato prossimo tense

VESTIRSI – FARSI – SPOGLIARSI – SVEGLIARSI – ACCORGERSI – METTERSI

Ieri mattina Paolo _____ in ritardo! Allora _____ la doccia e _____ in 5 minuti. Quando è arrivato in ufficio _____ di avere indossato una camicia sporca e due scarpe diverse, una nera e una marrone! Allora è tornato a casa, _____ e _____ una camicia pulita.

Answers:

Exercise 24.1:

I dress up: Io mi vesto

You worry: Tu ti preoccupi

He/she falls asleep: Lui/lei si addormenta

We put on make-up: No ci trucchiamo

You feel good: Voi vi sentite bene

They stop: Loro si fermano

Exercise 24.2:

1. mi; 2. ti; 3. si; 4. ci; 5. vi; 6. si

Exercise 24.3:

1. ubriacarsi.
2. arrabbiarsi
3. allenarsi
4. mascherarsi
5. guardarsi

Exercise 24.4:

1. ti sei pettinato
2. ci siamo allenati
3. mi sono addormentata
4. si sono mascherati
5. vi siete vestite

Exercise 24.5:

Ieri mattina Paolo **si è svegliato** in ritardo! Allora **si è fatto** la doccia e **si è vestito** in 5 minuti. Quando è arrivato in ufficio **si è accorto** di avere indossato una camicia sporca e due scarpe diverse, una nera e una marrone! Allora è tornato a casa, **si è spogliato** e **si è messo** una camicia pulita.

LESSON 25: CONDIZIONALE PRESENTE

One of the four finite moods in Italian, the conditional, refers to hypothetical events. The **Italian present conditional tense** (*condizionale presente*) expresses what would happen under certain conditions, and roughly corresponds to "would" in English.

Would you like to master the ***condizionale presente*** and express yourself in a more fluid and flexible way? Here is your guide. Let's start!

Using the condizionale presente

Listen to track 396

In Italian, the *condizionale presente* is used to:

- make a wish or express desires:

*L'estate prossima **andrei** volentieri in vacanza in Sicilia* – Next summer I would gladly go to Sicily on holiday

*Nicola **vorrebbe** tanto rivederti* – Nicola would like to see you again

- express opinions, ask questions and give advice or recommendations without sounding too direct:

*Se fossi in te, **chiederei** subito scusa a Nadia* – If I were you, I would immediately apologize to Nadia

*Penso che **dovremmo** prenderci una pausa* – I think we should take a break

- make very polite requests or offers:

***Potresti** abbassare il volume, per favore?* – Could you turn down the volume, please?

***Gradireste** del caffè?* – Would you like some coffee?

- criticize or disapprove of something:

*Mattia **dovrebbe** studiare di più se non vuole essere bocciato di nuovo* – Mattia should study more if he doesn't want to repeat the year again

- express a doubt:

*Non so se **andrei** di nuovo in quell'albergo* – I don't know if I would go to that hotel again

- discuss probability:

*Domani **potrebbe** arrivare un'altra ondata di caldo, le temperature sono in aumento* – Another heat-wave could start tomorrow, temperatures are rising

- pose hypothetical questions:

*Cosa **faresti** al posto mio?* – What would you do if you were in my place?

- report something you are not 100% sure about, or that you have doubts about:

*Secondo alcuni testimoni, i rapinatori **sarebbero** quattro* – According to some witnesses, there were four thieves

As you can see, the Italian present conditional tense can be used both in main clauses and subordinate clauses.

The hypothetical period

Listen to track 397

The Italian present conditional is used with the **imperfect subjunctive** (*congiuntivo imperfetto*) to express hypothesis in the hypothetical period (*periodo ipotetico*).

The **hypothetical phrase** is made of two clauses. The subordinate clause is introduced by **se** (if) and expresses a condition, whereas the main clause expresses a consequence. You can use this lovely construction to set up all kinds of situations, imagine what could be, and talk about something that might happen under certain conditions.

Have a look at some examples:

*Se avessi tempo, **andrei** in palestra ogni giorno* – If I had time, I would go to the gym every day (but I don't have time, so I don't)

*Se fossi ricco come il Sultano del Brunei, **comprerei** anche io 300 Ferrari e 600 Rolls-Royce* – If I were as rich as the Sultan of Brunei, I would buy 300 Ferraris and 600 Rolls-Royces too (but I'm not rich, so I can't)

***Investirei** in Bitcoin se offrisse buone prospettive di guadagno* – I would invest in Bitcoin if it offered significant advantages (but it doesn't, so I don't)

The subordinate clause can also be introduced by:

Listen to track 398

- **nel caso in cui** (in the event that, in case):

Nel caso in cui non poteste avere figli, **valutereste** *l'adozione?* – If you could not have children, would you consider adoption?

- **purché** (as long as, provided that):

Andrei volentieri a vedere la partita, purché non ci siano scontri tra le tifoserie – I would gladly go and see the match, as long as there were no fights between supporters of the two clubs

- **qualora** (if, in case):

Qualora ti venisse offerto un lavoro in Finlandia, cosa **faresti**? – What would you do if you were offered a job in Finland?

Remember that, in this case, *se/qualora/nel caso* and *cui/purché* always go with the imperfect subjunctive. Don't use them before the conditional.

How to form the *condizionale presente*

Listen to track 399

The ***condizionale presente*** is easy to construct in Italian. You just have to remove the verb's ending and add the appropriate conditional ending.

To make the present conditional of regular verbs ending in **-are** and **-ere**, take the stem and add the following conditional endings:

- -erei for "I"
- -eresti for "you"
- -erebbe for "he"/ "she" / "it"
- -eremmo for "we"
- -ereste for "y'all"
- -erebbero for "they"

Cantare (to sing)

*Io cant**erei*** - I would sing

*Tu cant**eresti*** - You would sing

*Lui/lei cant**erebbe*** - He/she/it would sing

*Noi cant**eremmo*** - We would sing

*Voi cant**ereste*** - Y'all would sing

*Loro cant**erebbero*** - They would sing

Listen to track 400

Vendere (to sell)

*Io vend**erei*** - I would sell

*Tu vend**eresti*** - You would sell

*Lui/lei vend**erebbe*** - He/she/it would sell

*Noi vend**eremmo*** - We would sell

*Voi vend**ereste*** - Y'all would sell

*Loro vend**erebbero*** - They would sell

As you can see, the *condizionale presente* has the same endings for verbs that belong to both the **-are** and **-ere** conjugation, just like with the *futuro semplice*.

To make the present conditional of regular verbs ending in **-ire**, take the stem and add the following endings:

- -irei for "I"
- -iresti for "you"
- -irebbe for "he"/ "she" / "it"
- -iremmo for "we"
- -ireste for "y'all"
- -irebbero for "they"

Listen to track 401

Dormire (to sleep)

*Io dorm**irei*** - I would sleep

*Tu dorm**iresti*** - You would sleep

*Lui/lei dorm**irebbe*** - He/she/it would sleep

*Noi dorm**iremmo*** - We would sleep

*Voi dorm**ireste*** - Y'all would sleep

*Loro dorm**irebbero*** - They would sleep

Not so bad, right? This works with all regular verbs.

Irregular verbs in the present conditional

The *condizionale presente* **irregular verbs** are the same as for the *futuro semplice*.

Both **essere** (to be) and **avere** (to have) are irregular in the present conditional. Their conjugations are as follows:

Listen to track 402

Essere (to be)

Io sarei - I would be

Tu saresti - You would be

Lui/lei sarebbe - He/she/it would be

Noi saremmo - We would be

Voi sareste - Y'all would be

Loro sarebbero - They would be

Listen to track 403

Avere (to have)

Io avrei - I would have

Tu avresti - You would have

Lui/lei avrebbe - He/she/it would have

Noi avremmo - We would have

Voi avreste - They would have

Loro avrebbero - They would have

As with the *futuro semplice,* verbs ending in **-care** and **-gare** have a change in spelling when conjugated.

Verbs ending in **-care**, like *cercare* (to look for), *praticare* (to practice), *spaccare* (to break) and *elencare* (to list), add an "h" after the "c," to preserve the /k/ sound of the infinitive.

Listen to track 404

Cercare (to search)

Io cercherei – I would try

Tu cercheresti – You would try

Lui/lei cercherebbe – He/She would try

Noi cercheremmo – We would try

Voi cerchereste – You (plural) would try

Loro cercherebbero- They would try

Verbs ending in **-gare**, like *litigare* (to argue), *pagare* (to pay), *negare* (to deny), *spiegare* (to explain) and *pregare* (to pray), add an "h" after the "g," in order to preserve the hard sound of the infinitive.

Listen to track 405

Pagare (to pay)

Io pagherei - I would pay

Tu pagheresti – You would pay

Lui/lei pagherebbe – He / she would pay

Noi pagheremmo – We would pay

Voi paghereste – You (plural)would pay

Loro pagherebbero – They would pay

Verbs ending in **-giare** and **-ciare**, like *parcheggiare* (to park), *danneggiare* (to damage, to ruin), *mangiare* (to eat), *rinunciare* (to renounce), *cominciare* (to begin), *cacciare* (to hunt), *intralciare* (to hinder) and *baciare* (to kiss), drop the letter "i" before adding the conditional endings.

Listen to track 406

Parcheggiare (to park)

Io parcheggerei -I would park

Tu parcheggeresti - You would park

Lui/lei parcheggerebbe - He/ she would park

Noi parcheggeremmo – We would park

Voi parcheggereste – You (plural) would park

Loro parcheggerebbero – They would park

Listen to track 407

Cominciare (to begin)

Io comincerei – I would begin

Tu cominceresti - You would begin

Lui/lei comincerebbe - He/ she would begin

Noi cominceremmo – We would begin

Voi comincereste – You (plural) would begin

Loro comincerebbero - They would begin

Here are some additional groups of **irregular verbs** in the *condizionale presente*.

1. In first group, the "a" in **-are** and the "e" in **-ere** gets removed.

Listen to track 408

Dovere (to have to, to must)

*Io **dovrei*** - I **should**

*Tu **dovresti*** - You **should**

*Lui/lei **dovrebbe*** - He/she/it **should**

*Noi **dovremmo*** - We **should**

*Voi **dovreste*** - You (plural **should**

*Loro **dovrebbero*** - They **should**

Listen to track 409

Potere (to can, to be able to)

*Io **potrei*** - I **could**

*Tu **potresti*** - You **could**

*Lui/lei **potrebbe*** - He/she/it **could**

*Noi **potremmo*** - We **could**

*Voi **potreste*** - Y'all **could**

*Loro **potrebbero*** - They **could**

Listen to track 410

Sapere (to know)

Io saprei – I would know

Tu sapresti - You would know

Lui/lei saprebbe - He/ she would know

Noi sapremmo – We would know

Voi sapreste – You (plural) would know

Loro saprebbero- They would know

Listen to track 411

Andare (to go)

Io andrei – I would go

Tu andresti - You would go

Lui/lei andrebbe - He/ she would go

Noi andremmo – We would go

Voi andreste – You (plural) wouldgo

Loro andrebbero - They would go

Listen to track 412

Cadere (to fall)

Io cadrei – I would fall

Tu cadresti - You would fall

Lui/lei cadrebbe - He/ she would fall

Noi cadremmo – We would fall

Voi cadreste – You (plural) would fall

Loro cadrebbero - They would fall

Listen to track 413

Vedere (to see)

Io vedrei – I would see

Tu vedresti - You would see

Lui/lei vedrebbe - He/ she would see

Noi vedremmo – We would see

Voi vedreste – You (plural) would see

Loro vedrebbero They would see

Listen to track 414

Vivere (to live)

Io vivrei – I would live

Tu vivresti - You would live

Lui/lei vivrebbe - He/ she would live

Noi vivremmo – We would live

Voi vivreste – You (plural) would live

Loro vivrebbero - They would live

2. The second group takes a double "r."

Listen to track 415

Volere (to want)

Io **vorrei** – I **would like**

Tu **vorresti** – You **would like**

Lui/lei **vorrebbe** – He/she/it **would like**

Noi **vorremmo** – We **would like**

Voi **vorreste** – Y'all **would like**

Loro **vorrebbero** – They **would like**

Listen to track 416

Tenere (to keep)

Io terrei – I would keep

Tu terresti - You would keep

Lui/lei terrebbe - He/ she would keep

Noi terremmo – We would keep

Voi terreste – You (plural) would keep

Loro terrebbero - They would keep

Listen to track 417

Venire (to come)

Io verrei – I would come

Tu verresti - You would come

Lui/lei verrebbe - He/ she would come

Noi verremmo – We would come

Voi verreste – You (plural) would come

Loro verrebbero - They would come

Listen to track 418

Bere (to drink)

Io berrei – I would drink

Tu berresti - You would drink

Lui/lei berrebbe - He/ she would drink

Noi berremmo – We would drink

Voi berreste – You (plural) would drink

Loro berrebbero - They would drink

Listen to track 419

Rimanere (to remain)

Io rimarrei – I would remain

Tu rimarresti - You would remain

Lui/lei rimarrebbe - He/ she would remain

Noi rimarremmo – We would remain

Voi rimarreste – You (plural) would remain

Loro rimarrebbero - They would remain

Listen to track 420

Produrre (to produce)

Io produrrei – I would produce

Tu produrresti - You would produce

Lui/lei produrrebbe - He/ she would produce

Noi produrremmo – We would produce

Voi produrreste – You (plural) would produce

Loro produrrebbero - They would produce

Remember that all verbs that end in **-durre**, like *tradurre* (to translate), *dedurre* (to deduce), *condurre* (to drive), *indurre* (to induce), *introdurre* (to introduce) and *riprodurre* (to reproduce), behave in the same way.

Dare (to give), **fare** (to do) and **stare** (to stay) add the ending to the infinitive:

Listen to track 421

Dare (to give)

Io darei – I would give

Tu daresti - You would give

Lui/lei darebbe - He/ she would give

Noi daremmo – We would give

Voi dareste – You (plural) would give

Loro darebbero - They would give

Listen to track 422

Fare (to do)

Io farei – I would do

Tu faresti - You would do

Lui/lei farebbe - He/ she would do

Noi faremmo – We would do

Voi fareste – You (plural) would do

Loro farebbero - They would do

Listen to track 423

Stare (to stay)

Io starei – I would stay

Tu staresti - You would stay

Lui/lei starebbe - He/ she would stay

Noi staremmo – We would stay

Voi stareste- You would stay

Loro starebbero- - They would stay

How to translate the *condizionale presente* into English

As mentioned previously, the **Italian present conditional tense** is usually translated into English with "would" plus the verb's meaning.

Listen to track 424

Se Roberto mi chiedesse di uscire, **sarei** *felicissima* – If Roberto asked me out, I would be very happy

Ci **parlerei** *io direttamente, ma non ho più il suo numero* – I'd talk to him directly, but I no longer have his number

However, it is wrong to think of the Italian *condizionale presente* as a direct translation of "would" and its myriad of uses. As you know, there is not always an exact one-to-one correlation between how tenses are used in English and Italian. Unlike in English, the Italian *condizionale presente* is not used to express habits in the past. The *imperfetto* is used for that:

I **would** go to work each day by bus – *Andavo al lavoro in autobus ogni giorno*

The present conditional along with the verb **dovere** (to have to, to must) can be translated as:

- "Should"

Dovresti *studiare di più* – You should study more

- "Ought to"

Dovresti *ascoltare con attenzione* – You ought to listen carefully

- "To be supposed to"

*Cosa **dovrei** fare?* – What am I supposed to do?

The present conditional along with the verb **potere** (to can, to be able to) can be translated as:

- "Could"

*Scusa, **potresti** chiudere la porta?* – Excuse me, could you please close the door?

- "May/might"

*Non spegnere il telefono stasera, Deborah **potrebbe** aver bisogno di chiamarti* – Don't switch off your phone tonight, Deborah may need to call you

The present conditional along with the verb **volere** (to want) can be translated as:

- "Would like"

Vorrei *proprio rivedere Ocean's Eleven /* **Mi piacerebbe** *rivedere Ocean's Eleven* – I really would like to see Ocean's Eleven again

Both "vorrei" and "mi piacerebbe" can be used to say what you would like to do.

To sum up...

Listen to track 425

- The *condizionale presente* is used to talk about events that would happen under certain conditions.

Se avessi più tempo libero, ***farei*** *volontariato al canile* – If I had more free time, I would volunteer in dog shelters

- It is used to make polite requests.

*Mi **accompagneresti** alla stazione domani, per favore?* – Would you please come to the train station with me tomorrow?

- It is used to give advice and express opinions in a less direct way.

*Se fossi in te, non **mi fiderei** di Danilo* - If I were you, I wouldn't trust Danilo

Practice as much as you can until you get the hang of it. The more you expose yourself to Italian and use the *condizionale presente*, the more this and other grammatical structures will become a part of you. A presto!

Workbook Lesson 25. Present Conditional Tense

Exercise 25.1: Translate the following sentences into Italian

English	Italian
1. I'd buy that game if it was cheaper.	
2. She would read more if she could skip her dance lessons.	
3. Marco wouldn't eat pasta even if it was free.	
4. We would help you tomorrow, but we are busy.	
5. Lucia and Matteo would marry if their parents gave them permission.	

Exercise 25.2: Conjugate these irregular verbs

	Essere	Avere
Io		
Tu		
Lui/Lei		
Noi		
Voi		
Loro		

Exercise 25.3: Complete the following sentences

1. Lucia si _____ in piscina se avesse tempo. (iscriversi)
2. Il mio motorino si _____ fermato per strada se avessi finito la benzina. (essere)
3. Quel camion si _____ solo se gli bucassero le gomme. (fermarsi)
4. Se potessi, mi _____ ogni volta che vedo mia zia Anna. (nascondersi)
5. Gino _____ in moto se sua madre non glielo avesse proibito. (andare)

Exercise 25.4: Choose the right option

1. Mangerei/mangerebbe la pasta se avesse fame.
2. Lucia accompagneresti/accompagnerebbe suo fratello a scuola se avesse la patente.
3. Noi viaggeremmo/viaggerebbero molto di più se avessimo i soldi.
4. I gatti dormirei/dormirebbero tutto il giorno, se potessero.
5. Scambieresti/scambieremmo la tua casa per 100.000 euro?

Exercise 25.5: Conjugate the verbs in the brackets

1. Se vedesse quello scoiattolo, il mio cane _____(abbaiare).
2. Se facesse un po' più freddo _____(nevicare).
3. Io _____(parlare) molto più spesso se non fossi così timido.
4. Secondo me _____ (camminare) molto più velocemente senza quei tacchi!
5. Io e Maura _____(dormire) meglio se il vicino facesse silenzio.

Answers:

Exercise 25.1:

1. Comprerei quel gioco se costasse meno.
2. Leggerebbe di più se potesse saltare le lezioni di danza.
3. Marco non mangerebbe la pasta nemmeno se fosse gratis.
4. Ti aiuteremmo domani, ma siamo impegnati.
5. Lucia e Matteo si sposerebbero se i loro genitori gli dessero il permesso.

Exercise 25.2:

	Essere	Avere
Io	Sarei	Avrei
Tu	Saresti	Avresti
Lui/Lei	Sarebbe	Avrebbe
Noi	Saremmo	Avremmo
Voi	Sareste	Avreste
Loro	Sarebbero	Avrebbero

Exercise 25.3:

1. Lucia si iscriverebbe in piscina se avesse tempo.
2. Il mio motorino si sarebbe fermato per strada se avessi finito la benzina.
3. Quel camion si fermerebbe solo se gli bucassero le gomme.
4. Se potessi, mi nasconderei ogni volta che vedo mia zia Anna.
5. Gino andrebbe in moto se sua madre non gli elo avesse proibito.

Exercise 25.4:

1. mangerebbe; 2. accompagnerebbe; 3. viaggeremmo; 4. dormirebbero; 5. Scambieresti

Exercise 25.5:

1. abbaierebbe; 2. nevicherebbe; 3. parlerei; 4. cammineresti; 5. dormiremmo;

CONCLUSION

Learning grammar is certainly not easy so if you were able to finish all of that by consistently learning every day, hats off to you! You did an amazing job and you should be very proud.

If you were not able to follow the daily schedule as recommended, don't despair. The important thing is you made use of this book to build a solid foundation for your Italian grammar.

We at Talk in Italian hope that you will continue to keep learning every day. Even just a few minutes a day goes a long way. It could be just listening to a 30-minute Italian podcast, watching an Italian movie or TV series, writing to a friend in Italian, talking to a native Italian speaker, changing your social media settings to Italian or reading the news in Italian... the list goes on.

We have other books available at the Talk in Italian website and on Amazon. Feel free to browse the different titles. They will help you solidify your knowledge of Italian grammar.

If you have comments, questions or suggestions about this book, you may reach us at support@talkinitalian.com. We'd be happy to hear from you.

Grazie, thank you,

Talk in Italian Team

HOW TO DOWNLOAD THE FREE AUDIO FILES?

The audio files are in MP3 format and need to be accessed online. No worries though; it's easy!

On your computer, smartphone, iPhone/iPad, or tablet, simply go to this link:

https://talkinitalian.com/audio-grammar-beginner/

Be careful! If you are going to type the URL on your browser, please make sure to enter it completely and exactly. It will lead you to a wrong webpage if not entered precisely.

You should be directed to a webpage where you can see the cover of your book.

Below the cover, you will find two "Click here to download the audio" buttons in green and orange color.

Option 1 (via Google Drive): The green one will take you to a Google Drive folder. It will allow you to listen to the audio files online or download it from there. Just "Right click" on the track and click "Download." You can also download all the tracks in just one click—just look for the "Download all" option.

Option 2 (direct download): The orange button/backup link will allow you to directly download all the files (in .zip format) to your computer.

Note: This is a large file. Do not open it until your browser tells you that it has completed the download successfully (usually a few minutes on a broadband connection, but if your connection is slow it could take longer).

The .zip file will be found in your "Downloads" folder unless you have changed your settings. Extract the .zip file and you will now see all the audio tracks. Save them to your preferred folder or copy them to your other devices. Please play the audio files using a music/Mp3 application.

Did you have any problems downloading the audio? If you did, feel free to send an email to support@talkinitalian.com. We'll do our best to assist you, but we would greatly appreciate it if you could thoroughly review the instructions first.

Grazie, thank you,

Talk in Italian Team

Made in United States
North Haven, CT
25 February 2023

33158359R00161